P9-DGJ-201

Reluctant Warriors

"... A land that flows with milk and honey" (Exodus 33,3)

"... A land that eats its inhabitants" (Numbers 13,32)

Reluctant Warriors

Israelis Suspended Between Rome and Jerusalem

Nathan Szajnberg

Copyright © 2006 by Nathan Szajnberg.
Copyright SACD: 175362 by Nathan Szajnberg

Cover Design: Dov Abramson and N. Szajnberg; Photo: Niv Calderon

Xlibris Corporation, a division of Random House.

Library of Congress Control Number:		2006908510
ISBN 10:	Hardcover	1-4257-3495-2
	Softcover	1-4257-3494-4
ISBN 13:	Hardcover	978-1-4257-3495-4
	Softcover	978-1-4257-3494-7

All rights reserved. No part of this book may be reproduced or transmitted in any form or by any means, electronic or mechanical, including photocopying, recording, or by any information storage and retrieval system, without permission in writing from the copyright owner.

Excerpt p. 21-2, Reprinted with the permission of Scribner, an imprint of Simon & Schuster Adult Publishing Group, from JARHEAD by Anthony Swofford. Copyright © 2003 by Anthony Swofford. All rights reserved.

Excerpt p. 22, Reprinted with permission of Toby Press, from Adjusting Sights by Haim Sabato (Translated, Hillel Halkin) Copyright 2003.

This book was printed in the United States of America.

To order additional copies of this book, contact:
Xlibris Corporation
1-888-795-4274
www.Xlibris.com
Orders@Xlibris.com
29132

DEDICATION

To these soldiers and their brothers and sisters, some of whom have given their lives for the sake of a Jewish homeland. To the Israelis who have built a haven for Jews dispersed since Roman times to gather into a homeland, Israelis who strive to maintain a democratic society, a productive society, who contribute intellectually and otherwise to humankind, even as these Israelis battle for safety and security.

CONTENTS

Conclusion: What are the *characteristics common to these men?* Death affects them profoundly: a certain sober, at times somber, quality about life; a more rapid movement towards intimacy. They have quiet certitude, without bravado, a core self-assurance; expect much of themselves and look to their peers for motivation without competition. They do not relish killing, nor soldiering, yet choose to be in close-combat units in order to have a sense of doing something substantive to protect others.

The effects of death and trauma on a society, are transmitted not only by those who see trauma, but also their intimates. We reconsider the reactions to trauma: that preexisting experiences, like previous earthquakes, *may* make us more vulnerable to trauma.

Israel's overall portrait is of a society militarized, but not militaristic.

The Israeli army is a governmentally—and societally— "sanctioned" transition to young adulthood; what are its advantages and disadvantages. What is the impact on a democratic society of a volunteer army? How do armies absorb, transmit and transform the values of their societies. 206

Acknowledgements

This too short section is most important for me. Many have helped this book's labor and birth. I thank the soldiers who spoke so freely to me, only to have their stories heard and told. They live good lives and risk their lives for the sake of others, while struggling not to take other lives. Now to those whom I can thank by name. I thank Bruno Bettelheim for teaching me to listen well; Myron Joshua, my dear college friend, a true kibbutznik, for helping me reach the first soldiers, checking on my Hebrew transliterations and reading too many drafts; David Valayre, a fine writer and editor, who has also written a play expected to open soon in Paris, *Quatre Soldats*, based on interviews in this book; Patrick (Pinny) Feigelson, the brother I always wished for, who is also an honest reader; Judith and Robert Wallerstein, for critical readings and to Judith who first suggested I write life stories; Marshall and Marlene Greene for warm friendship and support; Sonia and Lily Szajnberg for indexing and being my daughters; Michele Kaplan Green, for a mother's reading; Reuven Gal, a thoughtful soldier and colleague; Shlomi and Linda Ravid, fine kibbutzniks, at whose Hannuka party in 1999, I was set on this voyage.

Two organizations helped fund this long voyage. I thank the International Psychoanalytic Association's Research Advisory Board for its faith in funding me. I thank the Wallerstein Committee for continuing to support my research as a psychoanalyst.

Ra'anana, Israel, 2006

Introduction

Here are elite soldiers, kibbutz-born, battle-bred. Their stories reveal their minds and souls, and what has tempered and annealed their hearts. They are citizen soldiers all—officers or NCO's—who refused career military appointments and returned to civilian life, as much as one can be a civilian in Israel. Descendants of Isaac who, like modern-day Ishmaels, seek peace while pursuing the Leviathan of war. Or are pursued by it. They also search for inner peace.

These men and this author were transformed by the Second Intifada over a four—year period. I began this book in an era of hope following Oslo. In the political shambles after President Clinton's desperate and failed Taba diplomacy, it grew in complexity. I write today at the re-dawn of hope following Saddam Hussein's downfall, Kaddafi's "conversion," Arafat's death, Lebanon's Hariri murder. Much has changed since then.

A psychoanalyst by profession, five years ago I completed a book about American youth, their journeys, successes and failures, from birth through thirty. All but one of the 76 interviewees had navigated the inner turmoil of adolescence and young adulthood via the relatively pacific waters of college. During a brief visit to

Israel in 1999, I met an Israeli graduate student at a Hanukah party who asked me what I had learned about Americans. He listened closely, then quietly remarked how different it was to become a young man in the Israeli army. To understand Israel, he continued, one must understand its army. And so, a year later, in the fall of 2000, I decided at least to try.

Before I left, I returned to a book—Children of the Dream— written by Bruno Bettelheim, one of my teachers. More often cited than read, it is frequently misunderstood. He recounts the extraordinary job the kibbutzim do raising children in a communal setting. He demonstrates how different child-rearing methods result in different personalities. Bettelheim finds that kibbutz children are well-balanced with strong peer relations and a vibrant inner character. He predicts that kibbutz mothers would not tolerate many more years of having their children raised in the communal children's houses. He was right on target. In addition to severe economic factors, the movement by mothers to bring their offspring into the family home coincided with the kibbutz's near collapse as a social movement, ending perhaps one of the more successful experiments in socialism in the twentieth century. Once I realized that this historical phenomenon, this culture, was about to disappear, I knew the only way I could capture the experiences of the last group born and raised in the soil of communal settlements—who were also army-matured—would be to hurry to harvest their knowledge. Like grapes for fine wine, these boys absorb the flavor, the fragrance, the taste of the soil around them.

Moreover, the then prime minister, Ehud Barak, planned to shorten army service because peace was at hand. Since the Israeli Army has been so central to Israeli growth, development and identity, I had to act quickly to study its soldiers before peace transformed their swords into plowshares.

It turned out, no rush. Peace was not as forthcoming as hoped.

Why else this book, these kibbutz soldiers? The interrelationship between society's values, its socially sanctioned institutions for transition to young adulthood, and the institutions' impact on its youth. Child-rearing and culture are reciprocal. As you raise youngsters, so will they raise others, and, in this way, transmit a society's values. This is both true and not true. Societies such as modern democracies are sufficiently robust that they can evolve, grow, and change, hopefully, in healthy ways. For example, when the United States was founded in the 18th century, neither women nor slaves could vote. Yet the Constitution proved flexible enough to permit vital change.

In our thirty-year study of U.S. youth, we found that in this country transitions to young adulthood were not all the same. Although many attend university, their experience varies from Princeton to Long Island Community College. Americans may socially sanction, even value college, but it is often not an equable or consistent life experience; even not available for many youth.

Israel? Israel is a unique human "experiment." Barely more than a half century old, it was founded as a democracy, has grown exponentially, some tenfold, primarily through immigration. While situated in an almost third-world region, its expectations and lifestyles have more in common with Europe and the U.S., particularly in education. Yet, most of its youth go from high school directly into the army, an idea George Washington considered necessary for a democratic state. Until recently, the Israeli army was a highly respected experience for young people, especially those in the higher echelons of society, unlike most American youth, possibly excepting the South.

When so many citizens serve as soldiers, and continue in the reserves, how does the army affect its men? And how do these citizen soldiers affect the army and a democratic society? As a psychoanalyst, I focused on the inner thoughts, wishes, fears of these men of external action, more than on their actual military experience. You will hear their interior action, what they wanted to talk about. They feel most alive when confronting their inner struggles and dilemmas, the memories, the feelings, the need to recount losses.

In more than two dozen trips during the Intifada, I sought to interview these vanishing beings. How did I come to choose these particular young men? They are mostly kibbutz boys, who tend to become elite combat unit soldiers. They face the enemy up-close. Only three percent of the population, Kibbutzniks become 90% of pilots; 70% of paratroopers, and are over-represented as officers (and among those killed in action).

I select soldiers with the highest entrance scores. The army's elaborate testing program includes a composite score assessing ethnicity, demographics, school performance, and psychological testing, (the *Kabah* score). Historically, it predicts army success well, which in turn predicts post-army success. Despite highest scores and promotions, these soldiers had turned down army careers. I choose those in their late twenties, so that they will have had time both to experience civilian life and to reflect on their service.

Questions kept intriguing me: How do these citizen soldiers, residents in a democratic society, manage to be effective soldiers, yet maintain their humanity as men? How did their transition from adolescence to young adulthood influence their inner lives, their views of life and the tense, tangled world in which they live?

I listen. I hear a recurrent theme: their struggle between the poles of being a fine warrior—acolytes of ancient Rome's military—versus being a fine human being—descendants of Jerusalem. Rome trained fighters to conquer, to dominate; Jerusalem, these men believe, to protect its people, its land.

My questions persisted but my methods have to change with the ongoing Intifada. In the States I could interview individuals in one meeting over several hours, allowing me to complete portraits of their inner lives relatively quickly. During the Israel Intifada, when streets were vacated, and restaurants shuttered, the soldiers I met would not talk about soldiering or permit me to videotape them until they knew me, after I visit their homes, schools, cafes. We meet many times over four years. They want me to know their truths; stories bleed from their souls, like from stigmata, never-healing wounds. After informal meetings, then formal interviews, months, years, later, they called me. "I felt like such an outsider on kibbutz that I left. Now I yearn for it. Could we talk more?" "I remembered another death I hadn't told you about. We need to have coffee." "I want you to meet my fiancée, explain me to her." And so on.

In October 2000, I had hoped to attend the first International Child Psychiatry conference to be held in Israel. For the first time in its history, it is canceled. Instead, I immerse myself in the soil and toil of the kibbutzim that bred the boys I will meet, the better to understand them. Instead of attending conferences, I wear knee-high rubber galoshes. I work the fig and avocado groves of Kibbutz Glil Yam (Ocean's Wave), pick pomegranates, learn about cambium layers and pruning, transplanting the primitive limb swellings that turn into figs. On Saturday nights, I hose down the tiled floor in the kibbutz kitchen, listening to soldiers. It is here, a year ago, at a Hanukah party, that I meet the graduate student who directs me to an unanticipated many year Israel voyage.

*   *   *

There are moments I fear. Palestinians morph into live bombs in malls, on streets, at bus stops. Suicide bombers collapse the borders between soldier and civilian, between adult and child, between man and woman. Being frisked for weapons at malls, being asked whether I carry a gun as I enter restaurants is a constant reminder of the terror. It is annoying to be frisked; it is daunting to face roadblocks and bomb plantings; I miss some meetings. Often, cab drivers are intimidated when I tell them my destination.

Or moments intimidating. On Achad Ha'am Street, a short, charming road lined with elegant apartments and emptying onto a bustling boulevard, I hail a taxi to the Hebrew University, the Mount Scopus campus. I know the road, the trip perhaps a ten-minute ride. Suddenly the Arab cab driver takes a detour. He slows down, and after fifteen minutes we descend into a valley, where I can no longer see the hilltop campus. We are in an Arab village. Boys ride donkeys, women wear shawls, old men play *sheshbesh*

(Arabic backgammon) turn to look. Younger men stare. The driver stops, pulls to the side of the road. I tell him that I can't see the campus. He turns, looks at me and smiles, "You'll see it soon enough." When I take out my cell phone and begin to dial, he restarts the car. As we approach an Israeli checkpoint, I consider getting out, but I don't want to offend him. Around the bend, I spy a narrow road leading up to the campus. After this scare, I only take cabs hailed by hotel doormen. My American self dictates fairness—I tell myself, "Take cabs driven by Arabs." But now I look furtively to see if the driver is wearing a *kippah*, a Jewish skullcap, marking humility before G-d.

*   *   *

Where shall we meet?

In a jeep approaching the rim of Mitzpeh Ramon, stopping abruptly at the brink of a precipitous drop down many geological millennia, a highly decorated officer, now a professor with shrapnel-studded legs, responds dismissively that a "hero" is someone who has "shit his pants" under fire.

Under a blazing afternoon sun in the Negev Desert, beneath a flowering tree, with hovering heavy-bodied flies, I listen to a soldier on weekend leave. Shirtless, wearing billowing Bedouin trousers with a decorative colored stripe down the seams, he talks about the travails of basic training, why he refuses promotion to officer.

In a freezing guard booth, approaching midnight, next to the electrified gate in the territory of Judah, peering into the darkness beyond, I listen to a kibbutznik talk about growing up here, his rifle leaning nonchalantly against a wall too flimsy to protect us from the wind. He concentrates on me, even as he listens to the walky-talky, his cellphone ringing and the internal security phone jangling to be answered. Guest cars approach the structural steel gates, impatiently awaiting a once-over by this soldier.

I cannot get a cab to the West Bank near midnight. The King David Hotel hails a young Arab driver, who, after passing through the last roadblock, loses his way, enters a Palestinian village. As his face glistens with fear, I call my contact at the nearby kibbutz who directs us back on the unlit road to the electrified gates of the kibbutz.

To a physician colleague at the Ben Gurion University, I explain that I study soldiers nearing thirty because I want to learn about those who had finished their army service. The moment after I say this, I realize my *faux pas*. A drag on his cigarette, beard gristled after returning from his month duty in the West Bank, this father of three looks at the floor, responds, "What do you mean finished?"

While the settings change, in part because of the Intifada, my interviews continue to explore the "person" within the soldier. I ask about their childhoods and adolescence I also use the Adult Attachment Interview—an engaging, subtle way to understand their childhood relationships. Then, on to basic training, regular and officer service and reserve duty, with a summary of their current intimate and vocational lives. I find that I must shift my approach; some prefer to talk about basic training, even army, before discussing upbringing. My work is a kind of soul-spelunking, exploring carefully in dark caves, prodding gently, following caverns to see where they lead.

But deaths. These men had known more death by their mid-twenties than I had ever experienced by their age, than I had ever heard in our American study. My soldiers—and I now consider them research collaborators—want me to hear not only about their lives, but also about the lives of their *khevre*, buddies, who had been killed, as well as their other friends and relatives murdered. At times I worry that this book will become a memoir of the dead by the living who will not permit memories to die. "Remember them," they tell me over and over again.

*   *   *

During my youth, in the Viet Nam era, I got a favorable lottery number that precluded being drafted. I was lucky; I was not well-disposed toward armies. Now, I have much to learn. The function of armies remains similar across millennia—to attack, to defend. Their structure remains remarkably consistent since the Roman era. But armies differ culturally, varying from totalitarian to democratic nations, even among democratic states. To clarify how the army and the Jewish State are intertwined, brief accounts of the growth and development of the Israeli army appear in a later chapter. In some ways, these soldiers are like citizen soldiers following the American Revolutionary War: they know fathers' and grandfathers' battles, the details of tactics, the victories and defeats. It is living history.

Coming of age in a new society in which Jews were not only not a minority for the first time in two millennia, they are militarily, educationally, even economically strong. Bettelheim found that within two generations, the kibbutz and early Israel generated a new society and a new persona. The Eastern European immigrants, reacting dismissively to their centuries of subjugation, overt weakness and vulnerability, were determined to forge children who feel strong, secure, and are unapologetic Jews. As one Israeli soldier observed: "It is foreign to us, your American Jewish attitude of 'Don't do anything to irritate the goyim (non-Jews).'"

The Intifada is not simply a clash of cultures; it is oddly more complex, entangled. First, these Israeli soldiers are in an army that is a maelstrom of cultures, cultures compressed to a new identity. Soldiers train, mingle, collaborate, depend for their lives upon— immigrants from the former Soviet Union (many with attenuated Jewish identities); Moroccans, Yemenites, and Iraqis, whose parents and grandparents recall their flight from the pain of Arab subjugation; Orthodox Jews (of various flavors); South African, Argentine, North American, non-Jewish Druze and Bedouin, and, of course, the Sabra, the native-born Israeli. From these metals, the army, the society, makes a precious amalgam, a new culture, Israeli.

This Israeli army in the Intifada comes face to face with a culture deeply foreign, yet all-too-close. Israeli soldiers fight not only soldiers, but also terrorists. Israelis live and work among a Palestinian population, where it is not clear if an innocent-looking child is wearing a bomb-belt, if a woman in labor is feigning, preparing to give "birth" to the explosives strapped to her belly, if an ambulance is not furtively bomb-laden.

The Palestinian approach—using suicide bombers whose mothers pray that their younger sons will join the older "martyrs"— pits a culture committed to the primacy of life against a culture which extols the "assassin," who values his death over life. These Israeli soldiers are cheek-by-jowl with, as Tom Friedman wrote, "a cult of death."

*　　*　　*

The Intifada has taken its toll on these citizen soldiers.

As I read war accounts relating to the first Gulf War, and the Iraqi War, I notice that most are written by journalists—they are action-packed, riveting battle-oriented, even as they provide some sense of the soldiers. They reveal little about the soldiers' inner lives, their desires and dreams. How they became who they are, who they want to be. What is the nature of their intimacies (other than combat buddies). Here lies a major difference. My goal is to explore the effects of the war upon the outer and inner lives of the soldiers I interviewed. In doing so I uncover the remarkable cultural differences between armies.

Two brief excerpts will highlight how different elite forces from different democratic countries, different cultures, can be.

First a highly-touted account by a U.S. marine sniper, a "jarhead," from the First Gulf War. Here is how Anthony Swofford and his buddies gets ready for attack: . . . *We . . . drink all of the beer and watch all of those damn movies and we yell Semper fi and we head-butt and beat the crap out of each other and we get off on the various visions of carnage and violence and deceit, the raping and killing and pillaging. Viet Nam war films are all pro-war . . . pornography for the military mean; with film, you are stroking his cock, tickling his balls with the pink feather of history, getting him ready for his real First Fuck . . . We are afraid, but that doesn't mean we don't want to fight . . . . I want*

*ammunition and alcohol and dope, I want to screw some whores
and kill some Iraqi mother fuckers.*

Much of the remainder of Swofford's book details how
psychologically damaged he felt from his service. Ironically,
Swofford never fires a shot.

Now, listen to an Israeli soldier on eve of battle:

> We [the lieutenant and soldier] talked about
> Maimonides' view of individual Providence. If
> Maimonides really believed . . . that the world was
> governed by the laws of nature, how could God suspend
> them for a specific individual? Nature's laws applied
> equally to everyone.
>
> I gave him the answer I had been taught . . . .
> Maimonides' [approach] was that God's Providence
> sometimes extended to individual cases, but only with
> human beings . . . .
>
> We debated for a while. The second lieutenant pointed
> out inconsistencies in my position and I tried to harmonize
> them. One of his objections stumped me. I was mulling it
> over when he said out of the blue:
>
> 'The . . . attack will begin at exactly this hour of dawn.
> It will come from over there . . . I don't like it . . . if dozens
> of . . . tanks were to cross at this point, there would be
> nothing we could do about it . . . Don't ask me how we'll
> stop it. I wish this stint of reserve duty was over. The others
> call me 'the Philosopher.' Maybe they're right to make fun
> of me . . . I don't know who they think is going to save
> them . . . I don't like it one bit.'
>
> And he was gone.

I listened to my citizen soldiers for anything similar to Jarhead's
screed of head-butting, drinking and the exhilarating mixture of

fucking and killing. None talked like this. Perhaps I was missing something, so I asked explicitly about preparation for dangerous battles. I still heard nothing. So, I read Jarhead's account to several of my soldiers. They were shocked, stunned and even embarrassed—for Swofford. None had experienced anything like this, nor had heard of it. "Yes," said Eliaz, "We would get together and yell, 'Hoo-Haa,' before a tough exercises"; "Yes," Micha said, "My unit was known as knuckle-draggers for our aggressive chanting; "Yes," David admitted, "My unit had once been called 'Mao-Maos' because it once filled its ranks with immigrant Sephardi Jews" (like his father), who were not university-educated, unlike him. But none of my citizen-soldiers recognized the blood-chilling, crass animalization that the sniper-author claimed was de rigeur for his unit of elite soldiers. The soldiers in this book are not snipers; yet, all had the most elite hand-to-hand combat training, had seen death. And, unlike Swofford, all had fired at the enemy. And been fired upon.

*　　*　　*

Why this book? Why now?

Reluctant Warriors describes the last cohort from the communal child-rearing kibbutz or moshavim, extending Bettelheim's work. These men map their inner struggles: humane citizen versus effective soldier. They will tell you about the Intifada's effects upon them. After they speak, I shift from their inner lives to a larger focus, their society, and how their experiences are relevant for other societies.

In a democratic society, if most men are citizen soldiers, they will be affected by their army, and upon returning to citizenry, will affect the society and its army. This is one reason, I believe, George Washington insisted on a citizen soldiery. These men changed the army *while* soldiers. Ben Gurion expected the army to help build the nation—soldiers as farmers, border guards. What kind of nation is built by these men?

And what of other societies? What can we learn about ourselves from these soldiers The U.S. has done away with conscription; most citizens never serve, neither in army nor other societally-sanctioned program. What socially sanctioned institutions do we have to facilitate the transition from the adolescent task of establishing identity to the young adult struggle between intimacy and isolation?

These men, this book, and your reflections will begin to answer these questions.[1]

---

[1] Protecting soldiers' identities: a few words.

I try to balance the reader's desire to learn about these men and their inner lives with my desire to protect their privacy. I interviewed several dozen soldiers; twenty-four in their late twenties are the core of this book. I selected nine as paradigmatic for this group, each chapter telling one soldier's tale. I have disguised their identities, except for Eliaz Cohen and Nehamia Dagan, who have agreed to have names revealed. To disguise these soldiers, I have used techniques recommended by psychoanalysts, such as my teacher Paul Dewald and others. *Their names are changed, their family sizes, their places of birth and growth, their ethnic origins, their current professions and current family members and homes. I have also changed details of their army experiences: while all were in elite combat units, when I say that someone was in Golani, he is likely to have been in a different unit; when I say that a serious battle took place in Jenin, it is likely to have happened elsewhere, and so on.* In some cases, I have combined two soldiers' identities. *What has remained true is the portrayal of their inner lives.* I am grateful to them for their direct honesty and willingness to share their inner lives with you; I know that the reader will respect my wish to protect these soldiers' identities.

Wings on my Shoulders: Knight of Justice

Eliaz doesn't look like an elite combat soldier. He just is one. Short, maybe 5 foot 4 inches, nose hooked, curly top just tumbling over his ears, smiles dance across his face and evoke smiles. He adores his children, his wife. When I greet her two hours later—she towering over him—I see her light green eyes and recall the touching poem by Eliaz, describing the stream of a tear from the lake of her eyes. Eliaz, a poet, is editor of <u>Mashiv Ha'ruakh</u>, "(He) Returns The Wind."

Shaked, (Almond), now 4 1/2 sleeps on the living room couch in the tiny, remarkably neat kibbutz apartment when Eliaz greets me. We start late, around 9:30, so that he can get the four children to bed. His wife is at a kibbutz meeting about responsibility. But, Shaked isn't really asleep. His dad has told him that I, a dream doctor, would be coming from the States. Shaked turns to me, tells me excitedly about a dream. He has great dreams, great ones that excite him. But tonight, Eliaz, explains, we would sit in the kitchen, in direct eyeshot of Shaked and I would talk with Daddy.

When I ask about his preparation for the army, Eliaz starts with his dead Uncle, his patronymic. A poet, his language flows in both Hebrew and English.

*He is myth, he deserves to be. The story is brief, as was his
life. By twenty, Uncle Eliazer is already known by his family as
the "Knight of Justice," always doing right by others. In the Mitla
Pass Battle of Sinai in '56, Eliazer is a medic. Shot in the leg, his
officer tells him to stay back, be treated. But Eliazer is the medic, he
says his boys in the front need him. He limps to save others. He is
killed. The family is known as mishpachah shekulah; for this there
is not a good translation—perhaps an "orphaned family." This is
like a family's badge.*

*I carry Eliazer on my shoulders, just behind them, at the top edge
of my back, al ha'shechem.[2] Not just my name, his name, my name
after him. But also I am the oldest son, ben ha'bachur.[3] I feel that I
carry his life on my shoulders. And I can do it. He is not a burden;
his wings lift me. My uncle's memory is conscious, an awareness
and also a tension in me: could I put my life at risk for my khevre
(buddies) or not? When I was six, I was thinking about this.*

*But I always knew, I knew, that my younger brother in the same
battle would do the same thing—sacrifice his life for his buddies. He
looks like him. Like Uncle Eliazer, we both are gingy (red-haired),
but mine fades when I am six and his remains. I thought as a boy,
when my hair fades, I may not be able to be as much Eliazer as my
brother. His face looks like Uncle Eliazer's; Eliazer's photograph
in the house is a mirror for my brother. But I knew since I was six
that my brother is braver than I. We have many similarities—both
outgoing, strongly opinionated, yet humanistic; but he has shovev
(mischievous)—this charms people, they aren't put-off.*

*In kindergarten—I picture this in my mind, I have pictures in
my mind from when I was three years old—when I was six, we all*

---

2   Shechem, today Nablus, is also the name of the Biblical town where
    Dina, Jacob's daughter was raped; where Rachel, Jacob's beloved died
    by the roadside, and where Eliaz was dispatched for one month on
    a traumatic reserve duty in the Intifada of April 2002.
3   "Chosen son," who is expected to serve the priests of the Holy Temple—
    each word for this poet is carefully chosen, meaningfully laden.

boys dress to play like soldiers. Not just at Purim; we do this, most of the time. You know, the girls do Princess or Cinderella. We do soldiers. So, I put on a beret, Uncle Eliazer's beret, like this (he pantomimes with a little tug on the right, perching an edge over his ear and right brow a bit). *I make it like in the photo of Uncle Eliazer, the one on the mantle. I have red hair then. Later, when my red hair fades, I feel it is a sign that I don't deserve his name, couldn't do what he did.*

But *that* day, my parents and others come to school. *They see me in the uniform. I feel proud. They say, "We pray that you only play soldier and never have to be one."*

So this memory of when I was six has to do with what happened in the army when I was twenty. I am in a special yeshiva program: at 18, we spend 1 1/2 or 2 years studying Talmud, then serve in an integrated religious/secular combat unit, then return to Yeshiva. We go as a group, together. This is important for what will happen to me; to us.

What happens the night before *giyus*, recruitment?

Know, that the day of my *giyus* is the day of Rosh Chodesh of Nisan (the month of Pesach). The climax of the year. Not just Pesach, it is Spring, when within the dimming days of winter, the fragrance of life's hope rises from the moist fields; you smell the tendrils before the grasses emerges; the fragrance and warmth rises from the grounds—leavens your soul.

That night before *giyus,* I stay up most of the night at home. After everyone is asleep, I go to each room of the house to say goodbye—to each room. To each object I bid adieu: the books, of course; a light fixture; a leaded crystal door knob and its door; the glass shelf that held the radio; the standing desk for studying Torah.

I know this isn't rational. I know that the first weeks of Tironut, basic training, they wouldn't have us do any combat, I wouldn't get put in danger. But I feel driven to say goodbye, as if I might never return. Of course, I return, but never to the boy I was. Perhaps I was saying goodbye to him.

I feel a duality, a dueling in me.

At one pole, I feel responsibility: the Orthodox Zionist Rabbi Kook wrote of the Jewish soldier, that he fights for a State of ge'ula, redemption. When we left Egypt after 400 years of slavery, we were liberated and redeemed. This is whom and what I was defending, the redemption of the Jewish people. The _rav_ said that the uniform of the Jewish soldier is like the elegant, pure robe of the holy Cohanim, the Temple priests. Like them, we should represent purity and dedication, the purity and preservation of the Jewish people. That I am a Cohen, this meant more for me. This spiritual sense of becoming a soldier, of course, to an extreme, can become fascism. Even in righteousness, the middle way, temperance, is best.

The other pole of my inner duel is <u>catastrophe</u>: my soul doesn't need to go to the army! My soul wants theater, music, literature, the beginnings of poetry.

All this I feel as I bid goodbye to my rooms.

Then a strange happening as dawn's "rosy fingers" reaches through the window pane. I piss blood. Blood! I feel that my whole body is embattled. You know, we have an idiom of the early <u>chalutzim</u>, pioneers, that they were so powerfully dedicated to building the State, they pissed blood, so strong was Zionism in their blood. So, here I piss blood. This stops the first day of <u>Tironut</u>.

Yeshiva is odd soldier preparation. We <u>are</u> prepared for the army: which unit, the history of battles, heroes. But against this, it seemed, we were taught how to live holy lives.

Rebellion or Justice?

I strengthen myself through this. At twenty, I am two years older than most recruits. I go through basic training, really pass through it with a sense of perspective, a peacefulness, an inner smile. Early on, I feel another kind of duality: as I do all sorts of activities—athletics, running meaninglessly—I feel as if I am watching myself <u>and</u> others from an outside perspective, floating just slightly above things; like in Chagall.

<u>Some</u> of my commanders notice: I don't get rattled like the others, I don't become robot-like, terror-filled; I don't relinquish my humanness. They hate it.

For some of my <u>khevre</u>, my floating attention strengthens them; others are irritated. It is like a game that I play even as I don't play.

You know, with <u>Hesder</u>, we came into basic training as a group. This opposes the approach of the commanders in basic training. Two basic principles from Roman times the commanders use in <u>tironut</u>: divide and rule. Then again, I am older than some of my officers.

What bothers me most is seeing my <u>khevre</u> being humiliated (<u>mushpal</u>), broken. I recall my responsibility to my uncle, <u>mesoog ra'u'i</u>, to endanger myself for my <u>khevre</u>

Here is the strategy that I and two friends choose: we will follow any orders that were professional, not meaningless.

This is a thin line. The officers could experience this as rebellion (<u>mered</u>).

We handle it amongst the <u>khevre</u> like on kibbutz, my roots; we meet.

Some are dominant in the meeting. But I, I recall feeling that now I am following the mythical Eliazer, the Knight fighter of justice. Not rebellion, but justice.

Funny how I first realize this, in fourth grade. There is a fat girl in my class. Others tease her, call her names, chase after her on the way home; some boys take sticks and try to lift her skirt. I would always defend her, everyone knew this. Then one day, I tease her, call her fatty. My teacher is shocked: all she says is "You, Eliazer, the knight of justice?" I never forgot that; never did that again.

In the army, the officers know: first break the weak. In our meeting, the three of us said, "Look, look at him—one of the other boys—look, he is now a robot." We pointed to another, "He, he is almost a slave." The officers practiced abuse, <u>hit'allilut</u>. Then we lose our self-motivation; feel lost. You know, after a while, the group pushes others, pushes violently; "Go faster!" You give up the group friendship, our uniqueness.

At first, the group's reaction that night is silence. Nothing is said or decided, except we all agree that whatever the group decides, we would not tell the officers about our meeting.

One month passes. We work out a plan distinguishing the professional versus the unprofessional commands. What do I mean? You know: when it comes to shooting, maintaining the rifles, the condition of the tanks, we consider these professional. But, a command would suddenly come to run a hillside in 90 seconds, a run that we knew took two and a half, three minutes for the fastest runner. For what?

We meet again. Now, a few want to tell the commanders. We take a drastic move: anyone who rats, we put a kherem on, an excommunication from the group. For us, this is a terrible thing to do; it worked. We vote, it passes.

So, here is how it works. The group agrees that three of us would be judges in the field about which commands were professional, which not. We learn to read situations quickly, then signal secretly to the chinuch toran, the lead private, the one who leads the group in an exercise. In the middle of a shooting exercise, the commander barks, "Run this path in 1.5 minutes!" This would take the fastest 3 minutes and the clumsiest 4 minutes. We run . . . very, very slowly; we all arrive after the fat guy who finishes at 4.5 minutes.

The commanders aren't stupid. They figure out what's going on. They abuse us more. This strengthens us.

One of the group weakens. "Yoram," a friend of mine too. But he thinks, this is dangerous what we are doing. He is always tense; he is a Yekke (literally of German background; figuratively uptight). So, one day we see that he is about to pass the fat guy in the group. Two of the biggest guys in the troop grab Yoram's arms, his shoulders, hold him back. We all finish behind Big Benny.

But, now this feels to me cruel. We are deciding to be strong vis-à-vis the officers, but we are strong as a group against the individual. This feels wrong to me. Things are getting more complicated for my simple mind. Now, I feel we are abusing the Yekke. "I can feel freedom, but he not?" I ask myself. Finally, he gives up on his volition and joins us.

Our commander doesn't know what to do. He threatens. If we don't run faster, beat 1.5 minutes, for instance, then he would run us until we did. But, we say to him, "You can't run us all night, because you are required to give us six hours sleep; so only until bedtime."

The commanders call a few of us in, eight of the thirty of us. They have a proposal for our kvutzah. Usually, we get Shabbat off. Now, what this means, for instance, if you are stationed near Eilat, that after hitching home starting Friday, you get home in time to sleep most *of Shabbat, then hitch back after Shabbat. If you are Orthodox, you do noting but sleep on Shabbat; if you were not Orthodox, you might sleep, but could also go out with your khevre. So, the commanders say that they would have a competition among the kvutzot: whichever kvutzah is the fastest, the best would get a four-day pass for all thirty in the group. They figure we would go for the prize.*

Now, I say to myself: our motivation for being a good soldier should come from within. Like Rav Kook wrote, we would fight as a sense of obligation to the renewal of the Jewish people. What the officers suggest offends me: they want us to be motivated by an external prize. How capitalistic!

We meet again, decide that we would do our best, give it all, but refuse the prize.

And we did it! We prevail as a group over all the others.

It is humiliating for the officers at the ceremony. They called in the Lt. Colonel to give the prize. We step forward and announce that we would refuse the prize; that we gave our best only to be good soldiers. You know, physically, we weren't in such good shape; but we beat them all. While we feel embarrassed for the Lt. Colonel, we feel like prostitutes that they would bribe us so.

The commanders are shocked; the rest of the recruits, shocked. The commanders feel that we are jeopardizing the whole system.

Tank training takes six months: two months is basic training— what I just described to you; two months is getting acquainted with tanks and tank warfare; two months learning to fight, then we are readied for battle.

Here is the overall structure of manpower. Four guys, a tzevet, make a tank crew; three tanks make a unit (makhlaka) and eleven tanks make a plugah. To be effective in battle, you must be tightly organized so you don't get in each other's way. You fight as one.

The commanders who come through this experience with us in basic training are changed by the experience, to trust internal motivation. One commander in particular is a formerly religious fellow, now secular (Khozer b'sh'elah, one who returns to questioning). He falls in love with us. He says that our group turns him around.

Then something happens in our second two months, something within our kvutzah. A change within the group, changes me. A few guys take advantage of our approach, decide independently which commands to follow or not. One fellow doesn't want to carry his gun all the time in camp; leaves it behind by his bunk; another decides in the desert heat midday, that he would nap under the shade of the tank. This is one of the first things you learn never to do; don't go under the tank without informing someone. Only because one of the khevre sees him as the tank is starting, is he awakened in time.

I feel that the responsibility to address this is on my shoulders, since I started this approach. We could tell the Lieutenant about this, but agree to turn to the kvutzah; we are responsible for each other. Feelings run high: the kvutzah referrs to such activities as "criminal," endangering not only the individual, but also the kvutzah. Everyone agrees that we should have consensus about which commands to follow and which not; except one fellow. As it turns out, after we serve our 1 1/2 years active service and were to return to the yeshiva to study, he leaves our kvutzah.

Things begin to work in our favor. One commander decides to teach me a lesson, break me: he cancels my weekend leave for no substantive reason; my Lieutenant hears about this, reverses the decision so that I could go home; makes the sergeant stay on base instead. Later, the Lieutenant recommends that I should be advanced to mefaked.

But at the end of the second two months, we are given a week break before starting the last two months of training. We will be sent to the Jordan Valley to become serious fighters. And the story of our kvutzah and its overall success, our emphasis on internal motivation to train and become soldiers, spreads. We are euphoric. We do not know what awaits us in the Jordan Valley.

* * *

I go to Bekaa knowing that my last officer recommends that I be sent to officer training. I realize only near the end of my two months training that my new officers want to break my spirit as a "tankist."

Again, the Romans taught in military technique, to conquer, one must divide: divide and conquer. This tactic our new officers adopt: take the three of us who had organized our unit; separate us from our brotherhood.

Back then, I would say our commander was the Devil *himself. (Here, he laughs, he has a way of being charming about his travails.) A fine guy, a fine guy . . . But he had come from our Yeshiva, had left Orthodoxy, had a "thing" against Orthodox soldiers.*

At the time, I say näively to him that my last commander thought I would make a good officer.

My new commander is a big guy, strong. He leans towards me, very close, like this. (Eliaz leans over the table with a cold threatening pose, forehead bent and eyes peering upwards into mine.) *He looks into my eyes, grasps me by the shoulders so that I feel his breath's warmth. He says, "I will do this for you* very, very *hard."*

I don't understand this at the time. I think he means that he would work hard with me to help me become an officer.

Ha.

I'm a very strong person. Yet, he broke me a couple of times.

I am the shortest in the unit. You know, when your muscles are limited, your spirit has to be great. And, my officer tells me that he wants me to be the totchan *on the tank: load the cannon,* and *learn the machine gun,* and *use the internal and external radios. He says that he wants me to be "number one." And, in his usual style, when he sees me worn, exhausted, he leans towards me and whispers, "I will make you . . . like a tiger, a* tiger*." It is an impossible mission, I feel. Yet, I think he is complimenting me.*

The big event is when we were told that we are hosting some American visitors, many Daddy Warbucks. There are four of us in a Merkava. Since I am the smallest, I move around a lot, like a monkey in a cage. It is like Hollywood: bombing, shooting, noises, targets exploding; a good show, like Metro Goldwyn Mayer. There could have been that lion roaring at the beginning of the show. At the end, we all jump out, doff our helmets, hold them beneath our arms and stand at attention by height. The Americans approach, applauding, and one, a businessman, comes to me. Towering, he

pats me on the head and turns to the commander, saying, "You
must have picked this guy because he's small; good for a tight fit."
I laugh, as did we all.

My laugh is a force. I meet guys from my unit later who
remember my laugh. Once, I pick up a _trempist_, a hitchhiker,
a young soldier, who tells me that my laugh had saved him from
despair. It's a family trait: my brothers have this.

I even have this honor: being punished by my commander for
laughing. I ask, "How will you punish me for laughing?"

"You must write an essay about laughter!" he commands.

My brothers give me perspective on my experiences. About my
commander they explain that he is not really _the_ Devil, but a simple
guy, _am ha'aretz_.

But when the other units are sent to Hebron, an honor, our
commander keeps us in basic training. Usually a unit guards three
stations: he tells us to guard nine. We sleep four hours nightly; we
know that the Chief of Staff insists that all soldiers get six hours
nightly. Our colonel lives in a West Bank settlement. You know a
colonel; he has three "felafels" on his shoulder. One of the privates
writes to complain to our colonel about our treatment—that we are
getting only four hours sleep, guarding too many stations, being
held back from active duty—and, our treatment gets worse. The
commander starts us on arbitrary forced runs. We still laugh at how
we are being treated, but we have lost our sense of leadership.

The climax of our course is a three day trip testing our
navigational skills. Navigation is critical, especially at night. This
is a test of our team and is the first test of our commander. He fails;
he was smoking marijuana, I guess to relax himself. Well, he gets
too relaxed: he got us lost. But he blames me for the failure; insists
that I should repeat the entire course. Well, here my _khevre_ did help:
they write to the captain. I hear my commander arguing with the
captain. In the end, they compromise: I am permitted to pass my
course, am sent to an active _kravi_ unit, but the commander sends
me jogging the rest of the day. I have short legs, you see, but they
still reach the ground, good enough for running.

Finally, I am in a good unit, called <u>Yiftakh</u>. You remember him? In <u>Nevi'im</u> (Prophets), he was a bastard son, cast out of the tribe. Then, when Judea was being threatened militarily, they called back Yiftakh. Like Othello, he was an outcast, but a vital general. Yiftakh vanquishes in the battlefield and thanks G-d by saying that he will sacrifice the first living thing of his flock he sees upon his return. His only daughter is so excited to hear that he is returning that she runs from the tent, dancing, playing the timbrel to greet him first. You can imagine Yiftakh's horror when he sees his only daughter. He tries to renege on his pledge, but <u>his daughter</u> insists that he must follow through his word to G-d. She asks only a month to go to the mountains with her friends to sing and to pray. You know, there are <u>parashnuyot-perushim</u> (discussions of the passage) that point out that the text never says at the end that Yiftakh kills her—its ambiguous. I want to believe that like Abraham and Isaac, at the last moment, there is a reprieve. (Eliaz pauses here, looks at me hopefully: he is not sure whether this is convincing.)

So, that's the name of our unit. Everything is biblical in this land.

*   *   *

When childhood intersects soldierhood

He wants to speak about April 2002, serving during this Intifada, in Hebron, encircling Shechem. This was traumatic. But to explain his reactions, he needs to tell about where and how he grew up. Bear with us.

My childhood, its memories, its taste, invades moments of my soldiering. This doesn't always make me a good soldier. Perhaps a better man, but who knows. This is for G-d to judge. Sometimes <u>how</u> I was taught to behave as a child, as a young man, conflicts with what I am commanded to do. One example is microscopic, *to the outside world, but to me it is magnified. The second almost jeopardizes my unit. At least I think so.*

Abraham's sons

Here I confess: this year, when we read about our father Abraham, his expelling Ishmael, "divorcing" him from his family, casting him out with a skin of water and possible death in the desert, I felt a pain in my chest. A pain that I imagine Abraham felt. He had two sons and was told, first by Sarah, then by God, to send forth from his tent Hagar and Ishmael. Ishmael, the forefather of my cousins the Arabs; Isaac, the one who brought laughter to his mother, remained in his home and arms.

We Jews have lived or lingered in Palestine even after the Romans murdered some one million and others invaded Yet, our active ingathering and living together with the Arabs has been some eighty to 120 years. Almost thirty years, I have lived on the hills of Shomron and Yehuda with no fear, until the last half dozen years. Now, I tremble in fear as I travel the tunnel road to Jerusalem with my wife and four children.

I was born and spent my young childhood in Petah Tikvah; it means, "Opening of Hope." The Arab town of Malabas was a part of it. Even then, in the early 70's, Palestinians from the Shomron worked in our town in various services. Even in the Yom Kippur war, when my father is called up for army, we live without fear from our Arab neighbors. One of my first words, which I still taste in the back of my throat, was the "viuuu—viuu" of the emergency ambulances that ran through the town during the war. But it was a sound of excitement, one that I played with in my mouth; it was not with fear.

Our roads were bourgeois and calm. The Arab sellers would pass, some by foot, some pulling and old horse and wagon, calling out for sale in a heavy Arab accent, "Alte Zachen, Alte Zachen," the Yiddish words for old things for sale. Some of the kids in my neighborhood would call back teasingly, "Old Arabs, old and dangerous; Old Arab women, also dangerous, put them together and they have Old Arab children." Some of the old Arab sellers got angry.

Once, I am running with a group; they began jeering an Arab. As we pass him, one boy throws a ripe tomato at him, a tomato from the boy's lunch pail. I freeze in place, as if my feet suddenly grew roots. I watch. The old man wipes the rotten stub from his face, glares angrily at me, folds up his old clothes for sale, leaves. His look of insult in his eyes, I have not been able to erase from my memories.

These are prehistoric memories from Petach Tikvah. Then in the summer of 1980, we moved to "M'oorav", a moshav in the Shomron. From here, my memories are organized successively. My father joins the Yishuv night guard; sometimes he takes me, a seven year old.

M'oorav grows with us. We children feel as if we were American Indians, exploring our own wilderness: we count each flower, collect along the paths, watch the bold deer approach us, the butterflies. We flirt with snakes. We have basketball tournaments, hot dogs on the grill.

I wonder then, "Why are we guarding the fence around the Yishuv, against whom? Who decides who enters the guarded gate?"

We want to cross the fence to go out; explore the other side.

The fence advances as M'oorav grows. What was once outside, now becomes a part of our moshav. Suddenly it's not as interesting, the outside-now-within, as it had been when it was on the other side of the fence.

Sometimes we kids would make a "camp" next to the fence, peer on the world outside. The changing seasons make the year more meaningful; the plowing, the sowing, reaping and gathering, especially the date and olive harvests. We look with envy upon the harvests. Families upon families, Arabs, gather around the olive trees. Children and elders spread gray sacks on the ground; boys grasp long canes and beat the branches until the rain of black olives cease. Then, even after the olive shower, the teens climb the trees to pick the few olives that cling to their limbs, as if reluctant to be released.

Once, some Arab boys approach the fence and invite us to join. They signal us to follow and we find a hole in the fence. This becomes an opening in both directions. We go to the great almond tree behind the grocery on the outside of the fence. Behind the tree trunk is a small area where the Arab shepherds gather to drink from a faucet behind the grocery.

They call us their new friends. Remember how when Yakov returned from twenty years exile, he and Esau came together to bury Isaac? So I feel with my Arab friends.

After this first "infiltration," life changes. We bring more friends from the M'oorav, show them the hole in the fence; go to the almond tree. (You remember that my second son's name is "Almond"? So, now you know.) About 100 meters from there among the orchards of figs and almonds, we find an ancient well. The flocks are gathered there in the evening in the mornings; we meet more of these young shepherds. We hear echoing to us the nasal, mournful voices of the muezzin. At the mouth of the well, I met Hasan and Eli, twins from the neighboring village, who become my close friends.

The adults from M'oorav start to follow us children. They enter the life on the outside of the fence. On Shabbat eves they to hike around M'oorav. Once, twice during the week, the adults go with us to the linen store. The owner honors us with Tabulah and bitter olive oil.

Looking back, I stare at the memories, something primordial about those relationships. Something beyond words. There is an understanding that we are there, this is a territory to be shared by us; this is organized in heaven, immanent. This is during those years of war and peace in the Galil. We are hardly touched.

Whomever shames a fellow man

In basic training, I am stationed near M'oorav. Fatimah, an Arab woman from the village cleans our base; over time, she becomes part of the landscape of our unit, part of our staff.

One day, in the midst of a lecture on military tactics, our training commander, enters, calls down of the student soldiers, steps out with him. After a few minutes, he returned, his hand resting on the student's shoulder, sober and also with Fatimah. He tells us that the student had called her the "big boobed and fat bellied" lady, spat upon her.

The soldier, this fellow student, apologizes before all of and is given extra duty for the following week. And, he is assigned to Fatmah to cleaning duty for the brigade! The officer then apologizes to Fatmah and pats the soldier lightly on his back. He gives us a short speech that none forget:

"Beloved man, each of whom is made in God's image," he begins, "Whomever shames a person, is like spilling blood. Every man, even foreigners, every neighbor is our fellow man."

Isaac and Ishmael in Hebron

So what does this have to do with my being a soldier, you are wondering? I know that you came to hear about soldiering. In our April 2002 military actions during the Intifada, after the Park Hotel in Netanya is bombed by Palestinians, murdering families sitting at seder, my commander's words echoed in my head.

In Hebron, we are stoned by Palestinians, probably kids. My young officer shouts, "Chase them!" He begains running, yells, "Here they are! Over here!" We run over a ridge in Hebron, chasing with our tanks, then on foot as alleys narrow. A dubious battle, an impossible target, for these alleys consume its children, like a Moloch. Our officer is ablaze in anger. I think he is looking for some sacrificial victim, since we can't get the stone throwers of Ishmael. He shouts again, "Follow me!" and before we can catch our breath, we continue. In the army, you're told, you do.

We arrive at one alley. On the wall before us is graffiti in Palestinian Arabic with flags of PLO colors. "Ahah!", my commander raises his fist as if ready to punch someone. At the end of the alley sits an aged Arab on a chair surrounded by children playing around him. "Move!" and he presses us forward. Next to the Arab man rests his walking cane. Our officer's voice is shrill: "Who drew the slogans! Erase them!" The Arab points to his feet, then to the walking cane. His children begin gathering around him. I whisper to my officer, "Let's leave." He whips around to me, says nothing, but I understood that I should be silent.

"Now! You and the kids erase this!" I look at my officer, who now looks more like a young boy. "I don't care how you do it!" Then, then (it shames me to tell you this), my officer grabs the chair, pulls it from under the Arab. He falls. He groans, silently signals to his children. I have *to stop my self from pouncing on my officer. Now, all my upbringing, my youth in M'oorav, education in Torah, stand before me now; I feel I am being tested. To shame a man, is like to spill his blood.*

The children return with cleaning utensils; their father limps ahead, towards the graffiti. They try scraping off the paint. My officer and a soldier stand, amused by the situation. I see that the old man was about to fall. I take the chair, approach him. I reach under his arms, seat him.

My officer screams at me. My officer grabs me by the shoulders, "You maniac settler! What do you think you are doing?" But I don't hear him. Instead, in my ears echo with my childhood memories.

*   *   *

Shooting at the Birds of Nablus (or Shechem)

A second time, my childhood in M'oorav intrudes on my soldiering. This is not so simple.

In five minutes, I am promoted from Eliaz the soldier, to lieutenant, to major. At the edge of the Balata refugee camp of Shechem in April 2002, I find a time and a place for trauma on me, on my family on the Palestinians.

A few days later, we continue talking at Tmol Shilshom Cafe ("Day Before Yesterday Cafe"), Yehuda Amichai's regular place to write, read his poetry. The entrance doors are double, narrow. To pass in, even if you are slim, you have to sidle through, torque a bit, enter obliquely. In Amichai's corner, to the right, is the armchair, now offering up its stuffing where Amichai's arms once rested. It faces the doors, welcoming newcomers with these open, frayed arms. Three photos of Amichai sit above and to the left of the chair. An oak, carved round table holds two espressos and at its opposite edge, an upright chair, its upholstered, once-embroidered seat almost as frayed as Amichai's.

Eliaz's elfin head peaks between the doors, then he pivots right to join me.

Again, I think, "He is short, too short I think to myself to be an elite soldier." I notice his crown of curls topped by a *kippah*: this gives him almost a tonsured and cherubic look. His cheeks suggest angelical chubbiness, but he is not. He is solid, square to the ground, moves quickly and with certitude.

His smiles, his poetic plays with words, break through . . . even about Balata refugee camp.

I told you last, when the Park Hotel in Netanya was bombed on Pesach, when it pancaked on dozens of people sitting at Seder, I knew in my stomach we would have war.

Our fourth is born, our first daughter. We move into a new apartment in the kibbutz: two bedrooms. You know, Pirke Avot, states: who has built a new house, planted a field or just married should not go to war, for he may be killed and another man could occupy his house, lie with his wife, reap what he has sowed. Efrat (his wife) doesn't believe I will be called up, doesn't understand. I know I will be called up.

All the archetypes are there: house, wife, fields—places that hold you, contain you, of warmth, of growth, of hope and future.

But in its wisdom the Pirke Avot continues: if the people of Israel are in danger, even a groom on his first wedding night must go to protect Israel.

In its wisdom.

Worst is the day of giyus, (draft), waiting for call-up.

Efrat still doesn't believe. Erev Pesach, the first day in the new house and also Shabbat—a double holiday. I have to work on kibbutz. Oh you know, it is holiday, but this is kibbutz. One has to work. I request work in the small guest house, do the most mundane jobs: clean the floors, the toilets, scrub the walls—so I won't have to think about what I am doing.

Then I think. This could be the last day of my life with the children—why am I working, not spending the last few moments with them? Then, I debate myself (I do this sometimes). I decide that I should keep life as normal as possible. One thing is different, the children notice: I take my cellular phone along, a machine I loathe and avoid. It is only for army emergencies. I feel it on my belt, touch it. It stays silent. I see _khevre_ leaving the kibbutz, in uniform—first a few at a time, then in groups. I'm thinking, "When will they call me already?" I feel as if I have a mad puppy scrambling in my belly. I decide not to push down the feelings; I let them come forward, pay attention to them, stand up to them. I yearn for the phone to ring; it would be a relief. Once it rings, I have two hours to pack, and get to whatever base they order. Look, it's at most six hours from one end of the country to another and I live in the center, by Jerusalem; I know I can get to Gaza or the West Bank within that time, no problem. But what to tell my children and Efrat's reactions?

I get a "gift," a heads-up. One of the kibbutz members is in Army Intelligence. Sees my name listed for call up and where; tips me off; phone call unnecessary.

And then a funny moment from my two older sons. You know that my six year old has a speech impediment. He sees me in the uniform and asks, "To the army, abba (La'tzava, abba)?" But "La'tzava" (army) comes out as "La'tzaga" (play, performance). So, his younger brother, Shaked (Almond) hears this and repeats, "To the play, abba, to the play (La'tzaga, abba)?"

"Of course," I said. "I have this costume, like on Purim and I will ride in a tank, like Mordechai rode on the horse on Purim!" Denial—I use it. Whenever I call home, I tell them how the play is going, riding in the tank. When they ask about the noises in the background—the firing—"Just like Purim, we have noisemakers."

We haven't had such a massive call-up since 73. We know this way this was going to be serious, real fighting. Efrat cries; she's in shock.

I am living a myth, a bad myth. In Hebrew, we call this "t'ruf Yehudi," Jewish madness.

So, how I became a major in five minutes, you're still wondering?

We are stationed in Shechem at the edge of the refugee camp, a major origin for suicide bombers. Not Jenin, _baruch ha Shem_ (thank G-d). The disasters at Jenin with 23 soldiers killed, you know, came because the army _entered_ the camp to avoid civilian injuries, did house-to-house searches. Deadly.

So, our Colonel said, first, "Don't enter the camp!" Second, if ever there is *any* question of a face-off between Israeli soldiers and Palestinians; shoot, don't wait. You will see how this becomes my problem, when I become transitory major, a mini major: it is because of my background, growing up in a mixed Jewish-Palestinian village and my education to act respectfully to the Palestinians. I believe that we, descendants of Abraham's sons, shall live side-by-side.

Our job: keep the terrorists *in* the camp. That means, keep *everyone* in their homes. We too are imprisoned. Four days we stay in the tanks: four men in each tank; five in the lieutenant's. You know, you pee in a bottle? You sleep like this, crumpled where you sit. (He crouches comically, head below his knees, on the kitchen chair.) Except our lieutenant doesn't sleep for the first three days. He's responsible for his tank and four others, his *gurim*, puppies. Such words, *gurim*, humanizes the experience. We *are* like puppies, turning to our lieutenant's tank, snuggling up to it when needed.

My lieutenant comes to me, asks me to take his position for one hour so he can sleep. Nahum is great. There are two of us Orthodox in the unit—me, the Ashkenazi and Avinoam the Sephardi, also in my tank. Avinoam is a *bachur* (young fellow), my *totchan* (artillery gunner). So, Nahum says that he believes he will have no problems, since he has two "rabbis," Ashkenazi and Sephardi, in his unit. For an hour he will sleep and I will be "lieutenant," in lieu of him. O.K., I can do that. You know how "Fiddler on the Roof" starts in Hebrew? As Tevya enters stage left, pulling his milk cart—for his horse is sick that day—he announces, "Today, I am a horse." So, today, I will be lieutenant—for one hour.

Then, on the secure intercom, I hear that my major is going back from the line to consult with the Lieutenant Colonel. He calls to my lieutenant's radio. I don't think my major really hears that it is my voice responding, not my lieutenant's. So, now, I am a major, responsible for some 90 men and tanks, with a zone of responsibility. I am 28, a kibbutznik, a poet, and now a "major" in five minutes. I almost said "actor" instead of major. (He is chuckling here.) Like how Shaked said I was in a play; so I'll be an actor.

The *balagan* (commotion) always begins the same way, surreptitiously. Then it escalates, systematically. Maybe the Palestinians *"know" that it is only little Eliaz who was "major" for an hour. Anyhow, what you first notice is the little kids darting between the houses. At first singly. Then you see like shooting stars, zipping across an alley, or like ping pong balls, ricocheting from building to building. Sometimes you actually see the boys peer out a window or door, looking at you for an opportunity. If you do nothing, they escalate.*

I do . . . nothing.

What to do? Our orders are not to enter the camp, to use artillery and machine gun fire, at first over their heads. If need be, we call in the air force. But above all, keep them from organizing and transporting arms and men.

The Palestinians use the children as a test; for us it is a sign that terrorists are preparing something. Then older boys, maybe 15, 16 start appearing <u>with</u> the children. They begin to make noise.

My artillery man, Avinoam awakens, startled. He sits below me to shoot the artillery with two hands, like this. (He demonstrates: thumbs set parallel, facing upwards). He also can reach for the machine gun. He asks permission to shoot over their heads. Here, I have tugs in my heart from childhood, from what my Rav taught me about respecting and living with the Arabs; from how a classmate threw tomatoes at a 70-year old Palestinian with a cane at his rag stand, and how our Rav came out of the yeshiva to criticize the boys. All this swims up to my consciousness at that moment. I say, it is not yet <u>mutzdak</u>, justified. (The word comes from the root, <u>tzedek</u>, justice.) We were trained <u>tohar haneshek</u>, the purity of our gun, to be used only in self defense, I don't think yet we are at that point.

Avinoam sees me struggle. He says with a touch of derision, "You're like Rav Fruman." He's right. Fruman is a very Orthodox man, a poet and a settler and the rabbi of a the West Bank town, who negotiates with everyone, including Hamas, for coexistence. He dreams that Jew and Arab will live side-by-side. He tries to talk to everyone "<u>be'govah eyna'im</u>" (eye-to-eye, respectfully). Avinoam is right, and it stung me a bit. He catches me.

Nu, so of course, things escalate. The worrisome sign is when the "pregnant" women join the boys and teens. Always the same presentation: the pregnant women carry two heavy opaque black garbage bags, filled, dragging the ground. Now, I say to myself, then to Avinoam, "They too, like ourselves have been cooped up for almost four days. Perhaps, they are just carrying out zevel, garbage." But Avinoam looks up at me, I mean, throws me a look, and I know what he means. We know that ammunition and Rocket Propelled Grenades are transported in these black "Husky" bags by pregnant women. Here is tragedy, from the booby-trapped boy in Jenin who kills himself to kill our soldiers, from other settings, we push ourselves to remember that each child (or pregnant woman) is a potential terrorist. Now, I have a feeling of electricity in one part of my head, of danger; opposing this is all that I was taught by my father, mother, Rav, Torah, of how a man should conduct his life well. A paradox—perhaps if I hadn't been raised in a mixed village, I would not have such a conflict—and my conflict jeopardizes my unit.

Avinoam begs permission to fire—above the heads. "So what," he asks, "if I knock down a few pigeons? In the Arab shuk, they serve the pigeons as dinner; we could serve them dinner. Also, the Palestinians don't know from the sounds whether we are shooting above or at them—it scares them just the same."

The last "stone" is when I saw teen age girls in pairs carrying tzinorot, each maybe a meter, you know the large gauge plastic pipes for sewers? The girls are one at the front, one at the back, shuttling between buildings. This is not zevel anymore. From Intelligence, we know that these are used to transport both RPG's—lethal to tanks—or booby traps placed beneath tanks and detonated remotely.

"Now!" I command Avinoam. "Now, shoot at birds!"

With this, Nahum startles awake. He asks, "What, what?" I tell him what we are doing and he falls asleep, never remembering that he had awakened. But my major—the real one—hears our firing and calls. This time, when I tell what is happening, he realizes that it's me, mini-major Eliaz, not the lieutenant.

Once we started shooting, the Palestinians scatter; like mice, they either hide or escape the camps.

But, Shechem, once Abraham's home, is a deep trauma for me. This is the first time I see death up close. Before, I knew that when

I shot artillery, some died. But now I see death. And to my family, it is also a kind of trauma—we move into a new house the Shabbat of Pesach, I am called to war. For a month I am gone. The feeling is like the roof had collapsed on our heads.

You know the poem I wrote about driving through the security tunnels into Jerusalem safely, as if being birthed? Well, I was thinking not only of myself, but also when I was driving with Efrat and the children.[4]

Shechem changed me, changed my family, perhaps in a way so that we will never be the same, never completely shalem, whole.

* * *

His closing words pealed in my memory: for in the story of Jacob—as he is returning to see his father and mother after 20 years, fearing his brother—the passage closes, that he arrived shalem in Shechem.

---

[4] Ironically, tragically, that night, after we met, I learn that a mother and her two children were critically wounded on this road as her husband was driving. I learn about this as my friend, Myron Joshua, was traveling the bus home from Jerusalem. His bus was delayed by roadblocks. Since the bus was so delayed, it drops him off about a 20 minute walk on the unlit road to his kibbutz, around 11:30 p.m. Myron calls me and we talk as he walks back at one point almost stumbling off a cliff in the dark. He asks that I stay on the phone in case something should happen to him. As we talk about Franz Rosenzweig, Levinas, Walter Benjamin, above the nape of my neck is a gnawing concern—what to do if something happens to him? I am irritated that he goes to a lecture on coffee in Tel Aviv that evening, jeopardizing his life. I feel like a tenuous thread to safety (not even as thick as a lifeline, rather like the thin blue *techellet* of the *tzitzit*) on this phone, as if literally staying connected would protect him, yet knowing that this is a fiction.

Eliaz Kohen agreed that I could translate and publish four poems he wrote during the second Intifada. While Eliaz's earlier poetry is known for its Orthodoxy and erotism, and his active dialogues with G-d, these speak to his transformation during the Intifada. I thank Myron Joshua and Eliaz for assisting in translation.

The first poem some will recognize as a take off from the Shma prayer, "Hear, Oh Israel, the Lord is One . . . ." But, Eliaz now speaks to the Lord.

Hear, Oh Lord

(For Days of Awe)
Eliaz Kohen (Trans. Naftali Moshe Szajnberg)

Hear, Oh Lord, Israel is Your nation, Israel, is one;

And You shall love Israel, Your nation,
With all Your heart,
With all Your soul,
With all Your might,
And these children who are slain for You each day
Will be on Your heart
Study them sharply in Your vaulted heavens
Speak them:
When you sit in Your house
When You walk Your path
When You lie down and arise
Bind these as *teffilin* signs
On your hands (like neon blue Auschwitz tatoos) and they shall be as Frontlets between
Your eyes (like the sniper's clean shot);
And You shall write them (in blood) on Your *mezzuzot* of Your home
And Your gates.

This poem is a play on the traveler's prayer; it came to Eliaz as he drove, trembling within, with his children and wife, through the tunnels to Jerusalem. There is an open area, once a "shooting gallery" as one exits the second tunnel.

Traveler's Prayer: Through the Tunnel Road To Jerusalem

Eliaz Kohen, (Trans. Naftali Moshe Szajnberg)

May it be Your will
King, who listens to the needy;
Guardian over all breeches and hideouts
Save me from all hardship of the road

Walk me in Peace;
Escort me in Peace;
Guard me from all types of Stones,
Ambushes, blockades, shooters, infiltrators,
Evil-doers at road blocks, those death cursers;
From all hateful leers; tsunamis that swamp
The world.
(And in Darkness, add: Guard me from Night's evil intents)
That You will help me arrive to grasp my goal,
Alive. And in joy and peace
And, give me birth from the tunnel/orifice to Jerusalem
Listen to the travelers' prayers before you,
In mercy.

Eliaz sent this poem to me, written as he waited on the bus leaving Jerusalem, with his note appended, that it will not be his last poem.

Last Attack

Eliaz Kohen, (Trans Naftali Moshe Szajnberg)

In the clacking bus, I sit,
To be exploded,
I write my last poem.
Soon, all will rise in smoke
And launch, like Elijah's Fiery Chariot,
Dispersed in every
Direction, to be united,
To join thin smoke clouds
In the Heavenly vault, whisping into
Chimney ashes of Auschwitz days.
Below, of course, you will wail for me
A Keening will be raised, a lament
That one of the poets
(or the Rabbis) will shout in the bitter voice of a shofar:
"Where's the tongue, once quick with wisdom's pearls,
Now licking asphalt."
Before the grave is closed, you'll read (in my presence)
This last poem.
My whispered cry will flow forever,
Along with Rabin's Blood-stained "Song of Peace."

NATHAN SZAJNBERG

This is the first of a two-part poem, in which Eliaz engages with
Ishmael and his descendants.

Ishmael (and I)

Eliaz Kohen (Trans. Naftali Moshe Szajnberg)

Ishmael stones me
"Words"
He shouts
Stony words, "And where were you
When I was cast out with dawn, a skin of water?"
"Our sons,"
Shouts Ishmael
"Will writhe in our wombs (or scramble in our midst) and will
    serve one over the other
They will carry (Jacob's) ladders, angels, marry women
Stoning each other with memories.

*   *   *

When this soldier enters his tank, when he patrols his kibbutz
at night, when he surrounds Shechem, or pursues rock-throwers in
Hebron, Eliaz does so with these poems and dreams in his heart.

KNIGHT OF JUSTICE

Zionism, Shmionism . . .
I am for my Chevra.

I run out of videotape during our interview. Pinchas wants to walk with me to Radio Shack. I suggest, he could wait in the office. Read a magazine. He prefers company. At the store, he is delighted by the Zip Zaps — miniature radio-controlled rechargeable cars with replaceable, interchangeable bodies, mag wheels, whip antenna, and monster tires. He wants two, one for his cousin, so that they can play together in their apartment hallway. But, he won't buy now; he'd return to take his time (not mine) to pick the right models, right colors.

He is tall, topping six feet, balding and tightly-cropped remaining hair. He walks with military bearing, even though his midsection reveals he has been a civilian for a few years. He smiles readily, but when pondering, his upper lift rests heavily on the other. There is an edginess to some of his humor, which works well in Israel, but needs to be held back with American colleagues. Yet, a boyishness, a liveliness peaks through when he speaks.

My sister says that I still have the 7 year old boy in me, even now at 30.

A 7 year old boy?

In Jenin, my C. O. had me guard the body of a Palestinian criminal executed by fellow Palestinians. I had to guard it until one of our M.D.'s arrived to try to save his life. Otherwise, the Palestinians would return to defile his body. Meanwhile, I stand in the crowded alley of Jenin, Palestinians waiting like jackals to pounce either on this guy's body, or on me.

At fourteen, my father "graduated" from the Lodz ghetto, to Auschwitz along with three buddies. They hung together, only one shot during an escape attempt. My father is proud that he is the only one who was not branded, tattooed by the SS. He brandishes his forearm — clean, pure, his skin. He had decided he would die before letting the SS number him. His growth was stunted by Auschwitz, but not his moral stature.

Much of the interview goes like this, weaving from army, to Auschwitz, from Zip Zaps to morality.

We try to be the most moral army in the world, because of the Nazi experience. I told my father, I told him that I felt the opposite of what he did when German soldiers broke into their houses and took people out. The Palestinians know what they are doing, hiding among children and pregnant women; they know that it demoralizes Jewish soldiers. It's very hard at 2 a.m., pulling a suspected bomb-maker away from his screaming wife and crying children, who tear at your uniform.

But this is a decision only for officers.

The anger comes out because of the rules of engagement: you can't touch a boy throwing rocks, boulders; but after ten hours of stones, you can't stand it. Still, your officer says, "Don't respond."

An army can't fight citizens throughout history. You put an army into impossible situations.

Israel's attitude is to apologize almost always.

You Americans bomb 500 civilians in Afghanistan and the U.S. says, "It's war." Doesn't apologize.

I find at work (at the University physics lab), *I apologize for things when we shouldn't have to. But then I tell my boss, who is from India, that Israel is like the size of the Bay Area compared to all of the U.S. being like Arab lands. He is surprised. Israel had loomed larger in his mind.*

In ten years of (army) service, I never, never saw someone beat a Palestinian citizen. Their leaders treat them worse.

Midway through our first meeting, he becomes comfortable enough to confide that he carries a key fob with his unit's emblem. He bends forward, extends his palm, without handing the fob to me, not just yet. He explains all three symbols: *This is lightning (barak), then the rush of waves (ga'ash) which cross the javelin (ro'makh). They symbolize the three components of our force and also how we fight: Like a bolt of lightening, in overwhelming waves and the accuracy of a javelin to the heart of the enemy.*

Later, I see a photo of his tank, and the emblem of <u>Khativa</u> Seven in the foyer to his apartment, his helmeted head huddled next to a buddy's, out the turret.

I want to enlist at 14 in the residential army academy (p'nimia tzva'it). But my parents are shocked, my mother desolate that I would leave home. Instead, they ask me to enroll in the elite pre-university technical school (beit sefer han'dasi). My parents convince me of the advantages: beit sefer han'dasi had new computers, most graduates went into the technical service—communication corps, intelligence, electronics. But these didn't convince me; I wanted to be in combat. O.K., they even bought me new sneakers. I wouldn't hurt my mother and father, so I agreed.

From han'dasim high school for four years, you're supposed to go to four years of reserves (atudah, for "future"), then three years army service, then two years national service as an officer.

The reserves mean something different in Israel. You are given a few years to attend University, train during vacation and must maintain a 4.0 average; if not, you are called into active service.

But I don't know what I want to study during the four years of atudah, so I choose to go to the army after technical school.

My Kabah? 56. So, I pick the air force. But the doctor found a heart murmur and disqualifies me. Turns out to be benign.

The army sends me into a technical unit; signaling, communications. I won't forget that: three days after I finish my bagrut⁵, I am in the army.

I am sent to a 1 1/2 year course for officer training, that usually takes two years. Thirty people. It is attractive, because it is something new. There is a series of paths (maslulim): three months as a foot soldier, then sergeant training, then three months officer's training in Mitzpeh Ramon⁶, then three months in Khativa 7 in the Golan.

I like the people in the tank battalion. They treat me nicely even though this is the most famous tank brigade in the Golan. Avigdor Kahalani, you know him? In '73, against overwhelming odds and profound losses, he holds back the Syrians for days with minimal support. He keeps them from overwhelming Northern Israel. At one point, when he is trying to help the gunner aim. The gunner sees nothing out his sight: a Syrian tank was right next to them: the gunner just fired.

And I serve with his son, Oz, who is named after the battalion, you know, "courage." It gets into you. We feel we are the best unit (Khativa).

But at 18, you're so influenced by hormones; the only reason you'd do such dangerous things.

Others didn't want this assignment (armored corps): very hard work and less glory than paratroopers (tzankhanim). There is a kind of competition between foot soldiers and tanks.⁷ Also, many didn't want

---

⁵   Bagrut are the vigorous high school graduation exams; the word derives from the same root as "adulthood."

⁶   A hauntingly beautiful, desolate, multihued crater-like formation in the Negev Desert, perhaps forty miles due south of Beer Sheva. Physically, about a kilometer deep, geologically it descends eons.

⁷   Tanks were first used in World War I by the British, who were reluctant to develop these further. The first tanks were like something out of Jules Verne—huffing smoke monsters, which flattened trees and yet vulnerable to getting trapped in ditches. If hit by artillery, they roasted the men inside. The Germans quickly picked up tank engineering that the British lagged, to the German's benefit in World War II.

to go to the Golan, because you only get weekend leave every three weeks. And in the early '90's, the Syrians were a serious threat in the Golan. How serious? My commander wrote a sign on the border: "Not permitted for any <u>live</u> Syrian soldiers to cross the border." Today, of course, the Syrians are much more clever: they invade Lebanon and use the Hezbollah as proxy fighters against Northern Israel.

I don't feel danger while there. But I recall feeling relief of tension when I went home Friday night. Also the training. Training keeps you from recognizing danger.

I am offered another year, a career as an officer. I refuse. After four years five months, I decide to leave. Well, my parents pressure me to leave even as the army tempts me. The army would pay for all my University Bachelor's degree and give me a salary if I pay back with 1 1/2 years of additional service for each year of school. They even want me to get a Masters.

So, my father said, "I'll meet their offer and you don't have to do any service for me."

Look, it wasn't easy. My father is deeply proud of me. The Nazis would taunt him that Jews could build nothing. Instead, my father pronounces, we build not only tall buildings, but also an army. He takes visitors to the Azraeli twin towers[8]. He stands way across the street, my short dad. He cranes his neck and the visitors crane and he points upwards: "See what Jews can build?" Well, my father meant me too. I'm six feet; he's five foot one. He has to crane his neck to talk to me; and he's proud of it — I'm his Azraeli tower, my brother is the other tower. We are his "twin towers," never to fall. Tel Aviv is built on sand dunes; we, upon the Auschwitz's ashes.

But my cousin was killed in the Litani action in '78. His brother had been a hero in the '73 war in my same tank division. And my father complains that I rarely come home — only every three weeks.

---

[8]   These van-der-Rohe-like, twin towers sheathed in shimmering green glass, are the highest in Tel Aviv. After September 11, these twins became a place of anxiety among many Tel Aviv residents; an obvious target.

ZIONISM, SHMIONISM   ⊰55⊱

My mother? Well, she keeps reminding me that I broke my hand seven times when I was a child. She worries I would be prone to accidents in the army.

She didn't understand that <u>because</u> of those fractures I chose to be more responsible. I never got hurt in the army, nor since.

(Seven fractures?)

They started during the '73 war, when my father was away so long fighting the war. Thirty years after Auschwitz, now in his 40's, he was fighting for our lives. I think there is a connection.

Anyhow, it was really <u>my</u> decision: the army wasn't exciting anymore. For me, routine is very bad. I like science; each day isn't routine—always seeking, trying to discover.

Also, my friends are beginning to leave the army.

And I want my freedom. One week, after I left the army, I have an earring and I don't <u>have</u> to share everything.

But my best friends are from the army. Three in particular, I can call now from the US and say, "I need you." Nothing more I need to say and they will be here next day. I pay $300 monthly on phone bills, mostly to them. One is my commander, another was my sergeant for discipline. He's a Druze, the sergeant is the "bad guy," the enforcer. He once saved me from acting badly. He lives in Usfayah, near Kiryat Shemona, the upper finger of Israel. When he heard I was coming to study in the US, he drove four hours to say goodbye.

The best thing that happens to me in the army is my friends. We develop a lot in common: take responsibility, get angry at commanders who don't fight for our needs. You <u>know</u> these people, these friends.

We give our commander our word in the reserves: as long as he doesn't leave, we won't leave. His wife once said that she was jealous sometimes of his closeness to us. One commander, who lived in Netanya, heard that his buddy is building a little home in French Hill, Northern Jerusalem, not the safest neighborhood. He decides he will build a weekend hut next door and his wife said," Fine, you'll have weekends with your buddy."

Look, the army <u>can</u> ruin you, can eliminate your self-confidence—some guys commit suicide.

I grew up very protected, sheltered. I believe that your success or failure is driven by how you parents raised you and I was raised well. But, the army offers responsibility. By age 21, I commanded 50 soldiers—a lot of power and <u>a lot</u> of responsibility: to keep them alive.

*   *   *

No sooner does he talk about leaving the army, Pinchas returns; starts with his army beginnings, then gives a "tour" of the characters in different units, a typology of the guys in his and other units. The guys are what make his army, his experience.

My brother-in-law, Shlomi—well, my ex-brother-in-law—was wounded in '82. Shot on the third day of action. He gave me good advice when I decide to enter the army at 18. I really was tired of studying.

Shlomi taught me:

1. *the difference between officer and sergeant: officers come and go; your sergeant stays; stay with him;*
2. *physical preparedness—run, carry boulders, endure;*
3. *Prepare your dog tags;—one around your neck, another tied to your boot. If your head's blown off, they identify you by your boot tag. Your leg blown off? (A wry smile here.) Hopefully, your head is still on;*
4. *Clean and operate your weapon;*
5. *<u>Tohar haneshek</u>, purity of your gun.*

Purity? Means you use it only for defense. Like the army's name, "haganah," means "the defense."

I told you that I picked a battle unit. Easier was intelligence or electronics/communications. But I like challenges. And my parents always taught me: "Do the best you can, or don't do it." It was OK with them if I decided I didn't want to do something, but once we agreed, we should do our best. (Of course, if they asked me to do something, I never said,"no" to them; I took it as a challenge—a quiet challenge—and would do my best. I wonder if they knew that?) They never pushed us, although my parents did urge me to go to non-combat at the beginning.

Basic training was a shock. Look, I didn't know how to slice bread. And, while my high school wasn't snobbish, there were only sixty of us; we were well-mannered.

So, food in basic training! The first two days—starving, get nothing. People are grabbing food and I was used to waiting first for my turn, then to start eating together.

You wait, you don't eat.

I'll tell you about picking units. Especially with combat units, the soldiers have intense feelings of belonging; it is very competitive to get into elite units such as mine.

The Israeli army is not rich like the U.S. army: the US marines have their own planes; the US navy has planes too. We have an air force; we have tanks; we have infantry. The infantry needs tanks, they call me; they need planes, they call the air force. This makes us very interdependent; we meet often, get to know each other very, very well, including at 3 a.m. when we make or receive frantic calls from another Khativa.

There are two large, old elite infantry units: the Tzanchanim (paratroopers) and the Golani. Now, I am in the tank service in the Golan Heights; but the Golani brigade is named this way because of their service in the Golan in the '48 war. Each of these have their characteristics. The Golani infantry I work with a lot; they use our tanks on training and active battles. These Golani guys, they're hooligans. I mean not in a bad way. But they think that they can do anything; maybe overestimate their abilities and underestimate their required support. For instance, we have a meeting about an upcoming training. They tell me that they need four tanks for such-and-so many of their infantry. I ask them, "Really? Look, for that number, we usually send maybe seven or eight."

"No! We're Golani. We don't need no seven or eight!" He is offended.

O.K. So, I am not surprised or even bothered when at 3 a.m. in the midst of their training, I get a call, "Chaver, do me a favor. Send me another three tanks."

This got to be such a problem that we move the training sites closer to my base. Why? Look, to move tanks more than a certain distance, we need flat bed trucks. For flat bed trucks, I need to requisition. And we need to give Intelligence notice that we are moving tanks, so we aren't mistaken for enemy troops. Instead, we just decide to request from Central Command that the Golani field training be moved closer to our base: this way, when I continue to get the frantic 3 a.m. calls, we are close enough that the tanks could drive under their own steam. That's it.

You want to hear a story about Golani recruit? From my tank unit, we had a guy whose father had been in Golani, also an uncle and others. So, he refuses to be in tank brigade; picks up his gear, walks away. Nu, they put him in the brig. So, he says that he would serve the whole three years army service in the brig, unless they put him in Golani. This impresses Golani. They recruit him. Characters these guys are.

But amazingly dedicated. I am staying by Gil's, a friend's house, who is in Golani. In Beersheva, we had just hitched home from the Golan Heights. This is maybe 6 hours of straight driving, not counting the time to catch a tremp (hitch a ride). I was to spend Shabbat with him and the family; we would go on tiyul through the desert, where he grew up. We just arrive Friday night before nightfall. He strips off his shirt and is in his Bedouin cotton pants, flowing white with colorful decorations along the seam. I remember this clearly. He is drinking from a carton of milk by the refrigerator, his both parents so pleased to see him, they light the room from their smiles. His two brothers at the table reading newspapers—Hebrew, English. Then the phone. He is called to an action and must catch his unit near Haifa. Haifa! Still a four hour drive, straight shot if no roads are closed because of terrorists. No hitching to get him there. His father runs to the car and Gil barrels in with his gear, still buttoning his shirt and pants—you know we don't have zippers on the pants? I go along. I figure I would just go back to Golan for the Shabbat. So, his father is tearing up the highway, this professor of history, this staid fellow, a real <u>Yekke</u>.[9] *We get to near the embarkation up by Haifa and Gil sees the last helicopter beginning liftoff. He tumbles out the car, gear slung across his shoulders, full-tilts to the heli-pad and grabs the landing gear with his right hand, tossing his gear in with his left and as the helicopter takes off, pulls himself up into the "bird." By the way, his* <u>khevre</u> *in the copter watched, didn't give him a hand; they figure, if Gil could make it in, fine; if not, too bad. Real characters,* <u>Golani</u> <u>Tzanchanim</u> *also have a long, proud history. I learn personally about them, because as part of my officer training, I am rewarded with being attached to* <u>tzanchanim</u> *paratroop training for several weeks. I get my* <u>tzanchanim</u> *stripes; people admire these, women especially.*

Originally, <u>tzanchanim</u> *were used for "perpendicular flanking maneuvers." You know what this means? It's a contradiction: how can you attack from the flank, yet also hit* <u>en face</u>*? Only like this.* (He shows me a 3-D jump over the enemy, to its rear.) *But, you know what? Too dangerous to do anymore; hasn't been used since the '56 War. Now, you want to insert at the rear? Use helicopters. So, really, the* <u>tzanchanim</u> *continue to get paratroop training, but this is anachronistic militarily. They function as elite infantry. By the way, lots of injuries in parachuting: that's why they stop the refresher training by 35 years old, even though we serve in reserves until 50: can't do at 36 what you could do at 20.*

We spend the first three weeks learning how to fall. They don't take us up until the fourth week. The fall is where you can get hurt. So, for three weeks, we fall from different heights, in different ways. You are taught to release your harness under adverse conditions. A little wind is good; use it to get into a roll, break your fall; too much wind is adverse. They test us: five instructors grab the chute, drag us around, jerk us to-and-fro while we were supposed to get out of harness.

---

[9]   *A German Jew, who is generally law-abiding and polite and still wears ties to work.*

It's stressful, waiting for the jump; the noise of the planes; particularly night jumps. Everything is by seconds. You are most vulnerable in the air for 50-60 seconds. According to Geneva Accords no one is permitted to shoot at a parachutist while he is in the air: the Germans did it; so did the Egyptians. We can't depend on Geneva. So, we are dropped low. The plane is going about 200 mph. You need to jump out like this. (Here, he startles me with a pirouette as we are crossing Namir Road in Tel Aviv, Yarkon Park to our left.) *You kick your left foot, so, causing a clockwise rotation to prevent going into a counterclockwise spin that would result from a kind of gyroscopic action of your body as you leave the plane.* (Now, I hear the physicist.) *Then, about five, six seconds to open your chute, so you don't entangle the plane, nor get caught in its downdraft. If it doesn't open, about three seconds to open the auxiliary. Not too soon, or the auxiliary lines entangle with the main chute: then you become ground smudge.*

I go to Great America with my physics department. They want to bungee jump, but are to afraid to do solo. They have a bungee with three people harnessed together; raise you on a crane, then one person pulls a pin and you plunge down. Interesting plunge; initially you fall ventrally, then there is a brief moment when you incline nose down; at about one meter above ground, you get pulled back, then swing slowly back-forth for too long a time. Exciting enough for my colleagues.

Disappointing to me; does not compare to diving from a plane at low altitude at 200 miles an hour.

Tzanchanim wants me to switch to their troops in the reserves; leave my tanks. But I figure that with the annual jumps, I would get hurt, break a knee, a leg. I stay with shiryon, tanks. So, that's tzanchanim.

What did you learn in school today, dear little boy of mine?

But it wasn't how to jump from a plane, or how to command a tank brigade, or repair a tank while its on the run, that I really learned from the army.

Improvise, be independent, have goals, use minimal resources, stay close to your men.

What I __really__ learned? On Yom Ha'shoah, the nationwide sirens signal a silent break to remember the six million killed. We are in training with dozens of tanks, clanking, grinding, booming: then sudden silence, respect. Men leave the tanks, climb down, hands on their hearts. They point the tank guns into salute position: 60 degrees upwards. Complete silence. At the end of the silence, my officer says to me: __this__ is the army—__made of flesh__, not steel. Of course, I think of my father.

To improvise is the Palmach mentality. The Palmach was the army before the State was founded. Their idea: everything is unknown; time, a luxury.

Just out of training, my commander lost his leg in front of my eyes. He went into a minefield leading the troop; too sure of himself, he didn't take care about moving forward. I watch as he is lying on the ground, the medic staving off his bleeding to death—and my commander continues to direct the operation! That's not all, talk about improvising. He comes back after the hospital. He rigs a jeep so he can drive and shift the clutch with one leg. His tank? He fixes a ladder so he can mount one-legged.

Everything we are told to repair on the run, under fire. You never get enough time to get things in tiptop form. This is not always so good. Sometimes, I think that things are done shoddily, because we did things on the run. We have to be somewhere an hour away? "Fine, fix it on the way, or when we get there."

Look, never enough men or materials to do an operation. Improvise. You have 22 men and need to do an operation needing 16-18. You try to leave 4 in reserve, behind. But one gets sick, another is injured. You make do, somehow.

Improvise in little ways. We have two different radios to communicate: one amongst ourselves and one between us and the __mefaked__ (commander). But we are in a fire fight and the two radios are in two different tanks. I should run under fire from my tank, down to the ground, to the other tank to get to the radio to talk with my commander? Under fire? No. I just rig the two radios so that I could talk on my platoon radio and it automatically gets transmitted to the radio in the other tank, connecting with my commander. Of course, I rig it so that I would transmit to him only when I need to.

You see that on the floor, the shelves holding my model car collection? It looks sleek, modern, expensive, no? I improvised it. See the two end pieces holding it together? They sell at Ikea as stereo speaker holders for $12. I turn them around facing each other, buy two glass shelves, and voila*, fancy display shelves. This the army taught me.*

I learn to make schedules; clarify missions; define and focus on goals and always make it work with less people, time and materiel than you need.

And we train. We have a weekend free, but not able to go home on shabbat? I go with three or four colleagues, get maps, explore the territory, practice navigation.

Three to four months into my officer training, I feel *like a soldier. I have to organize my group to demonstrate war readiness. We get a score of 99. Now I am a soldier.*

The tanks, you have to maintain, care for, attend to. They're machines and will serve you well if you serve them. And inside, I feel warm, protected, safe, like a home.

But most important what I learned, what I got, was my friendships and closeness with my men. In the mess hall, there is a special table for officers. I never sit there. I fight with my men; I can eat with them.

Deaths

Roni, my cousin, is killed in Litani when I was eleven. His father had been in Palmach; carried explosives. You know how his father learned to carry explosives? Trained by the Nazis as a boy. The Nazis took Jewish boys to detonate mines, bombs—no big deal if the boys died. Roni's father didn't die; Roni did.

I couldn't understand why Roni's mother refuses to go the funeral. She sits shiva *(the seven day intensive mourning). I recall my parents getting the call at night and their crying all night, "But it wasn't a war; it was an operation." Like Roni shouldn't have been killed in an "operation." When I think of his mother now, I wonder if she didn't attend the funeral as a way of denying that he had died.*

Pinchas takes a detour, an important, complex one, first to his father in Auschwitz, then back to basic training, then into his childhood and family, suddenly plunging deeper, darker, into his father's life among the Nazis, before Pinchas returns to the deaths of two army buddies. His conversation, shows an unconscious elegance—his experience of death is refracted through the lens of his father's experiences.

I told you my father's history? He was 12 in the Lodz ghetto. When the ghetto falls, his family is soon exterminated, you know, murdered. He goes to Auschwitz with three other kids. They gang together to survive. He decides at 15 that he'd rather risk getting killed by the SS, than let them brand him.

For him, raising kids in the Jewish State was his victory. He is proud I went into a combat unit.

My father purposely marries someone who didn't go through the Shoah (Holocaust). It wasn't a conscious decision, he claims. But I think for an Ashkenazi to marry a Sephardi, an Iraqi, in the late 1940's was unusual. He wants his children to grow up as new people, Israelis, a different Jew.

I think that my father and I lived complementary lives: what he accomplished, I didn't; what I accomplished he didn't. He wanted me to be educated, because he didn't have an education. But, I'm jealous that he was a professional soccer player and I wasn't. He played for Hapoel Ramat Gan and Betar Tel Aviv. You know, the soccer teams are associated with different political parties. But my father didn't care about parties; he cared about soccer. When Betar changed from Histadrut to Likud, he just changed his party. Look, I know it was no big deal financially back then in the 50's to play professional like it is today. But, it is amazing to me that he comes from Auschwitz to Israel and plays professional soccer. Now do you understand why me and my friends would rush home from school and wait and wait for my father to return from work to play with us?

Then, we had a ritual. Every Thursday after work, my father and I walk to the toy store and I buy a matchstick car. But he doesn't just buy it. He gets on the floor with me to play with them. (Now I understood his excitement when we entered the Radio Shack store and he saw the Zip-Zaps; his need to buy two so that he could play with his cousin.) *Family is the most important thing in his life.*

Most of my accidents occur when he is at war or annual reserve duty for a month. A month felt very, very long. In '73, I was 14 months old; I choke on a pickle and my mother brings me to the hospital. Another reserve duty, I break an elbow at soccer. I break my hand five times in falls while he is away (my mother said seven; it was only five). I never cry. Funny, I don't recall feeling how much I missed him, or worried about him. But maybe that is how I would feel it—by breaking something.

You know how important was family to my father? In '79 he is told by his job to go to England for five weeks: he refuses. Switches jobs. He wouldn't spend five weeks away from his family.

Deaths, the Shoah Quartet, Auschwitz's Annual Shadows

Look, in retrospect I realize how much the Shoah affected my father and how he raised us. The four boys, all orphans hung together in Auschwitz and stayed alive that way. They were dedicated to each other. One dies during an escape, but together they keep each other motivated to live.

Ironically, an SS officer "saved" my father in the selection at Auschwitz. Mengele sends my father's parents for extermination; my father, only 15, follows them. The SS man yanks my father out of the line, kicks him in the ass, my father stumbles, head first, into the labor line.

He talks so matter-of-fact about concentration camp, but the Bowdlerized version, you know PG-13. But, on Yom Ha Shoah, he transformed.

We experience death differently in Israel. Death is so sudden, so often; they're routine. We're more aware of death, talk about it more, especially around the army. You never get used to death.

In the U.S. on Memorial Day, you have big sales, barbecues.

In Israel we build up to Independence Day. We start with two solemn days, Yom Ha Shoah, to remember those six million murdered in Europe; Yom Ha Zikaron, the day before Independence Day, to recall all those killed in Israeli wars and terror acts: a Jewish State with a Jewish State of mind: <u>al tishkakh,</u> never forget.

The day before Yom Ha Zikaron a siren goes off midday: all over the country, six million Israelis stop. Quiet. On the roads, cars stop. People leave their cars for silent respect—heroic stories told. It's more real to us that your American Memorial Day. For us, every family has war dead.

Are we more prepared for death? Is it possible to be more prepared for death? Maybe not. But we function better. Death is death. It hurts the same. You try to function as much as you can—everyday.

One question I ask my father. Three years after the Shoah, you are in Israel playing soccer, dating. How do you do such a switch. His answer? "You have to live."

But for Yom Ha Shoah, my mother prepares us for weeks. She reminds us: Daddy pulls into himself, cries. No TV or radio. We tiptoe around the house in socks. That day, the Day itself, was the only day I see my father cry. The whole day he cries for his parents, brothers and sisters, his buddies. He never had a childhood.

Later, we learn a trick: have guests over that day. My father is too shy to cry before guests. Now, his grandchildren come and he plays with them. But, I recall being jealous that other parents didn't have to go through that experience; jealous of kids with grandparents.

I wait for Yom Ha'Atzma'ut for the sense of release; liberation. It is my personal liberation.

My father refuses the German reparation money. He wouldn't give them the satisfaction of thinking that money could make up for murdering his family. Yes, we know that they said the <u>pi'tzu'im,</u> reparations, is for his slave labor in the camps; but he <u>feels</u> otherwise.

The big deaths before army were first my cousin in the Litani action. I am about eleven. I remember. His father had been in the same brigade. The Hezbollah knew how to be cruel. My cousin was blown up by an RPG, smoked. The army sent back his remains in a container, not to be opened. My cousin was buried. The newspapers publish each death, with a photo in uniform, so it's public. Apparently someone in Hezbollah read the Jewish obituaries, because they got his family's address. They sent his parents a photo of their son's severed head, on a bayonet, with a note, "You forgot something."

When I am sixteen, a man I called my grandfather, dies, suddenly, a heart attack. He lives next door. We build our sukkah there, you know the hut hung with fruits that you live in for a week during the autumn. Some of the fruits, like <u>bokser</u>, are hard as dried shoe leather. We have little room. He keeps my bike there, plays ping pong with me. He has fruit trees and insists he needs my help to pick the fruits: oranges, lemons, apricots, pecans. It is a small orchard—you know the Hebrew word, "pardes," from which comes the word, "paradise"? Well, it is my paradise.

I cry like I never had before. I see a change in my father. I realize that this man was also a father to him. Maybe every child yearns for a grandparent; mine dead, I found one next door, with a <u>pardes</u>, and then he dies.

The army deaths were few, but difficult. My leaders are good at keeping us from getting killed. Both know how to get us out of situations, although one was renown for getting us <u>into</u> bad situations. Well, when they both died, I take it hard.

I tell Benny that I would never leave the unit as long as he is the commander. Look, ideology, shmideology, Zionism, shmionism—what binds me to being a fine soldier is my <u>khevre</u>, buddies. But buddy is not a good enough translation. <u>Khevre</u> comes from the word that means to "bind things together." That's what we are, bound together.

Benny, he recommends, suggests things to us. We consult him, the way he trained us. We still talk about him now. He <u>always</u> has food in his hands, with a <u>shwarma</u>, he waves us right, with a <u>pita</u> and <u>chumus</u> in another hand, he waves left. Almost always food at the corners of his mouth, on his beard. If we have an intense strategy meeting before an important operation, we turn to Benny after an hour and ask, "Now we can eat?" Always, Benny said, "Let's eat!"

Navigating, he is the best. You have to *feel* the ground to know how to navigate. He is from infantry, so he really meant *feeling* the ground with your feet. Navigating in tanks can literally feel differently, in fact you can miss feeling the ground. With the tank you just use the odometer, a compass, a clock. But he takes us on training maneuvers. At night, we are to navigate an area, learn the prevailing winds, the smells. Benny lifts his nose out the turret to smell the fragrances, climbs down the tank, walks ahead, feels the ground, bends down to sift the dirt in his fingers.

And Benny always knows how to handle a *balagan* (fussing) from a senior officer. Once, we do a training, just training, but a competition between two units. The other unit moves faster through a field, while Benny maneuvers to be sure we don't get through a mine field, avoid sniper fire. The commander comes, dresses down Benny in front of us—"You weren't as fast as the other unit!" So, Benny responds—in front of us—"Better a live chicken than a dead lion . . . Sir!" Now, you know, this was a double dig . . . not just the chicken-lion, but also to call an officer "Sir" in the field (instead of his first name) is to insult him, treat him like was an American officer, highfalutin. Ha!

Also, Benny would listen to his commanding officer say, "Do this, that and also this, and for sure that." And Benny would say O.K., sure, *ha'kol beseder*, (AOK). Then he would turn to us after the officer left and say, "First of all, all of you calm down." He was always a smile, made fun of things. "Don't listen to him. Look, we'll do this and that, *chik-chak* (with a double brush of his hands . . . even with a pita) and that'll be enough." *Chik-chak*. That is Benny, the best soldier, the best, a *ben adam*, (literally, a son of Adam; figuratively, a *mensch*, a decent man).

A stroke takes him down. In his 40's. Sad, because the previous year he had lost a lot of weight. I am in the States when my *khevre* call me. I sit all night crying, listening to his favorite Israeli music. I spend the next few days talking with my four friends *in the army. I miss him today. We could always count on him keeping us from getting into bad spots and if that failed, getting us out of bad spots.*

Ayal we knew was going to get it. He looks for action. Gets us into tight spots. he gets us out of them too, but we are more tense when he is leading us. He lives in the territories, carrying a gun even when off service. He gets shot. Leading an attack, out front. Not surprised, but still a big loss; a night of crying and calling friends.

I just don't think its responsible to live in the territories with kids, like Ayal did.

∗   ∗   ∗

Between Palestinians and Settlers, I Chose my Chevra, (and the loss of soldier hood)

Now, we hear about his disillusionment and more clarity about his decision to leave the army.

You know how sailing between Scylla and Charybdis was treacherous? You could be shipwrecked on either shore of the narrow straits. They think it was between Gibraltar and Morocco or Italy and Tripoli. Only two reasons to sail through Scylla and Charybdis: to leave the Mediterranean or enter it. To leave, you penetrate the greater world, the Atlantic; to enter, you come to the heart of Israel. But what if you don't sail through Scylla and Charybdis, between settlers and Palestinians? What if you just decide to hell with it? This is how I begin to feel.

Here is sacrilege. But at some point in my service, I think of the Palestinians and the Settlers as Scylla and Charybdis: my unit isn't sailing through; we are expected to weigh anchor, protect Scylla from Charybdis!

Charybdis, I recall, was the churning waters that would swallow a boat. Ulysses listens for the roar to avoid shipwreck.

But Scylla was the silent monster with six heads on long necks. While Ulysses, hears, avoids Charybdis, Scylla's six heads slither out quietly and snatches up six of his men, consuming them alive: only their screams Ulysses hears. To Pinchas, the Palestinians are the roaring Charybdis to try to avoid. But the Settlers were like slithering Scylla, snatching at these unwitting sailors.

There is a change in me. I can't date exactly when. But, I recall that we talk in my unit in the late '90's that we care more for each others' well-being than for the settlers'. This isn't good, we agree: a soldier must protect civilians; protecting himself and his <u>khevre</u> should be secondary.

I keep being sent back to Jenin, the biblical Nablus. Jenin changes and I feel myself change. In the first Intifada, I had my first <u>milu'im</u> there. I had just started University when I was called up for 35 days in October. That blows my first semester. Then I got called back again in April '90 — my second semester goes to hell.

We are given different types of bullets for civilian dispersal: soldiers got rubber bullets — they look like this — (he holds forefinger an thumb perhaps a centimeter apart). *The officers are given plastic bullets to hurt only, not kill; but I was never sure they weren't dangerous.*

Now, imagine this. Orders are to shoot only if our lives are in jeopardy. So, you are with eight solders surrounded by about 500 Palestinians in the narrow alleys of the old city: people in the alleys, through windows, upon the roof, along parapets. If you don't shoot, they consider it a weakness and get aggressive. But what can you do with 500 people and rubber bullets? Sometimes we use gas grenades to disperse, sometimes that makes them more violent.

And our lives in jeopardy? If you want to shoot, your officer asks, "Are you sure they were shooting <u>at</u> you, not just over your head?" In the midst of this, it's hard to measure the distance between their rocks and bullets and your helmet.

Sometimes you do what you have to do. Once, we are called because an entire village surrounds a unit. We must rescue the unit. Look, the unit was supposed to complete an action during the night, *but they don't start until 5:00 a.m. The whole village is awake. So, what do you say to the other unit—too bad you started the operation? No, we save the unit. Later, the Army does an investigation; that's not for us. But, experiences like these help us realize we are caring more about our <u>khevre</u>, our fellow soldiers, than about civilians.*

A stronger example. We are responsible in the <u>shtakhim</u> (territories) to accompany a school bus in the morning. Now, look. We are told to be there, let's say at 7:30, we get there at 7:25, always. Then, one day we get there and the bus is gone, has left without us! It's just a damn school bus. Look, I know that the buses are armored, have special ceramic anti-bomb armor beneath its skin; has turkey wire on the front window; bullet proof panes on the sides (all scratched from stones, rocks, bullets). But, we accompany to ensure the children's safety. So, this morning the bus has left. Has left early. We start driving madly at maybe 50-60 miles an hour, when our jeeps are not supposed to go more than 40 miles an hour to find the bus, catch up. This doesn't happen only once. You think it is maybe a mistake the bus driver made? He plays games with us, with the children's lives.

Here is another that changed me, really changed me about the settlers. We are responsible to guard a settlement around the clock. Everything is fine until Erev Shabbat (Friday night), when my men call me from the entrance to the settlement. The Orthodox settlers won't let my men in, because they arrive in a jeep; driving on Shabbat eve means driving back on Shabbat. The settlers make a roadblock, a pile of tires and oil barrels to block the entrance! I arrived in my jeep with my sergeant—remember he is a Druze and we are close. I go to the head settler and tell him, we are responsible to guard the settlement and <u>they</u> are not to decide that on Shabbat we have no responsibility for them: of course, the terrorists are more likely to hit on a Shabbat or holiday; the settlers and we both know that. We are screaming at each other. I drive my jeep through the roadblock, smash it. The settler, a Sephardi Jew runs at me, says, "You Ashkenazis, too bad the Nazis didn't finish you all off in the crematoria!" We are nose-to-nose. Good that my Druze sergeant got between us.

(Good? If he hadn't?)
I was ready to smash this guy's face like I did the roadblock. Ashkenazi! Sephardi! I'm both!

So, I begin to realize that I was not caring enough for the settlers. Certainly, I wasn't caring for the Palestinians: they were ready to put their own children *in harm's way; they would plan "spontaneous" demonstrations, calling the news service beforehand; they were completely untrustworthy. I realized that I was now caring really to protect my men; they should go home safely to their parents, to their wives and children. This is not a good state of mind for a soldier, not a Jewish soldier.*

—

I won't tell you that *is why I left the army; I won't tell you that is why I accepted the post-doc in the States. There are other reasons.*

Partly also it is the state of mind in the States. Life is easier here; people are more pleasant. Look, the Israelis make fun of the Americans' politeness: "You Americans are fake; you don't really say what you feel. We *express ourselves more openly." At work, in Israel there is hollering, screaming and such. Since being in the States, I realize that almost every day in Israel, I was getting angry. Driving. My friends from Israel drive with me here and don't believe how easy-going I am; they are shocked that I drive through an intersection, expecting,* believing *that the cross-traffic will stop at the stop sign. "How do I know this?" they ask, "How can I be sure?"*

(He says all this as he is placidly cruising around the bustling University neighborhood.)

This superficial friendliness is not so bad, not so hard to get used to. People here respect your private time at home; no one calls me on evenings or weekends from work to insist I come in. Of course, I am a scientist; if an experiment needs to be done on the weekend, I do it. But, in Israel, someone would be hounding me, as if I wouldn't do it unless they keep calling me.

I'm a physicist, not a sociologist. But I think about how this happened, when it changed in Israel. For instance, because I have a Ph.D., working long hours for little pay, I am considered a freyer. *You know what is a* freyer? *It's a castrated rooster; cut off its balls, it grows more fat than muscle, stops crowing; good for making a* yo'ach, *a soup. So, anyone who helps out without asking for something back; anyone who has ideology—even ideals, anyone who is smart and isn't making lots of money—especially during the internet boom years—he's a* freyer. *A kibbutznik, by definition, is a* freyer. *You work for the government and not taking anything on the side—* freyer. *You follow rules, abide by laws—* freyer. *Here in the States, I realize that if I follow the laws and rules, I will be fine; in Israel I feel that if I don't cheat, first I will be taken advantage of; second,* frey-er!

I think this started in the early '80's around the time of Begin. Maybe also the influx of the Russian immigrants. Under Begin, we had a government that started bringing the worse elements of American culture, especially the greediness of unbridled capitalism, without the friendliness, the politeness of you Americans. The Russians come from three generations of a totalitarian government under which you should not trust the government, and if you don't "work" *the government, then you are a sucker and won't get what you believe you are owed. Ironic that some of these Russians come to a democracy with great freedoms, but still seem to have a belief that you have to manipulate everyone,* everyone, *to get what you think you deserve; that you are a fool to believe in the government or anyone's word, or to work without soaking your employer. But who am I, a sociologist? I'm just a physicist. It just seems that something changed, a change of values, of mind, in the early '80's.*

I tell my friends in Israel that at the age of 30, I feel like I have retired in the States: I work in a job that I love (as I did in Israel), but am respected, and I make a decent living without having to worm my way around rules or people. Here I am not a freyer; *I'm a* ben adam.

I will return. I miss home. But I struggle. I am changed by the experience in the States. I laugh when my lab or my University makes a five-year plan. Five years in Israel? We hope to plan for four months, maybe to the end of the year. Here, people plan weddings, bar mitzvahs more than a year in advance. In Israel, maybe four months; who knows what will happen in the interim, who will be alive?

In the army, Pinchas joins his father's shadows from Auschwitz and is victorious. His buddies become his teen-age father's buddies in Auschwitz. Pinchas learns his manhood and ability to be close to others, learns his strengths. He also feels his vulnerability, as he begins to find that, he wants to protect his buddies more than the citizens he should protect. He misses his family, he misses his buddies, he misses an old Israel and hopes to return.

A Soul in Limbo?

Five hours with Avi. I walk through the night, sit at a café for perhaps two hours until I can write notes about our meeting. I need time to recover from the heaviness of his memories—how a 20 minute fire-fight in a nighttime raid in Gaza darkened his life forever. Now, he believes all is vanity; only death is tangible. He is an embodiment of <u>Ecclesiastes</u>.

Earlier that afternoon.

We meet in a borrowed office at the Hebrew University, windows facing the Mount of Olives. The afternoon sun harshly pours in. Avi sits before the window. At times, the light creates a halo around him. I have to adjust the camera.

Avi is surprisingly different from his army photo. His full head of black hair is replaced by a bald pate, topped with a black knit kippah. His build is slight. He disappears in his Hassidic garb. A full beard, albeit carefully trimmed. It is hard to believe Avi is the former son of a most secular kibbutz.

You seem surprised. My hair disappeared after the Army. You expected someone bigger? The muscles also disappeared.

His black dress camouflages him against the black leather Knoll lounge chair. He is reclining. When I ask about his father, Avi folds his arms across his chest and shifts forward. *"As if on attack."* He then reclines, but does not relax. *"Like I'm on the defense. To understand me, you have to understand my father, my family."* His insightfulness about himself. This, however, has not been sufficient to heal his soul, I learned.

I grew up on a severely secular kibbutz, on the border with Jordan. (We will call it, *Mishmar Ha'Gvul*, border's guardian.) *I have become an Orthodox Jew, a Hassid no less. I decided on this before I met my Orthodox wife. I "converted" out of conviction, in rebellion against my kibbutz and mostly my family, not for marriage. In Hebrew, I am called a* khozer b'tshuva, *figuratively,"one who returns to G-d", literally, "one who returns to the answer." Sounds a bit pretentious to me.*

Like an ellipse, my life has followed two paths: the kibbutz and the army. But it is the army that turned my life around. More accurately, a 20-minute fire fight in Gaza, during my third year. I had 90 men, crack paratroopers, under me.

Jerked his life into a nihilistic free fall.

Yes, I know that to the outside world, I look OK. To the Hassidim, I am "a catch," a good religious Jew; to my business partners, a fine, acute businessman with impeccable morals. But, I'm straight out of Ecclesiastes. "Vanity of vanities; all is vanity"; there is nothing new under the sun"; and mostly, ". . . a time to live and a time to die."

A steel exterior; inside a core of cynicism rusts away.

Gaza

When it happened, it was so quick, so simple. It sent me into years of being lost. But, I realized that afterwards.

A major attack in Gaza, near Rafah, probably a proxy center for Hamas. I received order to mobilize. Move six units of men before dawn. Some I knew better than others: Tzvi from Odessa, insisting on his Israeli identity with the thick accented Hebrew; Eli unhesitating, a kibbutznik, always leading; Motti from Paris, who tossed away his Gauloises, proclaiming his independence from French culture. And then there was Khaval. Khaval was one of my lieutenants. He was soon to finish his four year tour of active duty. I never thought he was effective. We sheltered Khaval. A nice enough fellow, from a military family, hoping for a career. In the field, Khaval couldn't get through to his men. He said the right words, but his men didn't get it—couldn't move them.

I worried about sending Khaval out; briefed him through the night; offered to send someone else. But, he wanted this last action. He wanted it.

Central Command kept calling before dawn—get moving. I insisted, "We'll move when we're ready."

Was it Khaval's fault? Not likely.

It was an effective ambush. Within moments, I drove out to save them. Khaval was hit by artillery—cleaved like a log, head to pelvis. Motti was shot clean, through the neck—left smiling. Avi points to his own neck. Tzvi got one shot in the right forehead. Avi points to his mid-forehead, notices his error and wordlessly moves his finger. He wants to get this absolutely accurate, this memory of these men. Eli was carrying ordnance, bombs; nothing left of him.

Avi believes his life path is elliptical, but it may be linear. Perhaps Avi is following a trajectory through time that led him to a black hole—Gaza. A black hole that stretches and distorts his soul as he is drawn into a darker universe.

Kibbutz

By his upbringing, Avi is kibbutz—a child of the largely secular pioneer movement that sought to redeem the land.

Without Kibbutz, I would have stumbled, been hobbled by my fractious parents. "Argue" is not enough of a word to describe them. She wailed inconsolably; he bellowed; and I, from the beit yeladim, the children's sleeping house, could hear them at night. Maybe this was preparation for combat duty.

The youngest of four, I decided at eight that I would "divorce" my parents. I didn't tell them; I acted, acted decisively as I would throughout my life. Only on kibbutz could a child "divorce" his parents and still have surrogate families as I did. I knew I only had to visit them several times a week, one to two hours at a time after school—not even after school, after I worked my wonderful job in the fields beginning in third grade. I visited them in their minute single room, with a kitchenette, then dinner at the communal dining room; then to the beit yeladim for work and sleep. By sixth grade, I became close enough with two peers, that I would join them and their parents for the one to two hour parent visit several times weekly, still seeing my real parents at the khadar ha'ochel, not offending them.

My first "job" was to "help" Moishek, the tractor driver. Moishek was one of the kibbutz builders; from a rich American family, he would joke that he had "affluenza," an allergy to being wealthy. He loved kibbutz, but most of all, he loved the children. Perched high, sitting between Moishek's knees, I would "drive." The smell of spring plowing entered my senses, grabbed me. In Brooklyn, by Damrosch Park, I pause at the first fragrance of spring showers, moist earth, narcissus tendrils.

Fifth grade, the kibbutz kids got jobs after school and for every summer. The jobs were more significant to me than school. I did well in school, very well. But, I struggled with my father's stance about grades: my father's vehemence about grades was at odds with kibbutz culture. If I got a 96% on a test, my father demanded, "Why didn't you know the remaining 4%? Only 4% more you needed to know! Four percent more you couldn't know?" I felt a fiery magma ready to erupt (from my father and later from myself). Anything below 90% was disastrous. I would hide beneath my bed in the beit yeladim after a parent-teacher conference, fearing my father.

My father had joined Nahal on aliyah from Argentina; left college before finishing, to join the '67 war effort. (Nahal is a branch of the military that sends young soldiers to critical border areas to set up generally agricultural settlements and be responsible to guard the border.) But, he arranged with his Argentina University to "finish" his degree requirement in Israel. Then, lots of intervening, interrupting bureaucracies and events: the coup in Argentina, getting the kibbutz to approve time away from the fields to take classes (although most studying he did at night). Still, I recall for two years after my father finished his requirements, he would ask insistently upon returning home "Where's the mail?" Really, I heard it more like, "Where is _the_ mail?" the graduation certificate from Argentina. Two years, every day. I remember the anxious, insistent, tinged-with-anger tone of my father's voice.

Academically, I excelled, but my deepest pleasures were in the fields; my greatest dreams were of army; my ultimate dream was to return and live on the kibbutz, become like "blue blood" kibbutzniks, not an immigrant like my parents with their Spanish-tinged accented Hebrew; maybe become _menahel_, general manager of the kibbutz. I know the irony of my now being an executive in a capitalist, religious enterprise. Yet, I am surprised when I react with envy upon reading the kibbutz newsletter (which I still get): in bold letters it announces that Tzvi, a "blue blood" is now manager of a firm in Tel Aviv—nothing about me, about my being a business owner in New York City. Why, why does this bother me so much?

The blue bloods, I want to explain to you. Everyone was theoretically equal in kibbutz. But the blue bloods were recognized. A blue blood was someone whose parents and especially grandparents came from kibbutz, built a kibbutz. Yes, I knew that my father helped start the kibbutz, but he was an immigrant, an accent he had, no grandparents who had fought in '48, some of whom had died, buried on Mount Herzl's heroes cemetery.

Like the others, Avi teaches me a major difference about kibbutz "education," a difference first described by Bettelheim in Children of the Dream. In the US, we think of education in a more circumscribed, pedagogical, classroom-oriented manner. On kibbutz, education includes what we might think of as "character," "moral fiber," how to conduct oneself with others.

In school, the emphasis was on collaboration, helping others, not on grades, nor surpassing another. Here is a major difference between education in kibbutz and US. I had several types of teachers. One was called the _moreh_; a second, the _mekhanekh_; a third, the _madrikh_. _Moreh_—the "teacher"—comes from the verb "to point," like shooting an arrow; Moses does this when he thrusts a tree into the bitter waters. Literally, _mekhanekh_ means educator. In fact, he is a teacher and counselor together, a real mentor. He is responsible for *your behavior; how to become a "mensch" in Yiddish, a decent fellow or lady. The madrikh teaches, but is really a confidant, counselor, buddy. He is at the teen dorms most evenings. We talk about matters of life. He takes you on weekend or week-long wilderness hikes, to learn not only about nature, but also about your nature and how you treat your khevre (buddies).*

But learning to comport yourself begins earlier. In the beit yeladim, the children's house, the children had a metapelet, someone entrusted by the kibbutz to care for the children and to care for how the children treat each other. In junior high or high school, when we lived in dormitories, the metapelet was replaced by a madrikh. The word madrikh has the same root as derekh, a road: the madrikh's job is to help the teens on the path into life, of life. The madrikh emphasized the responsibility for each other and how more fruitful it is to have others upon whom to depend ("talui", to hang from). Moreh, metapelet, mekhanekh, madrikh, we kibbutz children were immersed in those dedicated to our moral and academic education.

At thirteen, I began to arise before dawn to work the fields, then went to school and returned to the fields after school. I looked forward to school breaks, when I could spend the whole day in the fields. My heart raced when I hopped a truck or the tractor with three or four friends to reach the fields before sunrise. A break for coffee around nine, a return to the khadar ha'okhel, the eating hall, for lunch, then a long stretch until nightfall. Sometimes, we would bring lunch along, so as not to leave the fields.

By fifteen, I was on my own. I realized how important I was to the kibbutz when there was another severe water shortage. A complex drip irrigation system, I'd mastered. I knew how much water each crop demanded and when. Nothing could be wasted. The kibbutz was told by the government of another cut in the water quota just when the wheat crop was most vulnerable. The menahel called me out of school. Could I arrange sufficient irrigation with the new cut? I did it. I felt quiet admiration flowing from the kibbutz.

On kibbutz, one doesn't trumpet achievements. Achievements speak.

Matkal

My parents helped build our kibbutz as a <u>Nahal</u> kibbutz in the Jordan Valley after 1967. As a child, I feared the <u>mekhablim</u>, the terrorist infiltrators, faces wrapped in kaffiahs. My word for this? Phobia. At nine, I knew about the infiltrators in Kiryat Shemona, who held children hostage, shot them to death. I chose the upper bunk in the <u>beit yeladim</u>, the bunk facing the window, so that I could keep watch on the local bus, to make sure that every hour when a bus arrived, no terrorists disembarked. I kept my eyes pried open past bed time, until the last bus arrived from Jerusalem at 11:00 pm, then closed my eyes. For a while, I slept with sneakers, so that I could leap out, run into the fields, should the <u>mekhablim</u> attack. Through the forest they would come.

I saw the "forest" Avi is describing. In fact, it is a small grove abutting the kibbutz cemetery. Some of the trees are younger than the teen-age soldiers buried there.

We have a tradition among the kibbutz youth. Upon graduating from high school, we gather at the cemetery, peers only, and bid each other <u>l'hitraot</u>, see you soon, in <u>this gan yeladim</u>, this kindergarten, where some of us would soon be "planted". A grim, realistic parting.

By fifth grade, I <u>knew</u> I wanted to join <u>Matkal</u>, the most elite combat unit in the army. <u>Matkal</u>, Ehud Barak's unit. They, under cover of night, attack high-level terrorist heads, then retreat. Minutes these attacks take, barely minutes. One doesn't volunteer for <u>Matkal</u>. One is chose (well before enlistment). Then after four months of grueling training, some remain. Of my recruited group, one fourth of made it. On the last day of my training, I completed a 40 km hike through sand and desert, carrying a stretcher loaded with an "injured" <u>Khaver</u>. Paradoxically, after successfully completing the training, on the last day I quit. Resigned from Matkal.

The first kibbutz son to join <u>Matkal</u> was one year ahead of me and from a blue blood family. I noted the quiet pride in the kibbutz and redoubled my determination to be the next <u>Matkal</u> recruit. The army testing begins in late adolescence. The army has a large dossier on each recruit: family of origin, culture, kibbutz *versus non-kibbutz, school grades. Then, it gives us tests, physical, medical, psychological, cognitive. All this results in a single score, the* Kabah, *which over years, predicts well a recruit's success and helps determine where you will succeed.*

I was recruited for both pilot training and Matkal. To be a pilot. This is the most *difficult position to achieve in the army. While kibbutzim represent less than 3% of the population, 90% of pilots are kibbutzniks; 70% of the most elite combat units are kibbutzniks, and so on. This has been a shift: more non-kibbutz Sephardic men—Moroccan, Yemenite, for instance—are reaching the elite units. I could choose between becoming a pilot and joining* Matkal.

Quickly, advice came from those in active duty. The most astute came from my chaver *in* Matkal: *even if you* want Matkal, *accept pilot training for the first few months of* tironut, *basic training. Too many of the Matkal recruits get hurt in* tironut, *then get dropped to a "'lesser" combat unit. Pilot training would protect me from serious injury. At the end of this four-month training, you decide to stay a pilot, or request a transfer.*

I did exactly this. Pilot training was exciting, but too removed from the ground, the land that I loved so much, that I was protecting. I needed to smell the land. And, as a pilot, I would fly alone; I missed working in small groups, a unit of 15-20 men, each breathing the other's soul (in Hebrew, the words for "soul" and "breathe" are related). I felt more alive, more connected, more whole with a tight-knit cohort. As in school, collaboration, not competition was central to the Israeli army. I knew that after several years' active service, I would be returning to reserves every year for several weeks with the same group until I was fifty. And, each guy counted.

Then an oddity happened. I started pilot training, requested transfer to the last few months of Matkal *training. The last task in* Matkal *is a 40 km hike: bone-aching, mind-numbing. Yet, I completed it. Then I requested transfer out of* Matkal!

Originally, Avi told me he was "tossed out" of Matkal. When I pressed him, he explained that he experiences his departure as being "tossed out," even though he was the one who requested transfer and his captain urged him to stay. He was the best recruit in that unit.

Now, I have a clue as to why I left; actually two clues. On the long hikes, I had too much time to myself. We couldn't talk. We had to simulate the silence of night attacks. My mind would go on and on. The most important attribute to being a successful soldier is don't think too much. My philosophizing began to trouble me. But now, I had no madrikh to talk with. No night time talks with khaverim in the dorms—they all fell asleep before reaching the sleeping bags; guys slept while hiking!

Second, my Matkal unit required thinking individually and minute hand manipulation. When Ehud Barak (former general and former Labor Prime Minister of Israel) was in Matkal, he and five others were sent to Beirut to kill a PLO commander. They arrived in pairs, two by rubber dingy, four over land. Barak was dressed as a woman and held hands with his "husband" as they approached the targets' house. Barak was kibbutz raised. But, I felt too alone, when I didn't have a group to work with. Also, I felt insecure about the careful finger coordination needed for some operations. I know that this was at odds with my excellent performance.

So, I got "demoted" to tank corps.

Two Early Crises

Avi experiences his transfer to the tank corps as a "demotion," even though the tank corps is regarded by most as a very elite unit. Although he may not willingly acknowledge their importance, Avi experienced two childhood internal crises that left vulnerabilities in his inner structure. Freud called this phenomenon nachtreglichkeit, what French psychoanalysts call apres coup: when earlier life trauma which may not cause severe inner life disruption, is later followed by another trauma that leaves severe disruption, sometimes catastrophic internal collapse.

I had two crises of ideology: the first in fifth grade and the second in mid-teens. The first, I realize now, followed my mother's severe depression. I, a child of seculars, began to feel philosophical challenges. Is there no God? How could the liberal socialists be so fervent about building in Israel, when they were so fervently against religious beliefs. What was my connection to my Argentinean grandparents? A thoughtful, patient teacher took on my questions: valid ones that needed to be discussed. We arranged special challenge dialogues: I would issue a challenge and my teacher was to respond. The crisis abated in a few months.

At seventeen, a year before recruitment, I faced a crisis that cut across several layers of identity: my Zionism, my secularism, even my dedication to the military. I continued to train from the military, running kilometers through the fields carrying boulders, sprinting carrying a "wounded" chaver on my back, testing how long I could hike without water. Now, my chaverim would encourage each other; when one dropped a stone, the others would turn back, encourage him to lift and resume.

But, I began to wonder the "why" of this. Partly, I knew this had to do with the right-wing government. How could I prosecute a war, when I disagreed with the government's policies? Then, I felt internal conflicts and how could I support West Bank settlements if by leaving them, peace might be achieved. But, I loved the meters of land of my kibbutz. I looked towards Jordan, across the Jordan River: desolation there. Desolation, which once was how my kibbutz appeared, before my parents helped plant orchards, fields of green. Across the Jordan River, I could imagine Sodom and Gomorra: cities reduced to ashes and salt. On this side, hyodroponic laboratories, succulent tomatoes grown in mineral media, a factory for natural beauty products from Dead Sea Minerals. I could taste a pomelo from the groves as I thought of them.

And Zionism. How could I justify the return to this desolate land? I knew intellectually that Argentina had periods of Jewish intellectual fervency, like Lithuania (from which my great-grandparents escaped); it also had notorious Nazis in refuge; Jewish teens like myself were "disappeared" over the Atlantic, after being kidnapped from their schools, neighborhoods. I argued both sides of Zionism — against myself.

And secularism? The kibbutz celebrated the secular holidays of Pesach, of Succoth, even a touch of Rosh Hashanah (Yom Kippur

*was too religious—no redeeming national or historical qualities).
They built Succoth to sleep under for the week, in the fields, at
harvest time. For Pesach, my* madrikh *took the group for a one-week*
tiyul *in the Judean desert—matzo they baked in the sun; water, we
found either in the deep wadis, percolating down from Jerusalem,
or beneath rocks, carefully filtering out the leaches before drinking.
From a Bedouin, I learned a second method for handling leaches,
which infest your esophagus, suck you to death: a thorny stem you
introduce to your gullet, thorns up; slowly withdrew and, abra
cadabra (*avura k'davura *in Hebrew), the leaches are punctured by
the thorns. This is done prophylactically every few weeks. In my
army training, I felt affinity for the Bedouin and the Druze, felt a
closeness to the desert Abraham.*

*But, an inner motor propelled me forward; even as my doubts
made this motor stutter, I never stalled. Until Gaza. Two people
supported me through my teen crisis: another madrikh, Shlomi, and
a female friend, Tal.*

*Not just any madrikh, Shlomi was the house Zionism historian
and intellectual, an autodidact who was not fanatical about ideology;
he was fanatical about the well-being and growth of the youth and
the kibbutz. As in fifth grade, Shlomi encouraged my challenges,
pressed me for more, taught me how my questions went to the roots
of early twentieth century Zionist debates: the "practical" Zionists
(Herzl) versus the cultural Zionists (Ahad Ha'am, "one of the
people"). A.D. Gordon, the East European shopkeeper in his 50's,
brought his family to Palestine and insisted that he work the land:
reviving the land would revive him as a Jew; Jews should not hire
anyone to work for them—they must redeem themselves through
work. At night, A.D. would write, for he needed to be in the fields,
or cleaning the chicken coops during the day.*

*Steadily, steadily, I regained an inner compass. My walks with
Tal helped. We were peers in the same grade since diaper hood.
We were friends without sexual charge (a phenomenon found less
frequently in U.S. culture, as one bicultural kibbutz woman taught
me.) She said, I was one of the deeper thinkers in our kvutzah,
group. She encouraged my thinking, questioning. She said that*

this kind of thinking will help not only myself, but the development of kibbutz ideology. I knew that Tal had a lover. A different set of feelings developed in me. Love, I would find elsewhere, later.

Tank Corps

In a Merkava tank, at least four are crammed together: driver, navigator, two gunners. In the captain's tank, there are five, with the captain suspended above the four men and able to poke his head out the upper turret to signal other tanks.

Tank corps feels better, more camaraderie.

As Avi tells me this, I can feel the gravitational pull of the Gaza fire fight—the "black hole"—becoming more intense as we get closer to the traumatic event. Avi now grips his temples. He leans forward, sighs deeply. He hangs his head back, cocked to the right, looking to the sky, closes his eyes. Later, he will confess that he gets severe two-sided migraines whenever he begins to think about the fire fight. He won't talk about it, except with his wife, Keren, and at her insistence. In six years, today is the first time he tells the story to someone other than Keren.

Tanks, like tractors, are good to you, if you take care of them. Take meticulous care of a tractor or a tank, and it will take you anywhere, do almost anything. During our maneuvers in the Negev, the sand would get through each cranny—into the gears, into the bearings. Through the front slit, a gust of silica would pelt your eyes at each turn, salt you inside the tank's guts.

Unlike Job in his Leviathan, Avi could navigate this tracked monster at his command, could silence enemy assault. And unlike Job, he had *khaverim*, close friends, in the belly of this beast. He then tells me how he began as a tank navigator. He was particularly adept at navigation, and navigation helped him overcome his "vulnerabilities."

As a navigator, I had to focus all the time—where are we? How can we get there quickly, safely? There is little time for ruminations. When I had to focus on the stars, on the surrounding landscape, I wasn't bothered by my own thoughts.

He excelled at night navigation. As part of his training, he had been sent in a jeep with his unit to train in an area for five days, moving at night. He prided himself on being able to navigate by the stars, by the prevailing winds. He could tell two unseen hills ahead from the breeze funneled between them; he could tell surrounding fields from the fragrance of the air, the desert wind. He knew invisible *wadis* by their watery borbourigmi.

Avi was promoted rapidly. As is true of the Israeli army compared to the U.S. and other armies, officers are far younger and are promoted from basic training. No one enters as an officer; no West Point or Annapolis. You want to be an officer? Start as a grunt, then your men may trust you.

Even for Israel, Avi was younger than most officers. At 22, he led a group of 90 men. At some point, Avi's *mefaked*, his commanding officer went abroad for special surgery and complications set in. As a result, Avi became effectively the *mefaked* for several crucial weeks.

I had never lost a man. I saw wounding in surrounding units. When I was on special training in Israel, a man in my unit was killed in a botched detonation.

But, I never saw a man die.

Until I heard that one of the Druze officers, a man unknown to me, mortally wounded. In emergencies, the cafeteria tent is converted into a MASH surgical unit. It is the biggest structure; the long tables easily become surgical tables. I choose to enter the cafeteria and watch the surgeons to the end. I wait until the officer died. Then. Then, I wait longer, let myself feel the feelings. I turn and leave. One of my soldiers asks why did I do that? I tell him, I wanted—no, I needed to see a man die to prepare myself for . . . well, I didn't know what for.

Motik

Gaza happened. Four men died, his men.
The unit was destroyed. We were destroyed.

After narrating the Gaza episode, Avi sits in long silence, looking away from me. Although it would cause enough of a trauma in itself, the Gaza fire fight is Avi's <u>après coup</u>: It shook the already shaken foundation of Avi's two childhood crises. Avi's shoulders slope forward as he continues.

Usually, after months in Gaza, a unit would be sent back to Israel for training—really for a rest. But the Intifada happened; the Pesach hotel bombing in Netanya, with thirty killed, 140 injured. So we were sent directly to Ramallah. We were destroyed. As acting <u>mefaked</u>, my job was to support my men: they were in tears. I didn't cry. For two years after I left the army, I didn't cry.

Look, now we were set-up for errors, tragedies.

The next death after Gaza, I expected. I was home on weekend <u>regilla</u>, a brief leave. The Israeli army is different than the U.S. military. Parents come up to your base for weekends; you go home for weekends; Israel is a tiny country—everyone knows people who have been killed, wounded.

So, I was on my girlfriend's kibbutz for the weekend when a jeep with my men came to get me. As they approached, I thought, "Uh-oh, someone caught it."

"Yankele," they said. He was one of my best men, one I had trained. A waste, a stupidity. A night time raid to get a terrorist leader. The target was on the family's roof in Jenin, in the casbah, the old city, cramped alleys. He was waiting for my guys on the roof, greeted the unit with a blaze of gunfire. He wasn't worth Yankele's death.

I climb in the jeep. We drive the road to the base, coming down Mishmar Ha'emek ("guardian of the valley"), my girlfriend's kibbutz. We pass Megiddo, I see the Egged bus arising from Afulah. I know it would have some of my men coming back from the weekend, so I stop the bus. The driver stops; no one complains. They tumble out; we sit on the road's shoulder overlooking the Yazriel Valley, at the brow of Megiddo. I remember the view, as they were crying on the roadside. Megiddo, the place Christians call Armageddon, where the final battle of the children of light versus dark would take place, the last battle before the end of the world. We cry like babies on the roadside. It is during the Hamsin, at sunset; there is a soft orange thickness filling the valley, arising. It's an oppressive heat that holds you, like you're wrapped in cotton batten. No breath.

A SOUL IN LIMBO

After that, I detached myself—I'm good at this. In the army, you do what you have to do to survive. At 22, I left. The army. They begged me to stay, "Another year, make a career of it." I wanted a family, a family life that army doesn't permit.

I went to Haifa University. I could have gone anywhere—Hebrew U., Tel Aviv—but I wanted to be away from everyone as much as possible. Two majors, I took, philosophy and economics. Everyone was surprised at philosophy, everyone except Motik. Motik was my bunkmate on kibbutz. Also my soul-mate. We were together in the army. He stayed for the career, took my unit. We used to spend long nights in army, talking philosophy, the meaning of life, the meaning of our activity. We were like Walter Benjamin and Gershom Sholem. Motik had quiet charisma. Everyone thought of me as the energetic leader, the <u>mefaked</u>. But, Motik was a true leader; he glowed from within. He rarely raises his voice. Men just follow him.

Without realizing it, Avi switches from past to present tense with Motik.

A sniper got him. Motik shouldn't have been there. He was at the front, leading an attack. It was a dangerous maneuver. Typical of him—he wouldn't send anyone ahead of him into danger.

Avi stops. I see a slight smile, a <u>rhesus sardonicus</u>, a grimace. I ask about this smile.

It is so simple. A sniper shot to the head. Death is so simple. What follows after, is a cataract of disaster, a waterfall of victims, whose lives change course forever. For worse. But death is so simple. Death is the purest truth there is; everything else pales. Happiness and joy are effable.

I was crushed. And the funeral was awful. I drove up with two army buddies in a tinny Suzuki. The army big wigs came, big shot politicians. They made a big deal of this: one of the most senior officers killed. Speeches, a big deal. We looked at each other. We just wanted to talk with Motik's family, his fiancé, Estee. She was an empty shell. When I started dating Keren, we had a special outing with a few friends including Motik and Estee. We went to Ein Gedi, (the oasis north of Masada, irrigated by waters percolating underground from the rain fall on the Judean hills, 150 years earlier). We hiked to one of the waterfalls, had a special ceremony of dedication to each other. I have a photo of Keren and I, arms around each other and Motik and Estee also embracing. We knew they would marry. Estee finally did, two years ago. But she married a man who was Motik's friend, who knew what her loss meant.

Motik's death changed me. When someone died, when things went wrong, Motik always said "Kadimah!" "Forward!" We had a responsibility to the living, to continue living. He died and I took his word into my life. It unleashed me from my internal torpor. Don't get me wrong. Everyone else saw me doing, always doing, doing, doing—two majors, a job, becoming religious. But inside, until Motik was killed, I was like the Hamsin—a heaviness that engulfed my heart.

I dream of Motik repeatedly, the same dream. I meet Motik on a tiyul (hike). He is walking towards me. He is smiling at me. As always, a smile. I ask him, "Motik, I always asked you 'What's the answer?' 'Tell me the answer.'" He turns to face me, opens his mouth, continues to walk past me, his opening mouth swallows him, and he disappears into the black hole." I never learned the answer from him. I miss him still. I would like my children to meet him.

Life and Movies

There are certain movies I watch twice a month. Alone, always alone. The same movies. _Apocalypse Now, Saving Private Ryan, Full Metal Jacket_, you probably know. But the one that I watch most often is _The Thin Red Line_. There are actually two versions of this movie about Guadalcanal in W.W.II. It's based on the James Jones book. One was in the 1960's and the second, more recent, maybe in the '90's with Sean Penn. My wife doesn't like that I do this. I suspect you would say that I shouldn't. But it helps me after I see them. O.K., some of it is watching the murder, the mayhem, the suddenness and senselessness of losing a buddy, or the guy next to you whom you may not know. But, I listen to the dialogue, the characters. In fact, I can recite the dialogue by heart; I do this under my breath. Penn plays the hardened NCO sergeant: he has a mean streak to him, under the guise of hardening these kids, he pushes too hard, sometimes. But, he also is dark, sees the meaninglessness of their activity. "It's all about real estate." "You in a hurry to die; your time will come soon enough." In the 1964 movie, when the sergeant saves one guy's life—a kid he had been hard on—the kid is surprised, goes to thank him. The sergeant takes the kid's last can of water, takes a sip, then spills the rest out in front of the other guys in the platoon. Says, he doesn't want them to get the wrong idea about him.

The lieutenant, a green guy, a lawyer in civil life, gets relieved by his war-mad colonel. Gary Busey plays him in the '90's movie. Fitting. Busey is the guy who cracked up his motorcycle, cracked his skull, damaged his brain, while riding his crotch-rocket without a helmet. As soon as he gets out of the hospital, he publicizes that he's going to ride again without a helmet. He plays his character to type. His colonel is a bitter son-of-a-bitch who's been passed up for promotions, been itching to get men into battle. In one confrontation scene, Busey insists from the rear that the lieutenant make a frontal uphill attack on a nest of machine-gun bunkers. The lieutenant refuses a frontal attack; offers to make a flanking approach over the ridge, which would take more time, delay the colonel. The lieutenant openly says that he has witnesses who heard him refusing the offer and making a counteroffer. He knows that under the circumstances, a frontal attack would cost him most of his platoon, a slaughter.

Busey is livid. Goes down to the front lines. Stands upright as the others crouch at a mortar attack. Takes the lieutenant aside and asks him how many men he is willing to sacrifice for a maneuver. Like the scene between God and Abraham over Sodom, but in a reverse manner, Busey browbeats the lieutenant—willing to lose ten men, four, one? When he is met with silence, Busey sends the men on a frontal attack and sends the lieutenant packing to serve as a judge advocate general: a nice kick upstairs, but you see that the lieutenant is wounded and that his men love him.

Can you see that I see myself as different characters in the movie? I suspect that now, I sound like the toxically bitter sergeant—a curse *upon the world and all that it contains—he is bad for his men, at some level, even as he will save their lives, even as I think I would be toxic to my children. Of course, I prefer to think of myself as the lieutenant. But I am not as good a man as he: I didn't refuse the order, I didn't revise the plans. And I see most of the career officers as being like the son-of-a-bitch colonel; and moments when I feel guilt for acting like him.*

Keren

I finally meet Keren while I am teaching at Hadassah Hospital in Jerusalem for a week. Keren has come to Jerusalem to spend a week's vacation with her husband. Avi has already spent three weeks in Israel on his own, his own vacation—in the army reserve.

They both give me a tour, starting from the renovated, virtually empty David's Citadel Hotel, once the Hilton, at the edge of the Mamillah neighborhood, its swimming pool shaped like a yacht with its prow facing the Old City across the Gahinom Valley. When you swim in the pool, water cascades towards luxurious condominiums, which, like the hotel, are "Intifada-vacant."

From there, we walk diagonally between the Arab neighborhoods of East Jerusalem and the architectural mélange of the Ministry of Industry and Trade—Greco-Roman, Renaissance, Gothic, Romanesque, Neo-Moorish and Maluk. Built in 1928, this building once was the famous Palace Hotel where the British "Peel Commission" sat and recommended the partition of Palestine in the wake of the Arab riots of 1937.

We climb towards Shlomtzion Malkah, towards Zion Square and suddenly descend into the *Nahalot Shiv'a*. The shops and cafes of the cobbled walkways and alleys used to be obstructed with visitors. Today, we are virtually alone. Some restaurants are shuttered. A lone jeweler, safe behind a buzzer-protected door, creates pieces for customers who never arrive. Again, the effect of the Intifada.

We sit at Cafe *Tmol Shilshom*, the cafe of the "day before yesterday," named after the wistful title of S.Y. Agnon's book. In a corner, some photos of Yehuda Amichai and the armchair from which he used to read his poetry aloud. Amichai died two years ago. David Ehrlich, *Tmol's* co-owner and an unreconstructed leftist, tells us he tried to bridge the gap with Palestinians during his guard duty in the West Bank last month. He gave them his home address and invited them to stop for tea some day. Now, he worries that his address may end up with in a terrorist's hands.

Once David has left us to ourselves, I ask about Avi's *milu'im*, the reserve duties he took a three-week vacation to fulfill. I am surprised Avi used his vacation to return to the army. As a US resident, he is free of the annual military duty, as to which Israeli residents are obligated until age 50. Why go back every year? Why go back at all? After all, his active military experience was devastating and he has little respect for the central command. He has also told me he does not support the current government's policies, especially in the territories. Why use his sparse vacation time to go on reserve duty, particularly during such a tense and life-threatening time as this?

For my men. I cannot leave them to someone else. I'm obligated to them. One day, I'm in business garb in Manhattan, on 47th Street; the next in army fatigues. My men see past the trim beard; they recognize me, their mefaked.

Keren interjects softly, "*What about the army refuseniks who just publicized their letter, refuse to serve* [in the Territories] *to protest government policy?*" Keren has inner fortitude and beauty that transcend her otherwise plain looks. Physically, she is Avi's homonym: lithe, narrow faced, sharp-featured. Like most Orthodox married women, Keren covers her hair with a fashionable shawl. Like them, she dresses modestly: a jean skirt; no baubles, a simple wedding ring, no watch, no make-up. What I can see of her hair has a boyish, even nun-like, trim.

The seriousness of their dialogue is impressive.

I can do more from inside the army than outside, says Avi. Israel is a democratic society, protected by a citizen army. However, an army is not democratic, nor can it be. For my men's lives, at times, I need to give an order and they need to follow, without questioning.

But there are opportunities to question effectively. Before a major operation, we sit, the officers, and go over the details with the commander: the goals, the motivations, and the battle plan. Once, I sat quietly as my senior officer presented an operation in the territories. Then the officers went over the details of how to carry out this action with no Israeli causalities. No casualties. They went on like this, perhaps an hour, then my mefaked summarized so that we would leave. But he asked again, "Any questions?" I asked them one question, well really two.

He poises his finger in the air, doing pirouettes, like a Talmud scholar making a singsong argument.

What is our aim? If it is to promote security for the Israelis in the area, then we should proceed.

His finger, still poised, pirouettes in the opposite direction.

If it is to show these Palestinians who is boss, who will control them, then we will defeat ourselves. My mefaked opened the discussion again. We went on for perhaps another ten minutes. My mefaked listened mostly. Then he turns to me. "You're right. We are canceling the operation." I do this for myself, so I can live with myself. I do this for my men, for whose lives I am responsible.

I ask about his sense of responsibility for his men.

Look (he often starts like this, getting my visual engagement), when I was on active duty, I was 22. Boys—not men—the families sent me. Eighteen even seventeen year old boys. These boys trust me. Their families expect that I will take care of them, return them whole. Now, some of them are closer to my age. They are married, some with children. I have a responsibility to return husbands and fathers to their families.

Keren does not appear fully satisfied with Avi's argument and confronts him. She has a personal investment: she doesn't want him injured, killed. A healthy and respectful *tête-à-tête* ensues between them.

Silently, I agree with Keren that Avi's soul is wounded. I agree with Avi that he is aware of this and is trying to recover. He feels too self-sufficient to turn to someone for help.

Later, when we are alone, Keren tells me more. Her grandparents and extended family were killed in the Holocaust.

Growing up in Brooklyn, in an Orthodox neighborhood, in retrospect felt like kibbutz; everyone knew the other, cared for the other. Her father was respected as a "go-to" guy, a "mister fix-it," everything is salvageable, nothing wasted. Other fathers were bookish; her father was a doer, with grime-etched fingers; her mother, quietly dedicated to her family. About Avi, she tells me she is dedicated to him. She respects him deeply. "He is a fine man, a reliable man, a good man." She believes he will be a wonderful father. Her seriousness and sincerity flows from her focused brown and tear-glistened eyes. But, she believes his soul is deeply wounded. She believes that Ha'Shem needs an agent like her on earth to help Avi heal. She hopes that I can provide this. She has never been able to convince Avi to talk to anyone about Motik and the others. When he told her about the research, that he might talk to me, she felt hope glimmer in her heart. But, Avi is "so stubborn, also so independent. He insists that he is doing this only for research."

A research interview? O.K., but no therapy.

A Soul in Limbo?

Limbo is a place where souls suffer for a time, because they still need to be cleansed from venial sins or have still to pay the temporal punishment due to mortal sins, the guilt and the eternal punishment of which have been remitted. Contrary to Proust—and more akin to the French title of his work—Avi is not in search of Rembrances of Things Past. He is in search of Times Lost (La Recherche du Temps Perdu). His soul is being purged in times lost. He is in a psychological state akin to limbo; suspended, temporarily lost, but (we hope) recoverable by the hard work of memory.

Avi has a remarkable, if painful, memory of the events that suspended him in the limbo of cynicism. But it is a cursed, Sisyphean memory, whose stone he rolls up to the top of his mountain, only to have it roll down. *"Comprendre c'est tout pardoner,"* goes a French saying—"to understand is to forgive." By understanding himself better, Avi may be able to forgive himself and move his life away from the dark cynicism of *Kohelet*, the Ecclessiast.

Paradoxically, Gaza's overwhelming trauma also is a screen that blocks earlier, troubling memories and feelings. Avi only has a sporadic, incomplete recollection of matters of the past, matters from his life preceding Gaza. He cannot see the defective foundation that was shaken by the 20-minute fire fight. To a certain extent, Avi's memory and life begin, return, almost end in Gaza.

It is obvious that Avi was connected with his men. Although he was overseeing 90, he experienced each of the four deaths personally; felt personally responsible for those deaths. He was conflicted about battling in Gaza, which is consistent with Gaza's place in Jewish history: a separate territory, unlike Hebron, Shechem (Nablus), Beer Sheva and Jerusalem, which form the spine of the Jewish kingdoms. Canaan/Israel, like embracing ribs, radiated to the west, towards the Mediterranean, and to the east, towards the Jordan River.

Avi's remarkable connection and efficacy with his men are direct products of his peer experiences from *kibbutz*. He, like others in this book, showed a profound, in-the-marrow, connectedness with his peers. This is qualitatively and quantitatively different, deeper than our American study[10].

Before the Trauma: The Fault Lines

In Israel, one learns more quickly—and unfortunately too much—about trauma. Freud believed that certain predisposing factors make one vulnerable to trauma. His daughter, studying children under the Nazi V-bombing in London, wrote that the children's reactions were proportional to the mothers' reactions to the bombings[11]. Lenore Terr differed. Beginning with her remarkable study of the Chowchilla kidnapping, she found that certain experiences are inherently traumatic, regardless of the

---

[10] Massie, H. and Szajnberg, N. *Lives Across Time*. Philadelphia: Xlibris, 2005.

[11] Burlingham, D. and Freud, A. *Infants Without Families*, London: George Allen & Unwin Lt., 1943.

parents' reactions. Bob Pynoos splits the difference in a very sophisticated and complex model: yes, events are inherently traumatic (the Armenian earthquake; the Kuwait invasion; the Northridge earthquake); but, subsequent experiences can maintain, amplify or diminish the subjective reactions, memories of trauma. Prior experiences may create fault lines, which may both effect vulnerability and create shears that follow the trauma, shears that channel one's life.

Avi's recounting of his life history gives us clues to vulnerabilities that predisposed him to collapse upon the occurrence of a traumatic event.

Avi's vulnerabilities are hidden behind the strength he developed through his kibbutz upbringing: its tight social fabric; its close peer relations; Avi's profound connection with his teachers (*mor'im, madrichim* and *m'chanichim*); and the parental grasp of other adults in the kibbutz: Moishek, his tractor "teacher;" Shlomi, his fifth-grade teacher, who welcomed Avi's questions about Zion, socialism; and significantly, the families into which he could "adopt himself" without overtly rejecting his family.

Avi designed his inner identity against his parents. Not overtly against, not completely consciously against; he protected them from overt rejection, criticism and could do so, in part, because of the kibbutz social structure that limited his time with them. Because he did not have to overtly reject his father (and parents), he was less laden with guilt, but only less.

Avi was determined to outdo, or at least equal, the blue bloods (and unconsciously, he outdid his father by leagues). He did not aspire to become a blue blood; he aspired to achieve as well as they did in the army and kibbutz, maybe some day become a mazkir (literally, the *kibbutz* "secretary," in fact, the manager). This need to outdo, to feel competition, is a legacy from his father, of which Avi doesn't seem aware.

He is conscious that he decided to "divorce" his parents in the early years, because of their acrimony. He recalls his father's towering rages (which he now shares) and his mother's hysterical crying. He has some sense of his own potential for towering rage, but redirects this: working in school, plowing mother earth, leading soldiers. But it is there.

Yet, a healthy part of him didn't want this acrimony, and he escaped into kibbutz and kibbutz families. This is both a successful adaptation, and a vulnerability. Yet again, he defined himself against his parents, an emotionally taxing task; one that takes ongoing energy to maintain. Always, always, even in his choice of wife, he tries to distance himself from his parents' acrimony. In one tête-à-tête at the cafe, I see that he has found a wife who is caring, yet has internal strength; they can discuss without the acrimonious argument.

How Was Avi Built?

Looking from the outside, we must speculate about Avi's internal make-up through his words and life. We must reconstruct Avi's internal "architecture;" his overall structure; the stages in which he was "built;" his strengths and vulnerabilities; his style and how well he can withstand the vagaries of fate.

Avi tells me that he has almost no childhood memories of his mother. Certainly, no caresses, kisses. Only what his mother tells him today about his childhood. In contrast, he clearly recalls his father's spankings and phobias. In the last few years, his anger at his father has erupted. Avi confesses that he now realizes that he could never return to kibbutz, because he is so angry at his father.

There are more hints to Avi's internal architecture. Avi, the boy, was like a sailboat on a tack, a steady keel in the water, his hand on the rudder; he had counterbalanced the ailments of childhood with the strengths from kibbutz (and some assets he took from his parents, unwittingly, such as his father's drive and persistence.) However, as an adolescent, Avi suffered three serious crises before the Gaza trauma. He did not consciously suffer from his childhood experiences prior to those three crises; but these experiences made him more vulnerable to the death of his men. Let us think of the later Gaza experience as an externally generated "quake" that knocked loose the internal structures rendered vulnerable by the prior adolescence crises.

His first crisis occurred precociously in fifth grade: a crisis of identity—doubts about his belief in socialism and the kibbutz ideology.

As best we can tell, this crisis occurred about the time of his mother's profound depression (although he doesn't recall her depression and only learned about it recently from his mother.)

Avi intellectualizes his felt crises. We can wonder whether, rather than feeling anxiety—about his mother's strength to care for him, to be there, about whether he could rely on her,—he experiences uncertainty about a more global "mother": socialism, Zionism, kibbutz. If we think of Erik Erikson's description of how in early childhood, we struggle with trust versus mistrust in our mothering world, we can better grasp Avi's profound anxiety in these terms. He could not trust that his "mother"—country was strong enough to sustain him.[12]

Precocious is a key word. In many ways, Avi developed abilities or experiences much earlier than most children—most significantly, his conscious decision at eight or so, to divorce his parents because of their acrimony. But, a child pays a price for precocity, at times. When a child is forced into precocity, he does so at the expense of other areas of personality, leaving vulnerabilities, such as losing a simple sense of trusting the world's benevolence, or feeling accepted simply for who you are.

His next crisis occurred in high school, as he was preparing seriously for army, around sixteen or seventeen. At the time, he questioned the ideals of socialism, kibbutz, and Zionism. He questioned those ideals so severely that his principal threatened to

---

[12] After the Lebanese War, for instance, there was a far greater incidence of "war neuroses," including psychoses, than in previous wars. There appears to be a connection between the societal support of and belief in a war effort and the impact on at least some soldiers' vulnerability to war neurosis. This may also be true in the American experience with the Vietnam war

expel him from the kibbutz school: "You don't like our ideals—go to regular high school." But Avi's skepticism jeopardized his leadership of the pre-army scout troop. (He credits both his parents with telling him to be sensible; to stay, finish high school for his future and to get into his desired army troop.) His mentor, Shlomi, welcomed all his severe questions. For Shlomi, Avi's questions were precisely what he would hope from a real kibbutznik—think critically about the ideology; don't accept passively. Yet, Avi jeopardized himself on the verge of his successfully completing high school—a pattern of identification with his father, who jeopardized his B.A. by leaving Argentina for the sake of his own ideals, but too soon.

These two crises were but tremors leading up to—in fact, setting the stage for—the third crisis: the rejection of *Matkal* after successfully completing the basic training.

Avi describes this third crisis as almost a collapse. In fact, he had a crisis of belief even before his breakdown at the end of his 40 km hike through the Judean foothills, bearing a stretcher and his "wounded" comrade, following the footsteps of his other stretcher-bearing comrade. There he was, almost at the pinnacle of his childhood desire: to be in *Matkal*, to achieve what only kibbutz blue blood achieved. Again—like his father. who sabotaged his college degree by leaving Argentina to become a Jewish "chicken-shit shoveler"—he sabotages his success. He confesses to me, *sotto voce*, that he was almost suicidal as he questioned the use of becoming a *Matkal* fighter, the meaning of Zionism, and why he was fighting. He felt the very foundation of his identity crumbling internally, while externally he was succeeding at every task. Avi reveals his feelings when he describes his quitting *Matkal* as "being tossed out from *Matkal*, and his transfer to an elite tank unit as a demotion. He needs to hold external factors responsible for his internal collapse. Avi unconsciously replicates his father's failure, (or is it failures): not finishing college, speaking a Spanish-accented Hebrew; preferring reading Spanish news, for Hebrew is still too hard. Even though, by his own standards, Avi has surpassed his father, like him he sabotages himself.

Psychologically, leaving *Matkal* and joining the tank corps is more suitable to Avi, and not only for the reasons we suggested earlier (being cozier with three or four khaverim in a tank; not preferring the individual decision-making of Matkal, nor the fine handwork of a guerilla fighter). The tank unit mimics Avi's psychological state: he too is heavily armored from his inner world, from his relationship with his parents, even as he leaves chinks in his armor or openings at the "turret" available to his khaverim and ultimately to his future wife.[13]

Avi was not built to withstand the Gaza "earthquake," a true trauma that would shake many Israelis, The deaths of his men in the ambush, and the death of his dearest friend two years later in another ambush were traumatic simply because the experience of death is traumatic. There is nothing weak, wrong, or problematic with Avi's reacting so powerfully to those deaths. However, the specific course of his reactions to those deaths—his unresolved melancholy; his belief that only death is real, tangible; his profound cynicism; his sense of foreshortened future; questioning the value of bringing children into this evil world, this world of vanities—were determined by preexisting cracks in Avi's foundation of trust and value in the world. In order to be repaired, the multiple weaknesses must first be revealed.

The kibbutz gave Avi a way to build around his vulnerabilities, to circumvent them; but it could not protect him from himself. As Avi moved towards the Gaza tragedy he carried within him both his resourceful circumventions and the vulnerabilities he was circumventing.

Like some inactive volcano, he now rests. Occasional wisps of smoke come from his emotional core, the hints of past eruptions. But, to some degree, he is spent. He is a businessman, but believes that his dead *khaver* would be disappointed in Avi's capitalist success. He sees his business success as vain compared to his self-assessed failure in Gaza. He is adored by his wife, who wants nothing more than to care for him and their children; yet,

---

[13]   (The Hebrew word for tanks, *shiryon* and the word for the muscles Avi says he once possessed, *shririm*, sound similar.)

he relishes hiking far from humans in the New Jersey hills or along the North Fork of Long Island.

The Future

Listen.

Avi leans forward, heavily, first, head in hands, then looking straight at me, eye-to eye.

Listen, the rest is no big deal. I finished the B.A. I thought about the dati (religious) stuff—I'm not meshuga. Who's more dati? Me or my socialist parents who left Argentina to build a kibbutz after a war in a forsaken corner of this land; left middle class homes to live in near poverty; my father who left the background of an educated family to work as a handy man or shoveling chicken shit? They think I'm religious? Well, it gives me a grounding. After the B.A., I met Keren. She was from New York, studying after her B.A. A year's study in Israel. I moved to New York. In Israel, I had the anniversaries of the deaths of both my men and my friends on my calendar. I'd go to each family every year, the day of Yizkor. I'd sit with them. It's my responsibility. I didn't realize how much this weighed on me until I moved to the States two years ago. I can't tell anyone it's been a relief to not have to go for Yizkor: Motik, Yankele, Eli, Motti, David, Khaval, Tzvi. Not just them; they're dead. Their families I sat with. Every Year. Look, it's a relief.

Keren is lovely. Her parents are from concentration camp backgrounds. I think that's why she worries about me, wants to care for me. She thinks I have trauma from Gaza; wanted me to meet with you. But I handle things myself. I analyze myself.

Business is nothing. After army, after deaths, this is nothing. My colleagues are so impressed with my ideas, my hard work, my getting things done. But, you see, I don't take this so seriously.

Maybe Motik would be disappointed that I am a businessman, a capitalist. But I won't do this forever. I need a base, an economic base. Money will permit me to do the things that are meaningful to me.

What things?

I am setting up a foundation named for Motik to fund research on desert agriculture, hydroponics, one of his loves.

Some day, when I'm rich, I will buy land, a farm, dunams (acres) in Israel. I will just go into the fields every day, smell the soil. You can't really make a living at farming. But those were my happiest days, happiest memories, being fifteen and in the fields before sunrise.

Will he have children?

Well, Keren of course wants children. I, I think, why should I bring children into such a fucked up world? I don't know how I will do as a father. I think of the mess that my parents did. My father insisted, starting when I was 8, that I had to play poker with him every day after school until I could beat him. He insisted I would learn strategy, keeping the cards to my chest, become a winner. I beat him when I was thirteen. Then I never played poker again. I hate it.

Well, I suppose I just might mess up my kids too. But Keren will be a wonderful mother.

# # #

I see Avi again, three years after the interview. He and Keren have two children. Avi had a look of hope, a glow in his eyes that I had not seen before.

Living Another's Life
(And Another's)

In the four-wheel drive Isuzu, doing late night guard around the periphery of the kibbutz, in the palpable thickness of a moonless rural night sky, bumping over unseen ruts, David tells me of his *gibush*, the crystallizing experience in his basic training.

For special operations exams, in Golani, they give me a bag full of sand to carry on my back. On top of the bag is a jerry can with water. The can leaks. I don't think that they know this—I hope they didn't. The water drips into the sand, then onto my back, as I run the course. This goes on for an hour, running to and fro. My shirt turns into sandpaper. My skin is raw. I come home, weekend leave. For two days, I lay face down and my mother oils my back. She rubs softly like this. (He strokes my left arm gently.) *It is not fun, the gibush, to crystallize into a unit. It does harden me, perhaps like crystal.*

This citizen soldier, this Golani brigade artilleryman/lawyer, is a father and husband, whose parents flew among the 50,000 other refugees on the "Magic Carpet" from Yemen to Israel. His receding black hair is tightly curled; light purplish halos encircle his dark eyes. Aubergine lips frame startingly white teeth. He speaks softly, almost a stage whisper, with remnants of the Yemenite breathy "chet," challenging my Western ears to distinguish from the soft "heh." I bend forward, listen closely.

This is our first meeting, at his father-in-law's kibbutz. He is short, like many other elite soldiers and I am surprised. I expected to meet to be a bunch of John Waynes. David will spend the Shabbat weekend with his wife and eight-month old daughter, Shira. Before we leave for guard duty, he feeds her patiently, having brought his mother's *jachnoon*, a timbali-shaped Yemenite bread that takes a day to make. He breaks off a piece, spreads chopped tomato and feeds it to his daughter. A piece of chicken too tough? He chews it briefly, then offers it to her.

He wants me to taste also; he pulls off a piece, suggests adding a bit of *s'chug*, a spicy-hot cardamon-coriander-cumin and garlic melange. He explains how his mother makes the bread: first, four rolled *ajin* bread-balls placed in a round pan, one egg between each and a fifth in the center, then baked at a low heat all night. The eggs emerge amber-toned; the bread, delicious. Others at the table peer to see how much *s'chug* I can tolerate; they caution me.

At nine, promptly, he rises. Now, I notice the gun in his belt. He kisses his wife, his daughter and heads to the corner behind the door. Suddenly, I see what I had missed when he arrived: his M16. There is no bravado in this soldier. He asks, would I like to join him for the four-hour guard duty; he's covering for his father-in-law.

I gather he wants to interview me before he decides to talk about his life. We hop into the Isuzu, spotlights mounted above us to scour the dark. Even as he drives, he looks directly at me, turning fully right, when he asks a question.

Why do I come during the Intifada when tourists have disappeared? I answer, in Hebrew, "Each Jew must be for the other." I see a nod of assent, a soft smile.

Why do I want to learn about Israeli soldiers? I tell him briefly about my American study; how none of the U.S. kids had been in the army.

What have I learned about Israeli soldiers? Here, I demur; I need to learn more from him and others.

He sounds a bit defensive about his reserve duty around Gaza, in Yehuda and Shomron. (I note that he uses the biblical names for the area from above Nablus to Hebron.) He describes hours of tedium, punctuated by moments of fear; being unable to trust the innocence of a child, who might be wearing a bomb vest (as happened with a fourteen year old at a check point); stopping old ladies trudging with unwieldy black plastic bags to check for rocket propelled grenades, and so on.

We drive the perimeter of the kibbutz in deep black silence. Periodically, he steps out of the four-wheel-drive, using a voltameter to check that the electric fence is intact, no voltage drops. The Isuzu's bright spotlights above the roof pierce the night. Yet, I cannot see what he sees. As he talks with me, his rifle nestling his right leg near the gear shift, I wonder how he can steer as he talks, how he can scan threats. Then, he stops suddenly—the car, the conversation—peers through the windshield where I see nothing. Only after he points, do I sense something: a movement, then a shadow, an animal, just outside the fence; perhaps a wild dog seeking refuge from the dark. Two years ago, by this fence, a woman was shot to death by a sniper from the Arab village opposite.

This Shabbat is peaceful.

*   *   *

A few months later, I return, teaching at Hadassah Hospital in Jerusalem. David calls Myron, our go-between, who introduced me to David: David will meet with me that week.

I prefer to visit the home, but it is too difficult to get a taxi to his moshav late at night after I finish at Hadassah, even more difficult to get a cab back. Via messages through Myron we discuss the hoped for arrangement. David ventures: could I see him in Jerusalem before Shabbat perhaps? I respond, It will be difficult, since I am teaching all day at Hadassah. David answers, *"If his research is so important to him, Nathan will find a way."*

LIVING ANOTHER'S LIFE

So, I find a way.

And, he telephones me Thursday morning. *"I will be in Jerusalem tonight, staying through Shabbat. I wanted to be sure how much you desire to do this."*

He will be at the Gates of Jerusalem (the Hotel's name is *Sha'ar Ha'ir*, Gates of The City). I finish teaching late, hop the bus with two valises and look for *Sha'ar Ha'ir*: The Hotel hasn't changed its name publicly; no one knows of it (including the slight, Ethiopian security guard at the shopping plaza beneath the Hotel). Even the neon sign atop has its former name, although it is unlit. Jerusalem seems to be going through a phase of hotel name changes; even most residents call the new hotels by their old names. By seven, I stumble into the lobby, confirm with the handsomely dressed Sephardic manager that this is the right Hotel. I fall asleep on a chair in the noisy lobby filled with adolescent girls, squealing greetings to each other. Here, I wait for David.

He wakes me gently and directs me with a smile to a mezzanine room overlooking the raucous lobby, where his wife organizes activities for young army women.

He has that quiet certitude about him. I feel as if I were talking with someone a decade older. I notice that while looking directly at me, at moments, it seems as if he were talking to himself, turning inward at critical moments.

I come from an Orthodox Yemenite family. For my father, studying comes first. Studying means Talmud, then come all other obligations. The army is a responsibility to be filled, but my father hopes that his sons would return to studying. Ironically, not one of us boys become scholars (of Torah) — only accountants, lawyers, businessmen. As a consolation prize, when my father retires, the beit k'nesset (a modest synagogue) gives him a small room where he and a few men can study. My father is slightly bemused that the rabbi puts up a sign on the door post opposite the mezzuzah: "No studying in pairs out loud." My father jokes, "Who do they think we are, academics, we can study silently? You best study Talmud standing two at a desk, arguing out loud." He is studying parallels between words in the Chumash and the Rambam's writings.[14] He gets excited over his discoveries.

I'll tell you my family's journey briefly. My mother and father were toddlers when they arrived in Israel. They were among the Yemenite Jews who upon seeing the Israeli planes that would take them to their homeland, recalled the biblical prophecy that they would be born home on the wings of Eagles.

My grandfather made a fateful decision for all eight children. In contrast to his brothers, my grandfather decided that to become Israelis, a new people, his children would be sent off to live and learn in the residential schools for some immigrant children, orphans, or those whose parents could not care for their children.

Because of this, we are at least one generation ahead of our cousins: while I and my sisters and brothers are college-educated, my cousins are not (yet): they stayed in the secure, but insular Yemenite community. Mind you, they are good people, but only now are their children achieving what I and my siblings have done. In fact, I married an Ashkenazi, a South African immigrant, with approval from my family (and my in-laws). One uncle cautions me that Ashkenazis are not real Jews, but for me and my fiance, he would make an exception.

At fourteen, my father sends me to study in Jerusalem, leaving my moshav near Makhaneh Aleph, a biblical place.

In boarding school, there is much talk about the army. Former students, now on active army duty, return for weekend leave, to visit. These guys are intoxicated (mo'rl) with being good soldiers.

A major way the army changes me: I realize that if I put my mind to something, I can achieve it. Before the army, I thought I would live in my village, become an auto repairman, or after awhile own a small business. After army, I know I should go to college. Then, I become a lawyer.

---

[14] *Chumash* is the five books of Moses, the Torah; Rambam was a 12th century physician and rabbi who wrote extensive commentaries on Jewish law.

LIVING ANOTHER'S LIFE

Later, I heard from others what David is too modest to tell me: he ranks fifth of 1200 on a national exam. But it wasn't until well into his second interview, I learn how deeply the army experience has transformed him. The interview almost didn't happen. On vacation with his wife, he asks to meet two nights before I am to leave. That night, they are marooned in Eilat—car trouble. The last night also happens late. He has to leave for Tel Aviv at five a.m., but, insists that after a shower, we start (at nine) and keep going until we are done.

I joined the Golani Brigade.

He looks up at me, sees my look of recognition (and admiration) then softly smiles. Golani soldiers once were referred to as "mao maos": good fighters, but not the brightest of stars in the constellation. In contrast, paratroopers are both good fighters and smart. In the '50's, the Golani soldiers are recruited from the poor immigrant tent camps. But by my time, Golani's image had improved.

Why Golani? Well, everyone at my school wants to join Golani, and my cousin is in it. Also, I have a more personal reason—a connection with my father. Maybe later I can tell you.

My cousin works to get into Golani. First recruited and trained as a food preparer, then in charge of supplies, he trains and appeals until he is accepted into Golani.

My Kabah score was 56, the highest possible. I could choose my unit.

I think it is better that I am a bit older than others who start at 17, 18. I feel older, more mature. You know, my officer commands us to run back, forth, back forth for one to two hours; others complain. I just tell myself, "It's one to two hours, then it's over."

During our short breaks, the young guys make themselves more miserable. The complainers complain to the others, who then feel worse. I, I go study Talmud, history during breaks; feel refreshed.

We have different branches in Golani: stinger antitank missiles, mines; special operations. I am sent to officer training after four months, basic training in Golani, then four months spent training, then another ten months—I don't remember exactly how much time.

The first twelve months, we are trained to think of each other as brothers, to shout "I will die for my brother." But, it isn't until my thirteenth month that I feel this.

In the army we have a hierarchy among the hova soldiers during our first three years, even though it's informal. New recruits are the "youth," then there are the "veterans" and finally, the "ancients". The youth have to do their own chores and also some of the veterans' chores. The "ancients" do almost nothing. I don't care for that attitude. All they do is look for opportunities to punish the youth. These "ancients" — remember, they are maybe 21, 22 — don't understand the idea of setting an example for the youth.

You learn quickly the army imperative to respect officers. Do not look into an officer's tent, see his bed. Do it once, and you get extra hours of guard duty. Twice, the same. You learn not to do it a third time. You walk around the back of the tent. You know, among the Bedouin, it is the opposite: to approach the tent from one of the three closed sides is an insult or a threat — they have have to approach from the opening which always faces East.

In my first level of officer training, making me a sergeant (Samal) I learn orders, how to fire, call in air support, call for help, manage my unit.

But, I learn something I am not taught. We are given many rules — for instance, at night maneuvers, to set off a light every minute, or if you miss a shot, readjust sites a certain amount. But I want to know the reason for the rules. I learn them and when I have to tell my men rules, I can explain the reason.

Also, I become known as someone who develops innovative techniques.

David becomes animated as he enters into a long discourse on triangulating a target using a sextant. Previously, he had been taught a more trial and error method that took one to two minutes for readjustment. He shows me how he worked out the mathematics. He is a good teacher, his hands articulating enemy positions and his unit's, his body torquing, even dancing.

*   *   *

Enough about sextants. I want to talk about Lebanon, about Eran, really.

About the event that transformed him, haunts him still. At first, I am confused as he starts with laser devices and dynamite. Where are we heading?

We have a laser device to interrupt the electrical impulses traveling the line between a detonator and its dynamite. Use this in convoys that anticipate ambush in Lebanon's beautiful, lush, deadly valleys. But you need to see the dynamiter as he hits the plunger, to interrupt the blast. Valleys make one blind.

I'm told that the Bekaa Valley is a premier heroin production center. Lebanon killed in many ways. The tarry, black poppy paste helped Syria and Hezbollah pay for its occupation of Lebanon. But this day, it isn't heroin that killed.

I would have been there that day, should have been, but for my officer's training.

Instead, Eran drives the rear car in the convoy. Since I'm not yet officer, I would have been doing rear guard.

The ambush is well-planned. Hezbollah positioned itself midway up the mountains; they know that ambushed Israelis go for the high ground.

Hezbollah waits for the entire convoy to enter the Valley. They aim at the first car, dynamite the second. The laser device now is useless. The officer is killed, his driver injured. Then, they dynamite the last car, precluding retreat, creating a double bottleneck, a Push-me-Pull-you of death.

Hezbollah turns the valley into a killing field, the flowing blood irrigating the red poppies.

But Eran, Eran Azuli (David wants me to remember his name, register it, *zachor*, he says), *gets hit in the back of his neck—shrapnel. Eran tries to tell the medic something hurt back there, but his helmet obscures the wound. Sent to the field hospital, he dies en route.*

Eran Azuli loved helping others. Puzzling; I wasn't that close to him before the death. Death toughens us. Me. From Netanyah, he wasn't wealthy. Netanya is a touch of North Africa, French-speaking devout Jews from Algeria, Tunisia and such. Sephardim, many are from communities established after the exile of Jews from the Inquisition in Spain. The villiage center, Independence Square, could be from a town in North Africa, or South of France. In the evening, late, families promenade; parents sit outside with a café, children play on the fountains, ride trikes, play tag. The people are simple, good. Eran was like me, a boy of the earth.

I visited his mother weekly for eighteen months. Whenever I get weekend leave, I visit her rather than my family; my parents understand, a mitzvah. After that, I visit twice monthly. Recently, I see her monthly. We talk about Eran, what he might be doing now. Three of us in my unit connect with Eran's mother. I've stayed longest.

Because he dies, I stop officer training. That's the real reason, what I didn't tell you at Sha'ar Ha'ir, what I didn't tell my father. I have three weeks left, maybe two, for the course. I request my officer to return me to my platoon in Lebanon. I tell myself, I would continue Eran's path, continue his life. He wasn't an officer. He was a soldier. This is enough for me, to follow his path.

Why did I do this? I still wonder. If I had been in Lebanon, I would have been in the ambush. Now I have a strong connection.

I ask him, "What do you mean, if you had been in Lebanon?"

I spoke to my friends who were there. What did they feel at those moments? What did they know, what did he say?

In my first rotation in Lebanon, before Eran, I meet death. A friend tries to run back to his tank; hit by a missile. I see his remains. I don't just see them. You know, if you're Jewish, every piece of flesh needs to be collected, even with tweezers, to be buried in one place. My officer knows that I am from a religious background: one of two in the battalion. He directs me to collect the fleshy fragments of my friend's body. I collect this former human, with a bag. I pick pieces of his flesh from the stones, from off the armor of the tank.

But Eran happens Thursday night. On Friday, I go to the Hospital morgue in Haifa to see him. From the front, he looks fine. His death is hidden in his neck.

The effect on my life? What death means. More than most of those I know, I seem to know more, more than I want to know. If

I hear about a death, even from an accident, then it's not just one man killed. His whole family dies with him—the pain, unable to work, unable to forget.

When I meet Chava (David's wife-to-be), she is returning from a lecture on death at the University. We are becoming a nation that is expert in death. You know how Saul Bellow writes that Germans excelled in two things: making cars and killing Jews? Well, we excel in high-tech and high-death.

Anyhow, before Chava can tell me about the lecture, I confess to her about Eran's death. My second date, I think, and I tell her about death. Can you believe that? Jewish courting. She tells me that with Eran's story, I teach her more about death than all her professor's lectures.

He sighs here, looks into the distance.

Why did I react this way; because I was so young? I feel part of his death.

"Do you feel guilty because you weren't in Lebanon?"

He looks up, smiles slightly, as if found out.

Yeah. I think so. All the time, I feel sorry of course I wasn't in Lebanon. Maybe that did cause me to leave the (officer) course, because I wasn't in Lebanon with my unit when I should have been. I never want to leave them again.

"Do you feel any sense of revenge?"

Not revenge, I don't think so. What for? Look, I am a soldier. I was educated to kill an enemy. Often, I didn't see the enemy I killed—artillery shoots beyond hills, into forests, out-of-sight.

Sometimes we are sent out for an "action"—to ambush, to be forward eyes behind enemy lines. We would lie for two to three days, always on the ground, never standing.

He demonstrates how to pee lying down.

Never did the enemy come. I guess they didn't read the rule book: we're waiting for you, you should come.

I want to stay at the end of my four-year tour. I don't. Would have been pushing my luck. As I am about to leave, I do exercises with the youth. I don't want all that I learned to die with me, I mean, to die with my leaving. I want to teach the younger. It was very dangerous, I realized, what I had been doing. But Lebanon was the real situation, real war.

"How did the army change you?"

It made me more serious. This is a difficult question. I know more the meaning of life. I have a different attitude to death, pain, friends. To a friend, you give him the all; and he gives you the all. Also, you know what you can achieve, if you want. You learn that everything in your head, you can achieve. If you make the effort. And everything you have, you feel is in correct proportion.

What do I mean, correct proportion? Look, if it's cold outside, you can wear a coat and still shiver and complain. Or, you say to yourself, "It's nothing, it's O.K."

You ask what it was like as a soldier to have to serve in Jenin, Ramallah[15]. I can be succinct: If I don't serve, don't fight well, first I will fall, then they will kill my family. I think first of my family.

* * *

Soon, David and I learn something hidden within him.

Two months later, we complete our meetings at his home at the edge of the Green Line, suspended midway between Jerusalem and Tel Aviv in the moshav, "*Miyuchad*," where he grew up.

I worry that our last meeting won't happen. As a psychoanalyst I know that as someone is about to breach an inner vulnerability, he or she may hesitate. Yet, I also know David—he will do the work. He invites me to his house for Shabbat eve.

I have to get to *Miyuchad* before Shabbat and complete our discussion well before Shabbat, so that he can prepare for Queen Shabbat. When I arrive, he is helping his wife clean. He insists that as his guest I must rest, not help. I watch as he upturns all the chairs on the dining table, "invites" the mutt to play outside, mops the terrazo floors, a continuous surface that is kitchen, salon and dining area and entrance foyer. He showers and changes into a

---

[15] In Spring 2002, after the Passover Park Hotel bombing in Netanya.

simple white open collar shirt, sleeves rolled up the forearm. He retreats for a period of quiet reflection. Then, he invites me to a separate room to talk. And he starts by talking about his children before he returns to himself, his father, his soldiering.

I am not Orthodox like my father, my brothers. I want my children to know that not everything has to be around religion. Being a good person, being dedicated to those whom you love and to your community, living a good life—these are most important.

But for me, everything good happened around religion. There were ten of us plus father and mother. After eating and blessing the food, then we would study Torah; after shul on Shabbat, we would eat, rest and have the day only for play and studying Torah. Learning, studying means the love of Torah. Studies at school were important, but different.

I told you there were ten of us: Yinon, Noam, Nama, Hadas, Tehila, Raphael, Avihu, Emuna, Nehama and me, Dov Chaim. Before, I didn't tell you that there is a story about my name; why two names. My father was in regular army for six years, three longer than required. But when my mother was pregnant with me in '73, my father is called up to fight in the Golan. For the women, life is much harder when the husbands and sons are called up to fight.

My father's closest friend, Dov Mizrachi, is front line against the first attack of Syrian tanks. Israel is unprepared for this. You probably know that Kahalani and his tank corps saved Israel by not retreating from the tenfold larger Syrian tank onslaught. Well, Dov Mizrachi is one of those killed. My father decides to name me after him. By tradition, he added Chaim, "Life," so that I would be the "Dov who lived." My life is to continue Dov Mizrachi's.

A strange experience I had in '98 when I am in the Golan with the Golani brigade. We are preparing for a special operation into Lebanon, against Hezbollah. I go into the small shul in the Golan to borrow a siddur to take into Lebanon. I'm not sure how long we would be there, maybe over Shabbat. So, I reach up, take down a prayer bookr. As I tip it downward, I see on the top edge is written a name—Dov Mizrachi. Still have it. Use it every Shabbat. Look, I don't know really if this is the same Dov Mizrachi. If it is, maybe before he went to battle, he left the siddur. But for me it is special . . . .

But what does this have to do with my army experience?

"What about the connection: your father losing his friend in Golan, you get his name; your losing your friend in Lebanon; your decision to live out both his and your lives?"

Dov quiets, and reclines, covers his face, and takes a deep breath. He sits up slowly, his hand slips down from his face, he looks at me.

You think it's possible? You think that's why? Why I reacted so strongly to Eran's death, decided I should live out both my life and his? You think that there is a connection between Eran and my father's buddy, Dov?

I realize that I felt I should have been there, with Eran, maybe instead of him. But now that you say this, I used to think, what a thin line was between Dov Mizrachi's death and my father's life. They both were in the Golan, but only one lived.

And I joined Golani.

*   *   *

I leave him for a few minutes in the room, to collect himself. He emerges for Shabbat eve dinner. I see that look of quiet reflection after our interview, as he discreetly takes his wife's hand, as he looks downward, almost inward, reciting the prayer of thanksgiving for a good wife—*aishet chail*—that begins, "A valorous wife is as rare as finding a pearl."

Kibbutz: How to Build a Reluctant Warrior

*I am about five when I first enter the bomb shelter. Our kibbutz
is near the Lebanese border; Hezbollah would often send "packages"
by airmail. I recall that I lose my* motzetz, *my pacifier, the first time I
go underground. The adults equip the shelters with the very same toys
that we have above ground; but they forget an exact same* motzetz;
they have new ones, but, you know, not the same taste.

*Yet, I'm not afraid, never afraid. I am surrounded by adults who
seem always to be laughing joking, with each other and always with
the kids. They turn one room into a "disco" for the teens, a revolving
reflective ball in the center of the room. We once spend a week
underground, hearing the thudding above and the laughter below.
I put all my trust in adults. But, when we emerge, I remember the
bloated bodies of dead goats hit by shrapnel, rotting gasses emit in
deep sighs, heavy-bellied flies hover.*

Peretz's glasses magnify his blue, lively eyes; his eyebrows dance
above the rims as he talks. He takes a break from the kitchen in the
chic Tel Aviv restaurant where he grills the fish, meat. He confesses
that he prefers to make simpler fare. In his first job at a "wraps"
place, he is so excited about the colors in his first spinach tortilla

wrap—the play of red tomatoes, tawny tehini, golden chicken on the green dough—that, before rolling-up the wrap, he carries it out to the cafe so the waiting customer can share his enthusiasm. I have been watching him prepare for dinner: his knife flies, cucumbers sliver, tomatoes fall in lacy rings, yellow peppers in angular haloes. He talks as he focuses on the food.

While he speaks about army, his life circles around kibbutz, his family's leaving, his return, his leaving and his yearning for kibbutz.

My family leaves kibbutz for Canada when I am in high school. My father is from Montreal, a nice middle-class Jewish family. He came to Kibbutz "Tzafon" when he was 17 for a summer; he stays 17 years, like Joseph in Egypt. Meets my mother there, who is from kibbutz, but Sephardi background; Syrian, of spicy temperament, red-haired, <u>charisa</u>. Over the years, my father gets too lonely for his family, for Montreal. Also, he never really learns <u>ivrit</u> well; sometimes he uses the wrong gender, occasionally refers to me in the feminine, <u>at</u> instead of <u>ata</u>. So, when I am 15, they take my brother and me to Canada. My sister has started Army and she is adamant about staying in Israel. She's now on Kibbutz "Yazriel."

I am miserable in Canada, miserable. I feel so different from the kids in high school. Please understand that now I see that they were nice kids. But then, they seem so immature: boys and girls playing games with each other; not being sincere, not really honest with each other. On kibbutz when we use the word "education," we mean not only academics, but also—even especially—social comportment, how you treat others, how you carry yourself. There is not a simple, correct English translation of <u>hitnaghut</u>, something like "steering or driving" yourself. Every adult on kibbutz considered herself or himself a parent surrogate—I had lots of "educators." Social comportment was not taught in Canadian high school.

When I turn 18, I tell my parents that I am returning to Israel, to army, to kibbutz. They take me to the airport; later confess to me that they had agreed not to cry at the airport, so as not to make it harder for me. But, I cry.

The kibbutz is ready for me. I am given an adoptive family who will join me for parent weekends at base camp and whom I will visit when I get weekends free. I have my same friends from school, although my sister has married and moved to another kibbutz. I get all the love I need in kibbutz.

Funny, because I had thought of myself as a troublemaker as a kid. In fact, they care for me. Returning to kibbutz returns memories, memories of growing up.

I guess, as a child, in school, I am trouble, want to be king of my class, compete, pick fights. I hear that someone wants to put me on medication for "hyperactivity"; my metapelet, Naomi, protects me from drugs, from everything. She gives me unconditional love.

What do I mean I make trouble? Once, In fourth grade, maybe, I am found smoking a cigarette in the bushes outside school. Imagine, puffs of smoke arising from the shrubs during snack time, and, I, thinking no one would notice. Both my mother and metapelet speak with me. They aren't mad. My mother is almost relaxed, but firm. I feel I had hurt, disappointed her: haven't smoked since.

Another time on a Friday, I am upset about something—can't remember what. I decide to run away to Jerusalem. Picture me, all of 11 years old, trying to hitchhike four hours to Jerusalem. A kibbutznik sees me outside at the road; gives me a ride around for a while, then returns to kibbutz. Naomi reassures me. I decide then that it was important to listen to her, be like her.

When on kibbutz, I thought I was "violent," but I learn that this word means something stronger in English, in Canada. "Violent" on kibbutz means stealing vegetables from the garden, driving the tractor late at night.

When I turn fourteen, the kibbutz moves us to the Teen Homes. This is great. We have much freedom, which we abuse: some are smoking, others drinking, joy-riding on the kibbutz trucks, tractors. The kibbutz is very tolerant.

But if you skip school, the madrich would send you to live with your parents. This cures us quickly of truancy.

Because of our group, our rowdiness, the kibbutz committee votes to move all teens back to live with their parents until 18; they want to control us more. We start an action, organize, petition, finally demand a meeting with the committee. They back down. As soon as our class graduates, they change their policy, close the teen dorms.

Small memories of how kibbutz prepares me for army. We get responsibilities early. Third grade we get jobs, love them. I want to herd the goats, a fine challenge: you get to know all different parts of the kibbutz; follow the seasons where the best grass is. And I get to be outside. The goats are good company. Now, when I eat goat cheese, I think of my goats. They have rectangular pupils, you know, and a look of kind curiosity.

Can you believe? When I am 12, 13, they let me drive the forklift to load the pallets of potatoes! I could have hurt someone! How do they know to trust me?

We start with responsibilities young. At nine, not only do I herd the goats, but also go with a donkey and wagon and buddy to harvest grasses for the ponies in the zoo. We have a little zoo for kids; call it the Garden of Eden. Now, I visit and it's tiny. Then, we would go there on Shabbat with my family and I marveled: boulders are great mountains to conquer; mountain goats with scimitar-like curved horns—shofars-to-be; ponies to pet, ride, of course, a peacock who struts about, keeps to himself except to unfurl his tail, like a braggart.

So, harvesting grasses is a special job. In fact, I go with another nine year-old, but we have two eleven year olds, who are supposed to teach us how to use the <u>chermesh</u> and <u>magal</u>—what you call them?—scythe and sickle. You use the scythe in large areas, but not near a fence—could gouge it. For this, you use the sickle. They are to show us how to lead the donkey, load the wagon with sheaves, like in Joseph's dream. In fact, the eleven year olds are bullies, smack us on the backs of the head for nothing. We tell no one, but one day a teacher sees and stops them and tells our parents. My father talks with the boys. They stopped. I have a mixed reaction. First, I am embarrassed that my parents find out: thought I should be stoic, handle it myself. Eventually I feel relieved; we become friends with the eleven year olds.

We we turn eleven and have two nine year old assistants, we treat them well. And the fun, the fun of riding back, one of us on the grasses in the wagon, and arriving to feed the ponies; the ponies knew, greeted us. Great.

At thirteen, I get promoted to work on irrigation and sewage. You know how precious is water to us: we use sparingly and watch its waste. You know the buried drip irrigation system was invented in Israel? But sewage also is important: we build the early water-reclamation pools for plant irrigation. (The Arabs down the valley accuse us of storing poisons to pump down into their olive groves; I remember when one of our khaver kibbutz brought the Arab sheik up to the pool. The khaver pulls a tin cup from his belt, bends down, scoops up water and drinks. After that, the Arab ask if we would build such a water recalamation pond for their village.) During droughts, we distribute big plastic bins for under the sinks, open the traps below the sink to collect water for hand-washing or dishwashing. Then we go house-to-house to empty the waste water; use it for the flower gardens. The men have us check the faucets for drips and repair them; just need new rubber washers. Boring then, but now I know every drip is important.

The water people taught me at thirteen how to drive the new Jeep. Myself. Before this, as kids, we would sneak into the parking shed to drive a truck. Because we are short, this takes three kids: one clutches, one brakes, one steers and accelerates. The clutch is stiff. But now, at thirteen, I am a sanctioned driver.

I guess they _did_ know enough about me to permit me the forklift when I was fourteen. But, hand—harvesting the potatoes, the kibbutz hires Arab women. I recall them, bent over, digging, rooting around, popping out the potatoes. I suppose for them, it is good work, good pay; but as a boy, I feel guilty that they do the hard work and I on a forklift. I am confused, though, since labor with the earth is so important in our studies about the building of Israel, in the stories about building the kibbutz, which we hear from the grandparents who built this kibbutz. How could they ask Arabs to do some of the labor? Confused and uncomfortable. At harvest, the students are allowed skip school to work the fields. _Kef_ (fun).

I grow up surrounded by fields. The kind of work you _do_ is important. At twelve, thirteen, you are given one day weekly off *from school to work. I love, I <u>choose</u> at fourteen to work in the fields, planting, pruning, tilling. I love getting up before dawn, drinking the botz ("mud" coffee) with the older men, working until nine a.m., returning to the common eating hall, our nails and hands encrusted with earth, having breakfast, returning to work the soil until night fall. In the dining hall, maybe a nominal rinse of the hands, but no scrubbing: earth-encrusted hands are a badge of true work, of honor.*

Parents Promotions; My Disappointment

Before I was born, my father worked the avocado fields, planted many of the trees, especially avocados, harvested rapidly by hand before the fruit dropped heavily to rot. But, by my childhood, my father gets promoted to manage the new pool; my mother the guest house. Look, today, I understand that the pool and guesthouse are big moneymakers for the Kibbutz, their first venture into capitalism. I would hear form other kibbutz members what a great job my father does, arranging for special events, attracting non-kibbutz guests. My guess is that the money he makes for the kibbutz helps support our wonderful fields. But as a boy, I am disappointed, a little ashamed that my father didn't do <u>real</u> work, agriculture. I feel badly now, but please understand the culture of kibbutz and my view as a boy. I have surrogate fathers who drive tractors, plant, harvest, make water reclamation ponds, have earth-encrusted hands: from dust to dust, in a manner of speaking.

Now, for me, is a the good thing about my father's job; he has a kibbutz car assigned to him. Listen to how I think as a fourteen year old. You know that on kibbutz, all cars are communal, you have to sign up far a car for a few hours, sometimes days ahead. Priority is given for kibbutz use, not personal trips: you can sign up, then, get trumped. But, my father's assigned car meant that he can use as he wished. This and basket ball brings us closer until he takes us away from kibbutz. You see, (when I am) about twelve, a coach for the local city team sees me dribble, dunk, move down the court during a kibbutz game. I have always been agile, fast, good with the hands and feet. He invites me to join the serious team in the nearby city. My father is dedicated to me: drives me to all practices if I miss the bus; arranges for pool parties for my teammates; goes to my games to watch me. I feel closer to him then than ever in my life—before or since.

*   *   *

Kibbutz to Boot Camp

Here is how I think kibbutz prepares me for army: I never feel threatened, even when bombs drop. On kibbutz, I always feel calm, even in danger. And I have a kind of optimism: if you let things fall by themselves, they fall in the right place. I never feel lonely. Finally, for the army, it is good not to be selfish; selflessness we are taught on kibbutz.

I return to kibbutz in January and into basic training by March. Basic training is a big shock, a shock. The _Bakum_, the major gathering center, is huge, chaotic. You get your uniform and are told: make your three choices about unit. I pick antitank and later get it. But it feels like the slave trade; each unit bids on you. Then you wait for 2-3 weeks to start something. Meantime, they have you wash dishes, cut grass, wait. I have a physical exam; the Russian doctor says something is wrong with my eyes, which would exclude me from an elite combat unit. Here is where knowing someone in Israel can be helpful. My mother has a friend, a nurse, who works in the army. She says if I ever had a problem, to come to her. So, I do. She insists that the doctor who examines me is not an eye doctor: I should get an appointment outside the army with an eye specialist. Which I do. My eyes are perfect. I appeal to the army and get my placement.

A trick I learn with a buddy in the _Bakum_: we wander about with nothing to do except dishwashing, mowing. But, if you walk in a straight direction, as if you are going someplace, as if you are

KIBBUTZ: BUILDING A RELUCTANT WARRIOR   ⸱123⸱

busy or about to be busy, no officer bothers you. We walk looking determined; it works.

For the army, I want a combat unit. I twist my ankle the week before basic training, but no problem. I get placed in an antitank unit.

Here's what I learn they look for in basic training: 1) be unselfish, help others; 2) be honest; 3) be like anyone else, don't think of yourself as more special. Also, I don't take the officers' threats too seriously. I know that the army requires that we get 5-6 hours sleep every night. So, if I get an impossible task, I don't make a big deal; by 11 p.m. I know I will get to bed. My officers do well by me.

My biggest motivation to do well was to get a pass home for Shabbat. It is so restful on kibbutz. I become blue Saturday night. We have a special phrase in Hebrew for the feelings on Sunday morning, when you have to return to army: sh'vi'zut yom aleph, or sh'vur zayin. Now, this is translated as the "blues," but its literal meaning is something like "being broken on Sunday." I feel broken as I anticipate leaving kibbutz to return to duty. Once, I lose my weekend pass: on the shooting range, I fire one too many bullets, get punished. Never again, I waste a bullet.

I told you that I got all the love I needed from kibbutz. Not quite honest. You see, once my family left, once I return, I am no longer a ben meshek, literally, a "son of agriculture"; figuratively, I am "orphaned", my family had abandoned the kibbutz. I feel like a guest and like a guest, I feel that I have to watch myself more closely; when the other youths want to do something special, they might approach the kibbutz for funds; I don't feel comfortable doing that; I feel that I have to behave more diligently. I feel on the periphery, as I have ever since.

I graduate at the top of my plugah of 90 guys. My proudest moment at the ceremony ending basic training is when my officer hands me his beret to wear, to keep his beret; I still have it on my bed stand. My adoptive kibbutz family and my sister are there.

For this, I become the radio carrier for the officer. You get to be in front, you know what's going on, you learn from your officer and you keep in good shape; back then, the radios are heavy.

Why do I do so well in basic training? I am not sure. Can I brag to you about it just a bit? How come I stood out so? I never break down. Even the 40 km. hike from the Jordan river through the Judean Hills to Jerusalem with a back pack, with rappelling in the wadis, I never break down. The excitement of going home helps. It is a lot of honor.

I remove my medals whenever I approach kibbutz on weekend leave. To show medals is immodest, would make me look like a braggart, make my friends uncomfortable. On kibbutz, doing is what is important, not showing-off.

* * *

Army to Hebron

I realize that I thought, sometimes, that army is like a game. These officers, they can be just like me, not so different. And like a game, there is a sense of unreality and predictability: if you do this, then that happens. Even the officers' harassment: I think of it as an educational game. Army life is so extreme, it felt unreal; kibbutz was always real for me. What I brought from home to make army easier was my sense of humor and my commitment to selflessness.

With the Intifada, my antitank unit gets reassigned to foot soldiers, to the territories, almost entirely.

There is supposed to be a pattern to army, before the Intifada: basic training a few months, then eighteen months service, then additional training, then to the borders to protect us. But the Intifada changes all that.

There are different kinds of sergeants. I am promoted within my platoon. In Hebrew, sergeant is segel, which is the root for m'sugal, "capable." So, the word segel means you are capable of leading men. Now, I am leading both younger guys and guys who had been my peers. But, I am assigned to sleep in the officers tent. I miss sleeping with my platoon.

NATHAN SZAJNBERG

Cleft Self

Serving in the territories I feel cleaved, like a lightening bolt that strikes a tree: split vertically, left standing. I have a David "me" and David, "the Sergeant," whom I don't like as much. I do the best I can with him.

Hebron, I wonder, "Why are we here . . . It's completely different, different country. Very confusing." Scary: who is an enemy; who not: which boy, which apparently pregnant woman, who could kill you.

You know about Hebron? It is where Abraham finally settled, where the Caves of Machpelah[16] is, where Abraham and Sarah are buried. But now, it has tens of thousands Palestinians and a few thousands Jews. They took it, the Palestinians; let them have it.

I had trouble with the settlers, tense with them. They considered themselves pioneers, a special word in Hebrew, associated with Ben Gurion, those who came in the early 20th century, drained the swamps of Huleh, shared a single egg for breakfast, died of malaria or Arab raids in '29. But these settlers harassed us, would throw stones at us, hit us if we carried out our responsibilities. Our orders were at times unclear, except never open fire on Jews, even if you think you are being shot at. This changed after Baruch Goldstein.[17]

I was in Kiryat Arba when Goldstein killed those Arabs and was killed. I think that the army called in half its forces to Hebron to prevent rioting; every few yards there was a soldier. It worked. No riots.

Still, some of my soldiers objected when I said to use non-lethal force against settlers—tear-gas, beanbags shot through a special gun; they couldn't bring themselves to do anything aggressive to fellow Jews. I reassigned those soldiers.

---

[16] Machpela, means "couple", as both Abraham and Sarah are buried there.

[17] Goldstein, an extremist, militant Orthodox Jew, gunned down Arabs in a mosque and was then stoned to death by the crowd. Some religious settlers still visit Goldstein's grave to honor him.

Here was one of our jobs on Shabbat in Hebron: to block streets so that the religious Jews in Kiryat Arba could walk to the Cave of Machpelah and back. Now I saw the whole picture, why there was so much tension with the Arabs.

We were in the middle. It was very depressing.

After Goldstein, I was sent for a one-month course on how to handle violence. I just couldn't shoot at boys throwing rocks, even if they were lethal. I just couldn't shoot.

I begin to do the minimum: make sure <u>not to put my soldiers in harm's way</u>, and to <u>protect the civilians</u>. That's all. I'm not angry with the government: I feel disconnected—seeing suffering people.

I do become angry when I see friends from kibbutz losing compassion. Look, you go on a road and set up a road block in a few minutes. You use those nails, you know, the big ones to puncture tires if someone won't stop. Then you ask to see ID cards, papers. By the rule book, if a man doesn't have all his papers, you are supposed to turn him back or detain him, teach him a lesson. We build a temporary jail, just a cage from fence material, next to the camp. It is too hard for me: I share my pita and felafel with the guy.

Death, and What Dies Inside

My unit is lucky; no one killed, no one seriously hurt and we don't see any mean things done to civilians. I hear stories. My officer is from Golani brigade, an old and very elite fighting unit. He was a great person. But he says that some of the guys in Golani acted terribly. Once in Nablus, he saw a fellow soldier kick and slap someone. Some of the guys taunt the Palestinian men whom they suspect are paramilitary.

What do I prefer to do? Sometimes, they call us out from the territories for a special operation. You know the "engineer" Yichi Ayash? He was the Palestinian who would build various bombs to kill civilians, plan operations. He would make those bombs for the suicide bombers that were packed with nails, ball bearings, so that they would kill and maim more people. He would coat nails with rat poison so that victims would bleed more. A despicable fellow. Well, the army gets information that he might be traveling in a certain area; we are sent to dig in for 3-4 days. A stakeout. You find a ridge, build a berm that looks natural from the road, cover it and stay underneath with a few guys watching. You pee in bottles, eat what you carry. If you spot the guy, you either get him, or call in an attack. This is interesting, the adrenaline pumping. It is scary, don't get me wrong, but it is what I prefer. The army finally got him: load a cell phone with Semtex, I think; his father calls him and the phone explodes his head. A fine end for this "engineer" of destruction.

Here is what happens to me around death. You ask about deaths of friends, soldiers. I say that we were lucky that we lost no one from my unit. People say to me that we must have done a good job, I must have been a good sergeant; I don't believe that—just luck. But someone from my neighboring kibbutz does get killed, blown up while I am on a training in the Desert on a Jeep. I get a call on the radio to come back to base immediately; I have a phone call. This is weird, I feel; how anyone could find me. When I get back to base, I speak to a girl friend from kibbutz that Moshe has been killed, I should return immediately. I am amazed that my friend could track me down: it is supposed to be secret where I am deployed. In some sense it is a blessing in Jewish tradition: burial takes place within 24 hours; almost no time to think; just do, go through the rituals with others. I recall when I get to the bus station from base camp, already Moshe's photo and story was on the front page. We are a small country: not a sparrow falls from the sky that God (or at least the news) doesn't know. A small country.

But, listen to what I do, what has changed in me. I get back to my kibbutz—and I go into my room. I don't go to Moshe's funeral. Unbelievable for me. Moshe has been my friend in the last years of school before we left kibbutz.

I get to kibbutz. I think to myself, "After all the trouble my friend took to track me down, after Moshe is my friend for three years, I should have some reaction." Nothing. I don't feel much. I stay in my room; go afterwards with some Khaverim to get a drink, ask about the funeral, then to the kibbutz cemetary, where boys are planted.

But, I think that my _sh'vur zayin_, my Saturday night blues, starts after Moshe. Yes, after Moshe.

*   *   *

A Weapon: Humor Against Darkness

You know one way I manage? I laugh, usually at myself. A story, starts grim, ends funny.

An important job in Hebron is to guard, tail the school bus each morning and evening to make sure terrorists didn't hit the bus from behind with explosive-packed SUV's. Timing, distance are critical. Before the bus leaves, we scour the roadside for bombs. Most mornings, find some, get them detonated by another team, then head back to the waiting school bus. These aren't like your yellow American school buses. They have turkey wire in front to deflect rocks and bulletproof glass on the sides that become scratched and hazy with time. How hazy? To turn left, the bus driver has to open his window to peek out; to turn right, he opens the doors to take a gander. The bus has a layer of ceramic cylinders that deflect shrapnel: developed at Kibbutz Kfar Etzion. With angled mirrors at the end of long poles, we check beneath the bus for bombs.

Now, we are ready to leave.

There are strict rules. We must stay a certain distance behind the bus, close enough so a terrorist can't squeeze in, enough distance to stop in emergency. The driver is instructed never to go more than 40 km/hr; we can't move safely at a faster speed, and so forth.

As sergeant, I sit on the back gate of the Jeep, facing backwards: I am the first to see oncoming threats. Picture this. I wear my pack, about 40 kg. and cradle my gun, for this mission an M16. My driver is good; he knows how to follow, has to follow closely.

Suddenly, I later learn, the bus driver takes off with all the kids, maybe 70 km/hr. The road is marked at 50 km/hr. My driver hits the pedal to catch up. And I? I am now tumbling head-over-heels off the back of the Jeep, Palestinians lining the road, gaping. Of all things,

I'm thinking, "How silly I must look to them, all bundled, grasping my M16 and rolling away from the Jeep, like a tumbleweed in a Clint Eastwood's "The Good, the Bad, and the Ugly." I think, "How can I do this without looking foolish before them (the Palestinians)?" I sit up in the road, smile, rise, turn around and ran after my Jeep, as if I could catch them;, like a Charlie Chaplin, I am thinking. Of course, my men can not turn back from the bus.

When it happened, I laugh to myself; now when I recite it, I am not sure it is as funny.

*   *   *

From Soldier to Chef

The army affects how I see life. I have the sense that I am making news: what I do, my kibbutz, my family hear on radio. I want to act in such a way that they are proud of me. I also feel that by being in the territories, I know more truly what is going on there.

Most of the Palestinians just want to work the land; most are poor, struggling, except for the Tanzim[18], who drive black, tinted, armored Mercedes. Now, the settlers, I can't understand. Except because of them, we can't have two separate countries. I do my job, I protect them, their children. I just don't feel close to them. Ironic, because someone else could look at me and say: "You grew up on kibbutz at the Lebanese border; Arabs tried to kill you; your parents and khaverim were determined to stay." I guess there is something about the border that I rationalize: that was OK, but the territories not.

---

18   A branch of Arafat's crack paramilitary organization. Later, journalists were to expose the rank fraud and diversion of moneys from various European countries and the US, towards corrupt members of Arafat's crew, and even tens of thousands monthly to support Arafat's wife and daughter in the toniest arrondissement of Paris.

The army begs me to stay for career service, at least another year. I can't do even another year. My friends are leaving to Nepal, India, Central America, wherever. Some hike treacherous trails in Peru; others veg-out with some dope and mantras in India, far from Jews and Arabs. We want to get away from the state of tension, not necessarily the State of Israel. I won't return to Montreal. But my brother moves to Miami, opens a restaurant. My father loved to cook, so too my brother, and I learn that I love it too. I told you, I get so excited making a meal, that I bring it to the customer to see before it is finished, to see the beauty in the colors, the symmetries, before cooking: the various colors and textures; avocado's tints of green on the red tortilla; red onions with inner rings tinged pink; three types of lettuces and the olive oil or sometimes tehini drizzled on top. We have an open kitchen; I can watch the customers' reactions.

*   *   *

I learn something about myself after the army when I go to live a few months in Jerusalem. For a few months before that, I am a couch potato at my sister's: she is very patient, tolerant. But I need to sort out my thoughts. I decide to go to business school in Jerusalem and to work in a restaurant. School is tedious. The restaurant, well you know how that has gone: it's my career. Jerusalemites, you know what they are like: imagine the attributes of a typical Israeli—tough, direct, yet open—and multiply those by ten to get a Jerusalemite.

But, here is what I notice about myself and have been thinking about while talking with you. I stay on the periphery. I stay on the periphery and watch people, what they do, how they act. I choose a strange neighborhood in Jerusalem: on the border of <u>Meah Shearim</u>, the "hundred gates," the very, very orthodox. This neighborhood was founded years ago, before the State, on the week of the Torah reading of Isaac. In that reading, Isaac is said to plant wheat and to reap one hundred times what he planted. They name the neighborhood after Isaac's reaping, I think. But there are also poor students and others in <u>Meah Shearim</u>. I remain on the border of several different *groups. And I kind of like it; and I don't . . . . always being on the border of others.*

Isaac as a farmer differentiates himself from his father, Abraham, and successors, who were herders. The farmer must stay in one place, commit himself. So too, perhaps those who started this neighborhood: they were committing themselves, planting themselves to stay.

But, me, I'm no father Isaac. Since army, I keep moving around: Jerusalem, Miami, Tel Avi, yet never feel rooted.

As a boy on kibbutz, I felt that there was something different about us. When kibbutzniks go into town, I think of myself and my <u>khevra</u> as special because we are from kibbutz. It is a good feeling.

But, this periphery feeling is not so good now. I think that since we left kibbutz, even though I came back for the Army, I have never had a home . . . . I'm sorry, I don't know why I crying. Excuse me a moment . . . .

I am no longer a <u>ben meshek</u>, a son of kibbutz. Look, is it my memories of kibbutz or I am I really missing something that is still there? I don't know. I am a little afraid of always remaining on the periphery. I meet a wonderful woman in Miami: she is nice, spontaneous, open, has close friends. But she is not Jewish. I am completely not religious, but being Jewish is who I am. Wouldn't it be ironic if I were on the periphery of my own family: if I marry and have children and I am the only Jew?

*   *   *

I went back for a visit since I last talked with you. The kibbutz. Well, they offer for me to stay in the guest house. I refuse. My mother ran the guest house; it's for tourists, visitors. But I don't want to be a tourist. So, what do I do? I make like in the army; get a sleeping bag and sleep in the fields. My kibbutz family and others ask me to stay at their home. But it is not the same. I feel not a part of the kibbutz, even as I desire to be there again.

O.K. I miss kibbutz.

###

Two years later, I visit Peretz at his restaurant digs. He is now married. He and his wife went to visit his old kibbutz. She fell in love with the kibbutz. They are moving there within the year.

After a Mother Burns: Armored Man; Life in Tanks

I first meet Aviv, whose name means Springtime, on the brow of the kibbutz hill, the barren, unbuilt, unpopulated side of the hill that faces the <u>Sh'veila</u>, the expanse of beautiful, fertile plain in the distance that stretches towards the Mediterranean. It is night. Tel Aviv's lights twinkle afar. The quiet worries Aviv. The Intifada has started. He points towards the Arab villages on the other three sides of the kibbutz.

Too quiet. In peacetime, the Arabs shoot their guns in the air. To celebrate: weddings, births, funerals, who knows what else. But, our Intelligence says that when Palestinians are preparing for serious war, Arafat's security forces send out orders that ammunition must be saved, not wasted. Quiet. Worrisome.

Aviv is tall, reaching six feet, close cropped hair on an oversized leonine head that makes his shoulders seem too narrow to hold such a head. He has a mole on his left cheek, an infrequent, but broad smile. His hands are large, move carefully, slowly. Dresses plainly, but not as wrinkled as some kibbutzniks.

If we come back to kibbutz, and if kibbutz agrees, Chen wants to build on this side of the hill. She says that the kibbutz has turned its back on the Sh'veila. In the Sh'veila we also have our largest fields, where I spent some of my best years of work.

You are going to Jerusalem tomorrow? I heard that you want to talk with soldiers. I want to talk with you. I will drive Chen to work and have to stay in Jerusalem. We'll enter Jerusalem from the south, through the two tunnels, into the "shooting alleys" from Beit Jala. Drive with us.

This Israeli directness takes getting used to.

Emerging from the tunnels, If I crane my neck, I see Beit Jala to my right, above us; Israeli cement barriers offer intermittent cover from any snipers above. A chancy trip that they had driven every day until they moved into Jerusalem.

Now parked in front of the King David, even with two wheels over the curb, traffic squeezes by us. But, Aviv is focused on talking with me. He speaks quietly, urgently, seriously.

My major concern (at the beginning of the second Intifada): *men are no longer motivated to serve Milu'im (reserve) duty; this is a loss of commitment to the State of Israel. I want to tell you about this.*

I said I would return.

When I do in a few months, I visit their miniscule flat in Jerusalem. I am prepared to learn about army, tank corps in particular. But, I am not prepared for his mother's death by fire.

Immolation

I was thirteen when we moved back to Israel after my parent's two years abroad as <u>shlichim</u>[19]; in time for the Jewish holidays. My mother is a kindergarten teacher. On Hanukkah, my mother is preparing a play with the children; its zenith is to light their

---

[19]   *Shlichim* are representatives from Israel sent to Jewish communities around the world to collaborate on Jewish culture, teach about Israel. Often, the *shlichim* are from kibbutz, although not in Aviv's case.

homemade menorah, each candle a bit taller than the height of a kindergartner. This is in a barn outside the classroom. She pours oil in each branch. Oil and wicks, for she wants the menorah to be authentic. It is during the rehearsal. She and the children are alone. She keeps trying to light the wicks; won't ignite. She pours lighter fluid directly onto the oil; the flames sweep back, ignite her. I want to believe that she runs outside to protect the children, even knowing this would fan her flames. So she runs outside. She is like a human torch. She rolls in the dirt; is hospitalized with severe burns.

One month she is hospitalized with eighty percent burns. She dies.

I remember. I remember this: sudden quiet; no hollering, no commands from my mother; my father passing between hospital and house like a shade; people visiting in hushed tones. My aunt stays a few months, cooking, cleaning; she would sweep the dust into a pile, then, <u>under</u> the kitchen cabinet. I remember this as something my mother would never have done.

A wierd period ... all of a sudden you're alone ... from a previous era when everyone knows at every moment what the other one does.

Within months, we move to kibbutz. My father has always wanted to live on kibbutz. With five children, he thinks it best now. He picks Kibbutz "Ritzini." Established after the '67 war, it is a young kibbutz.

How did this young man overcome such an experience? Did he? We will learn that both kibbutz and the army are healing experiences for him. Only years later, after he marries, and after the death of a leader whom he loved, does he realize, experience echoes of a belated mourning.

When I return, the Intifada is heated.

Aviv and Chen now live in a corner of Jerusalem that, until recently, had not been terrorized. The "Cafe Caffit" attempt in the German Colony ruptures the quiet which once dwelled in this cosmopolitan neighborhood. At this corner cafe, "guarded" until recently by a waist-high swinging door, a waiter, a former Sayeret matkal[20] guerilla fighter, grows suspicious of the thin, perspiring fellow in a bulky overcoat on this warm spring day, who had ordered only a glass of water, no ice. Pushing the suspect out on to the sidewalk, the waiter tears the wires from the man's sleeve, subduing him until the police and bomb squad arrive. The bomb doesn't explode. But, fear does. Parents once permitted their teens or children to walk to a candy store, or cafe on the main Emek Refa'im. Parents now proscribe such ventures. Emek Refa'im, "Valley of Ghosts," is now empty yet haunted at night.

I hunt for their place. The cab breaks down some 100 meters from their street. Their "house" is past the dead end of a side street. You reach a "T" in the road, an empty, rutted lot on the left. Parked cars tilt gently with the unpaved terrain. You face a wall. Cross, turn right, walk along the wooden wall. I look for #19, their house; but no building after #21, just rubble. You might find a gate; there is no number. Enter through the gate, into a narrow, gardened, perennial pathway along the side of a main house. Built onto the house's hind part, climbing up its shank, is their house. It sits like the haunch of a crouched animal. An improvised picnic table, wobbly, sits in the walled garden, outside the kitchen window. It totters; assorted wood shivs are scattered about the legs, as if from day-to-day, different levelers are needed to keep the table steady.

Inside, their home is perhaps 500 square feet, meticulously spare, narrow, like a two-story Pullman car. The ground floor is a kitchen and sitting room, terrazzo throughout. Sculpted against the far wall, terrazzo steps emerge from the floor, like some M.C. Escher image, as if the floor and wall's flatness pop into three dimensions. Stairs, no bannister, wide enough for one, lead to a bathroom, then a bed room, the size of a walk-in closet. The "closet" itself is a pipe rack in the hall at the top of the stairs, wedged between bathroom and bedroom doorways.

---

[20]   Sayeret Matkal is an elite undercover unit, generally working in secret in the Arab population. Ehud Barak, a former Prime Minister, had been in Sayeret Matkal.

NATHAN SZAJNBERG

His wife's warmth enlarges the place. She has left for us homemade honey cake, tea, walnut-studded rugelach. Freshly cut daisies in a glass, center table. Then she dons a straw sun hat and leaves.

Like mother . . . like son

Above the couch is a deeply hued Rauschenberg-like painting by Aviv's brother, an artist. Unframed, stretched canvas has colors of clotted blood, ochres, layered as if with a spatula.

Takes after his mother, Aviv says, *unlike myself.*

He seats himself, back to the art.

But Aviv is more like his mother than he realizes. He empties his pockets to sit more comfortably, unclips two phones from his belt; places them on the coffee table.

You wonder about the two cell phones. One is for my wife and business, the other for the men in my division. Yes, I am in reserves, not on active duty now. But my men must be able to reach me for even personal matters at any time, all year, day or night, on or off-duty. If I care for them, even in personal issues, I am better able to lead them. When they're called up for milu'im, they are more likely to come without asking to be excused.

I refused an army career. Here is a contradiction. I refuse a career, but my first post-kibbutz job is to test officers' coping and decision-making under simulated battles. Our biggest customer is the Israeli army. But other democratic armies are now interested in the work. Also, while I was on kibbutz, after my required service, I spent three to four months a year on milu'im.

You want to hear another contradiction? My required army experience was indifferent to me. I refuse to continue milu'im in my well-regarded Research and Development officer job. When sent to a field unit of tanks, I approach the mefaked, wearing my mud-spattered clothes. I am met by a mud-spattered mefaked, sleeves uprolled, above the elbow, a fellow kibbutznik. And for the first time, I become invested in the army.

Another contradiction. I think I lived through my mother's death and my father's emotional evaporation, thanks to the kibbutz; but I leave kibbutz feeling despair about its future, even though I yearn to return to its fields.

He presents with a calm fortitude throughout. He listens carefully, doesn't interrupt; reflects on questions, at times asks himself whether he has answered a question thoroughly. A quiet certitude pervades all three hours of our interview, as I had sensed in previous and subsequent less formal visits. Even as he talks about his mother's immolation, he is quiet, reflective, yet puzzled at his reactions.

Puzzling, I know, that what should be the central event of my life, my mother burning to death when I was 13, still affects me so little. A freak accident, a painful death, a profound change in my life. We had just returned to Israel after living in Australia for two years, where my father was a shaliach, a representative from Israel to the Jewish community.

But before that, I can tell you some about my family. A fifth generation Jerusalemite on my father's side. My grandmother still lives in the original home, with a cistern in the house. I am the oldest of five; we move a lot until my mother's death.

My parents are itinerant teachers, gypsies. They follow the immigrants of the poor to Israel. A new Moroccan town of immigrants in the Negev? They move to teach school there. Next, a development town near Arad, overlooking the desolation of the Dead Sea? Move there to teach. Called by the government to bring Jewish culture to an Australian Jewish community? On their way. My mother is the dynamo; she could have been a power source for the secret reactor in Dimona, if there is one. We wouldn't have needed nuclear power. Determined, she has the voice of a drill sergeant, barking orders without a bullhorn. She makes the decisions.

My parents are diametrical: mother is demanding, an organizer, dominant, aggressive, a shouter and a good cook. Yes, a good cook. To this day, I meet people in Jerusalem who stop me to comment on how well she cooked, different cuisines.

I like a photo of my father and me on a motorcycle, maybe I am five. My father is quiet, very quiet, not strong nor demanding; he floats with life. A job changer, he was earlier in life a grocer, printer, then after several failures, a return to teaching.

Until, we are sent to Australia on <u>shlichut</u>.

Australia is wonderful. I love my nanny, Freda, in Australia. An aboriginal, Freda lives with us, wakes me every morning, cooks my favorite breakfast: oatmeal studded with raisins, topped with cream; raisin toast with grape jelly; hot chocolate with mini-marshmallows and whipped cream. Then, she sees me off to school. I love her, recall her warmth. This is my first experience of such nurturing, unintrusive, all-accepting warmth. From my mother, I get my drive, persistence, and, yes, demandingness.

On weekends, Freda returns to her bus village. My parents drive her; I ask to stay with Freda. They don't permit.

My childhood is great. We have a color TV in Australia, although I don't understand the accent all the time.

When I am twelve, my parents worry about the quality of my education in the Australian public school, that I would be behind academically on returning to Israel. They decide that I would go to a Jewish boarding school in Sidney during the week. This is a compromise; I had told them that I wanted to return to Israel and I would go without them. I mean it. I miss Israel.

Boarding school is great. Why? The other boys and I do pranks; we steal chocolates from the cafeteria. I don't learn much. But, no one is on my case.

Whom do I mean by no one? My mother. She upsets me. Rules she has, such as not drinking milk until I finished the whole meal. She scrubs me in the bath tub; scrubbing like Macbeth's wife, unable to clean off some unseen filth. Boarding school is a relief from that.

Then, back to Israel. She dies. We move to kibbutz.

Kibbutz

Kibbutz "Ritzini" is a young kibbutz. For me, it is great.

But my father lives like a ghost, cannot run the household.

I run my brothers. How can they still stand me? I used to make their lives miserable. For instance, at the funeral, one of my brothers refuses to come to grave as my mother is being lowered in. I shame him and he comes.

At fourteen, I decide I would work in the fields.

The kibbutz refuses. It is tough work, I am told. They say I am too young, I have to attend school. I insist. I suspect that the kibbutz caves, because my mother had died and they feel sorry for me.

After a few years, the good children of the kibbutz work in the fields, following me.

My experiences are very physical, visceral: eye-searing, white fields of cotton; yellow sunflowers, heads seeking the steps of the sun through the day; driving tractors through mud, getting stuck; jumping into the mud to pull out the tractor.

I am good at responsibility. I leave before dawn to watch the sunrise in the fields, feel the muck, watch the plants grow . . . eat with the guys. For me, holiday is work . . . I want to smell the ground in the morning. By fifteen, I am an expert in irrigation; pruning; I learn to cut part-way into the cambium layer to slow a tree's growth, or to hasten it. I marvel how figs sprout, like green lumps from the branches, ripen, and if not harvested, split open like stars at the bottom, glistening prey to hovering fruit fly clouds.

School? I do the minimum to pass so that they won't call my father. Half the year I work, half I learn. The whole holidays are just work for me, which for me is play. In the summer, I refuse camps; I want to be in the fields.

Now, I sound soft-spoken. Then, I was like a drill sergeant at home. I take over the household; have to; my father becomes more ghostlike. This goes on for three years, until he finds someone to marry. He leaves kibbutz, but my brothers stay when I go to the army.

From Pilot, to Almost a Paratrooper, to "Jobnik"

This young man is the first of the boys raised on kibbutz to enter as a pilot. How does he make the transition from a boy bereft of a mother (and effectively of a father), who thrived in the fields, to becoming a soldier? His first path has setbacks. His account, brief.

Unlike most young men, I don't think about, nor plan for the army. My father was in army intelligence, so he didn't talk to me about the army. I am the first boy from this kibbutz to go to army, so I have no older friends to advise me.

I am recruited as a pilot, but want to join my friends in tzanchanim, paratroopers, so I opt out of the air force.

Then the doctor in the army says that I have a bone malformed in my foot; it would preclude me from jumping from planes. I argue: how could I be recruited for the air force, the most rigorous physical and psychological screening, yet not be qualified for tzanchanim?

This time, I don't prevail. They send me to research and development. As far as I was concerned this was being a jobnik, a desk job. My father tries to console me: that this is a prestigious job, like his in army intelligence. But I don't want to sit at a desk while my buddies were in the field. Jobnik is a derisive term in the army; for guys not good enough to be in combat. I become the worst soldier; I don't care. It is good that they didn't send me to command men then; who knows what would have happened. They put me in Tel Aviv, in an apartment. I do a good job; I just don't care. What is research and development? Once, I am sent to the field, because of malfunction of artillery shells; soldiers are being injured. I evaluate the weaponry, resolve the problem, write a report, save lives. Look, I know that what I am doing is meaningful to the guys in the field; I just don't want to be doing it, sitting and writing reports. I have a jolly time in Tel Aviv; good night life, girlfriends, much freedom.

But I don't hitkhaber, connect, with the army. Like school.

You know Hebrew, how words have three-letter roots, relate to each other. So, hitkhaber comes from the same root as khaver, a friend, someone with whom you are bound, like a book's leaves. This I miss with army, a deeper sense of connection. I feel bound to my buddies, not to army. This comes later, in milu'im,

Interlude: Kibbutz to Paris

I finish, do officer training, take discharge, and escape back to kibbutz. Here I am given full management responsibilities for the sh'veila fields—at twenty-two. At first, I return to my love, work hard, enjoy it. My brothers now work the fields with me until they get drafted.

But I also supervise older men, some in their forties. Some won't work hard. I try to get the kibbutz to transfer them to other jobs. Not only did the kibbutz committee refuse (always committees, committees on top of committees, they have), but the _menahel_, the manager upbraids me. He says that I am not being in the spirit of the kibbutz; should accept these workers' efforts as they were. You want to know why today the kibbutz loves the imported Thai and Philippine workers? They are quiet, work hard, don't fuss. Yes, they are less expensive, but that isn't the only consideration. On kibbutz, the strong are to support the weaker. But, I can't tolerate those who were "weak" because of laziness.

I am offered a year off to travel after army. I don't take it at first, but after two frustrating years in the fields, I leave.

Most army buddies go to far-flung places: Nepal, Tibet, Central America. In a town in southern India they even have beach huts with Hebrew welcome messages.

But, I choose Paris. An aunt lives there. But I decide on Paris mostly because of the images of Paris from movies: its urbanity, its light, its cafes, its cosmopolitan air. I land at Charles DeGaulle, hop the Metro, then to my aunt's, who lives in the outskirts, near the Bois de Boulogne. But, I get off at the wrong Metro stop, some four kilometers away. Here, my navigational skills and the night sky work together. I hike the four kilometers using the stars as a guide to her house.

Two days later, I get a job as a mover from a fellow Israeli. So wonderful, moving someone's house. Amazed, I am. You arrive in the morning, coffee cup still on the table. After several hours, you pack them, move them and by afternoon, coffee can be served in the new house. I find this gratifying. I would make a coffee for the people to have when they arrive.

Then I become a cab driver for the rest of the year. I like meeting my fares, practicing French, driving them around Paris, or to Giverny. I would walk them from Matisse's House, avoiding the crush of the arriving tourist buses, along a gravel path to the small guest house where Matisse's foreign guests stayed to study with him. In the back, I show them the one-room studio, used, smeared palettes hanging on

ARMORED MAN; LIFE IN TANKS   ∴143∴

the wall. Then, I would sit with them in the front yard of the guest house, recommending the <u>tarte</u> <u>tatin</u> and an espresso.

But one of my quiet pleasures is to drive to the airport, near it, really, and watch jets taking off and landing. I still enjoy this. It's like watching a ballet of lumbering Leviathans, suddenly flying. When finished with a 10 or 12 hour shift in the taxi, I drive to Charles DeGaulle, watch planes. Today, I go with a buddy and we fly lightweight, single man aircraft that hover just above the land. My wife doesn't like this; too dangerous.

After a year, I return. My brothers need me.

Our father finally leaves kibbutz after remarrying. Two brothers remain on kibbutz; a third is in army, but keeps a room on the kibbutz.

My brothers feel that some kibbutz members question their ideological commitment to socialism and the kibbutz: after all, their father had left. I thought that perhaps our father's abandoning the kibbutz (after benefitting as a widower with five children in tow) led some kibbutz old-timers to question the <u>sons</u>' commitment. Bothers me: because my father leaves kibbutz, some members question my teen age brothers' commitment. What is this?

I rent a flat in Jerusalem; bring my brothers to live with me for the next few years.

I attended Hebrew University, easily accepted after my glowing military recommendations. But, now, I confess, my dismissive attitude towards education in high school takes its toll. A son of two teachers, I realize I had missed basics to understand the course work. I transfer, finish at a technical school.

I was shortsighted about school as a teen. I wanted to live in the fields. Today I love learning: I read military history, decision-making under stress.

Milu'im

Then I get called-up for first milu'im. It's before this Intifada; not so worrisome. I am reluctant, drag my feet. Every year until

I am fifty I would have to go for one month to milu'im; I couldn't bear the idea of desk work.

But the army, bless them, forgets about my physical anomaly. In error, it sends me to join a tank unit. Not just any unit; Kahalani's '73 brigade, the 77th.

Still, that doesn't impress me at the time. Army is army, I am thinking.

I purposely go to my first day dressed in my field duds, muddied boots, blue kibbutz shirt with sleeves rolled. I am mud-spattered; even living in Tel Aviv, I would get to the kibbutz fields for planting and harvesting.

Then I see my officer, sleeves rolled-up, mud spattered boots. I know *he must be kibbutzniki.*

My first meeting with my reserve officer impresses me. I am moved by his actions, presence, straightforwardness, honesty and his few words (The Hebrew is punchy, dugry). *Not like I am doing with you now, talking so much. My officer's life is filled with doing, not talking.*

He sees I am reluctant.

"No problem," he says, a wave of his hand. "No problem, you will spend the day with us, meet us. After today, you want a transfer, no problem."

A clever officer.

We shake hands, talk crops, irrigation, soil, tractor models. O.K., so I'll stay for a day.

And the next day. And a month passes; I realize how much I deeply respect these men. Many are still serving together from the '73 war. Many have refused promotion to officer, because they want to stay together with their khevre. *Again,* khevre *has no simple American translation. Yes, it could be "friend," perhaps "buddy." But I told you, it is being bound together.*

And I become bound to them.

Milu'im has been wonderful, other than the fighting. Once a year, you leave your regular life—a lawyer, kibbutznik, mechanic— and for a month you are with buddies you have known for years and with whom you trust your life.

When my commanding officer retired recently, I worry: who would replace him. But I see that his peers have transformed into leaders. Now, even they are beginning to retire, nearing fifty. I have been urged by them, including some older than I, to take promotion. I am concerned that the unit might not maintain its cohesion. New recruits arrive. The culture of hard work, dedication, protecting each other, continue. In all my years with them, in all the actions in Gaza and the West Bank, we have never lost a man. So, I take promotions, provided I could stay with the unit.

I have learned much about tanks. Can I tell you?

This is too tempting an offer. I am now about to learn more about tanks from Aviv than I have ever known. While other soldiers have talked about the armored service, none have spoken with such depth of history and knowledge as Aviv. I also suspect that I will learn more about his inner life by taking in his enthusiasm about his tank unit. So, I listen.

Tanks: The Israeli Merkava and Protecting its Men

I will tell you about tanks, since we have time. Since 1979, we have made our own tank, the Merkava, possibly one of the best in the world. A tank has three major functions: mobility, firepower and protection. Until the Merkava, most tanks were made emphasizing firepower and mobility. The Merkava is designed and built emphasizing protection *and incorporating protection into the systems of the tank. Here is simple math: most tanks use 50-55 % of their weight in protection; the Merkava, 75%. And much of the impetus to redesign tanks comes from the grievous losses of men, particularly from burning in the '67 and '73 Wars. In battle, burns cause 26% of injuries.*

You know that if you are in Israel, history easily begins several millennia ago. So, Merkava means chariot. We learn from our successes and losses. When the Egyptians had second thoughts about releasing the Jews from slavery, they pursued the foot-worn Jews by chariot: God made the chariots' wheels fall off and drowned most of the Egyptians, save the Pharaoh, so that he could attest to God's strength. Later, the Judge Deborah defeated an army of ironclad charioteers by engaging them in the North on a field after drenching rain: the charioteers' wheels got stuck in the muck and the Jewish army defeated them. She sat atop Mt. Tabor and directed General Barak to attack in the valley: Barak means lightning.

Tanks are a recent military invention, first used, reluctantly by the British in W.W.I (fired by a British Jew, by the way), then embraced and used brilliantly by the Germans in W.W.II. Because of Israel's small size, being surrounded by enemies, we need to attack aggressively and definitively. In the history of warfare, many if not most wars were won by time and attrition; that, we can't afford. Tanks are a central feature of the Israeli army, along with air cover.

Maybe the major impetus for defensive armored equipment came after the Arabs ambush and murder nurses and doctors with supplies en route to Mt. Scopus after the so-called cease-fire of 1948. But its use as a major battlefield instrument is ramped-up in two experiences. First, in 1952 and 1953, Lt. Ben Ari during training exercises breach "enemy" flanks with tank attacks. Ben Gurion decided to allocate more resources for tank brigades. Then, in 1956, to Moshe Dayan's surprise and dismay, the tanks of Major Shmuel Gonan not only attack Kusseima in the Sinai, but sweep through the Deiku Pass to attack three Egyptian brigades, _then_ race to the Canal in 100 hours. _Now,_ the army puts money into tank hardware.

But there is a crisis in November 1964, when the tanks in Tel Dan in the north perform poorly. Some believe the blame lies with the Centurion tanks. Israel Tal, who later creates the Merkava, studies the situation and critiques poor discipline in battle. Know this: the real "armor" in battle are your men; the equipment must protect and match the man.

Now, I will tell you how '67 and '73 contributed to the creation of the Merkava, then I can tell you about the Merkava.

'67 is the easier story; '73 is more "heroic," that is, too many more died.

In '67, we have three tank divisions under Colonel Shmuel Gonan, each headed by Yoffe, Tal and Sharon. You know about Rafah, at the southern end of Gaza, where there is much news *about deep tunnels and arms smuggling from Egypt? Well, this was a major military battle site and the first significant victory. Tal leads the battle against Rafah. Lieutenant Kahalani, of whom I'll tell you later in '73, leads the assault of the 77th Battalion of the 7th Brigade. In four days, they defeat the Egyptians in Sinai and travel 100 km. Kahalani is burned badly in his tank; 60% of his body; a year in rehabilitation. Major Ehud Elad, leading his charge standing up in his turret—usual for Israeli tank commanders—is decapitated. But, after the air attack on grounded Egyptian planes, tanks make the '67 war.*

Tanks also save Israel in '73, but with great heroism, at great cost and just barely. You recall how we were unprepared for the attack on Yom Kippur? This, despite warnings and indications from Egypt and Syria. The U.N. observers watch hundreds of tanks hurl past them towards the Golan. The Syrians are fierce, well-trained soldiers. They are driving Soviet-made tanks, including the most recent T-62's, and they have infrared for night driving. In the North, Ben Gal is stationed with a too small unit, maybe fifty tanks. I will tell you about the south, the Suez Canal in a moment.

The Syrians are halted at Kuneitra, where we have an antitank ditch. We are stationed above and our turrets could aim downwards, below 180 degrees; we slow their advance. But by the third day, exhausted, Ben Gal is fighting to the death. Just then, seventeen reserve tanks arrive with Avigdor Kahalani. Kahalani describes in his book—which we all read—how he narrated the battle for his men, urging them along. By the ninth of October, he positions his brigade on the heights and shoots the Syrians to shreds in the Valley of Tears.

They are on their own, because tanks are overwhelmed in the Southern Golan under Rafi Eitan and on the Suez, a disaster. The Syrians have easier terrain in the South; they outnumber the Israelis ten to one. They destroy the Barak Brigade. Some reserve tanks run up the steep Golan Heights and push back the Syrians. Air attacks follow on Syria, including their Defense Ministry.

The South, on Suez, is still painful to discuss. We had built our own Maginot Line, the Bar Lev, along the Canal, and it is as successful against the Egyptians as France's Maginot was against the Germans. The Egyptians attack with forty-two brigades, cross the Canal. Some 100,000 Egyptian soldiers, perhaps 1,000 tanks, attack three Israeli armored brigades, of which one-third survive. We send two tank divisions under Adan and Sharon to counterattack, but lose 260 tanks. And the Egyptians first use powerful Soviet antitank missiles. The Soviets and the U.S. had been using the Middle East as a testing ground for new military technology for decades.

Sharon crosses over to the east side; overwhelms the Egyptians, surrounds their third army and heads north. Then, a cease-fire is imposed.

So, how does it affect the army, the tank corps?

You know that Golda Meir resigns after the '73 fiasco, as does Moshe Dayan. The Agranat commission is established to examine what went wrong; they come down critically on poor IDF intelligence, and incompetent army leadership. After Golda Meir, Begin becomes prime minister, the first time that Labor lost leadership of the government.

And Tal prevails on designing a new tank, the Merkava, that would put protection of men above all other criteria.

This is what the Merkava is like.

Bear with me. After the history I bring you inside the tank.

The crew is at the center of the tank, including the driver. The tank systems protect the crew. Tal believed and showed that if you protect both the crew and the tank, you can get the tank closer to the target, thereby increasing mobility and firepower: he turned previous thinking on its head; instead of emphasizing mobility and firepower, with protection as an afterthought, he thought of the burnt men in '67, '73, and knew that by protecting them, he makes them more formidable.

(As he talks about burning men, about Kahalani's near-death, I think of his mother aflame. I say nothing.)

And firepower. The Merkavas are made with 120 mm high-pressure guns that have minimal dispersion: at 1,000 meters, the shells disperse less than the gun diameter.

Tal protected the tank with modular and reactive armor. Reactive armor, when hit by an enemy shell, explodes <u>outwards</u>: we used these on Centurions in Lebanon. But modules were a Tal *innovation: if you have new armor, you can pull off the old panels, put on the new.*

Crew protection comes from more interior space and a low rear entrance. If we are hit and need to escape, the hatch is safer; if we need to rescue infantry, the hatch is easier. And the crew cabin has no contact with fuel or oil, making it safer from fire in case of a hit. Munition containers are fireproof to 1,000 degrees.

That's the machine.

What makes us effective are three components: first my men, second this tank, and third our strategy of massed and preemptive, rapid attacks, with innovation at the front. The last principal has been with the Army since its inception.

Maybe I told you too much about tanks?

*   *   *

Motze Chen B'eynav

My third visit to see Aviv, I miss him; called up on the massive mobilization after the Park Hotel Passover bombing in Netanya. He is somewhere in the West Bank, perhaps Jenin, perhaps Nablus. I am not told.

But Chen, his wife, hears that I am in the country; she is surprised, as few Americans are around. Asks me to visit while in Jerusalem.

A close friend, whose daughter is in Army Intelligence, hears that I am heading to Jerusalem, suggests that I stay away from public places. Difficult to do, as I am heading by bus; the central bus station in Jerusalem, a new building, is like a fortress. Chen means "grace." This name, given at birth, she has grown into; she shows a graciousness in her manner, modesty and generosity in her spirit. She speaks candidly. To the degree, as Plato wrote, that we seek a mate to make ourselves whole (again, in his myth), Chen teaches us about Aviv. Here are some excerpts.

I grew up on Kibbutz "Zohar," in the North. I meet Aviv on a teen kibbutz get-together. I am fourteen; he, a <u>madrikh</u>, then eighteen. That weekend, I recall how I like how he treats us so respectfully, yet protectively. I also think to myself, here is a man I can trust. Also, he <u>is</u> quite handsome, no? (I notice her blush.) *I decide that weekend: this is the man I want to marry. I know that fourteen sounds young, but, remember that Juliet was not much older. I am too shy to speak with him at the time; only told him of my "decision" after we married.*

I had heard the story of his mother; the kibbutz movement is small; stories travel.

We meet again when he returns from army. I am now eighteen. Now, I can show interest. He actually is shy; surprised that I remember him from four years ago. He confesses that he noticed me at that time, but thought I was so young. We begin to go together. Although, I start my two years of army service as a teacher, the country is small. We often see each other on weekends. We marry when I am twenty-two, almost done with teachers college.

My English I got from my mother who taught English, keeps English books in the house and insists I practice. A heavy English dictionary she would often snatch (snatch you say, right?) from the book shelf in the salon whenever she had any question about a word. Doesn't matter if we are in the middle of dinner, or changing a diaper; if we are unsure, down comes the tome. From this I also get good shoulder muscles, possibly.

My grandparents helped found the kibbutz. My father's father was killed in 1948. This make this kibbutz special to me. I loved my childhood. The oldest of six, I help raise my siblings and their friends in the children's house. Early on, I want to be a teacher, care for children.

But, I will also tell you about fears.

My father, among other jobs, runs the kibbutz security. We are a border kibbutz; this is a serious responsibility. We often had drills, lock-downs, practice as if infiltrators are attacking. I recall as a child hearing about the infiltration by terrorists up North, who killed the captive children. Drills are taken seriously.

But one drill terrified me. One night, men dressed with kaffyas[21] *wrapped on their faces, carrying Kalishnikovs come to the door of our house; break in. This is a drill to test my father's ability to handle security, protect us, notify the rest of the kibbutz. I am terrified. I hide in my bedroom, behind pillows. After this, I make a plan: how to pile my clothes and pillows by the side of the bed, beneath the window, so that I can hide, should real terrorists come.*

I have a recurrent childhood nightmare, I think after this drill. The terrorists wearing kaffyot over their faces, streaming behind them in the wind, tear through the forest on motorcycles, shooting. The forest is behind the kibbutz cemetery. I awaken.

For years, I prefer not to sleep alone (with so many siblings, this is not a problem; in the army, I have bunk mates). But after marrying Aviv, I no longer fear, even when he is away.

*   *   *

I will tell you a fantasy I have now. I enjoy this, I do this. I sit out there (she points to the small perennial garden bordering her house, facing the rickety table with shivs) *facing the wall lined also with flowers that Aviv planted. I bring a glass of tea. Early in the morning I do this, before going to work, often before Aviv awakens. I imagine that I am a princess of this kingdom. The flowers, ants, flies and bees are my subjects; sometimes birds in the arbor. I grant them their every wish.*

She turns to me, a silent smile on her lips. She says:

Soon, we hope to have a child.

After visiting Chen, I cab to the central bus station. To enter, lines (or what passes for lines in Israel) snake down the block. When I am reach the metal gate before the doorway, I am searched several times before entering; I am asked if I pack a gun; my back pack inspected on a table; a wand passes over my body. Then, through the doorway, my back pack on a conveyer to by X-rayed, and the careful eyes of inspectors sweep over me.

---

[21] Arab head dresses also used as masks

Yet, I take with me Chen's stories, and her imaginary princess-dom, which shed a soft glow of hope over this journey. The opening phrase on this section is Hebrew, and translates literally, as "found grace in (one's) eyes," as she does.

Leaving Kibbutz, Returning, Leaving and Returning

After marriage, at Chen's urging we return to kibbutz. She wants to raise the children there, having grown up on kibbutz herself. I agree, provided I could have an impact on the kibbutz's economy, future. I am clear in my mind, to distinguish the social and economic aspects of kibbutz: an impossible task, for they are like thatch. The social aspects are the relationships among kibbutz members: who is "in," who is "out," who's a veteran, who's not. But the protection that a socialist ideology represents — to each according to his needs, from each according to his ability — prevents isolating social from economic spheres. Here is how I learn this.

I leave the fields, give up on managing those who would not work. I ask to work with an innovative inventor. An odd fellow, a loner (except for one "friend" who ends up sabotaging his efforts), he has cobbled together a machine to detect hidden explosives, including Semtex.[22] He and the kibbutz think it would be useful at West Bank roadblocks, airports, and who knows where else. I do some calculations, insist that we could increase the income eight fold in three to four years by expanding its uses, licensing agreements and marketing. No one believes me, but they leave me alone.

I achieve the goals. I look at other opportunities for the kibbutz. I am good at putting together apparently disparate programs synergistically. The kitchen is losing money? The high school dorms are not used over the summer? The field school for visiting high school students is in the red? Put all three together and you have a program for week-long retreats for families looking for guided outings in the

---

[22] Here, while I fictionalize the invention to protect identities, the real man's invention was seminal in another field

Judean Hills. Make the kitchen kosher and you and do catering for surrounding communities' weddings, births, bar mitzvoth. (Some of the khiloni (secular) guys object to the kosher part.)

But, each idea runs up against a committee after committee. Social relations prove more powerful than ideas for growth, prosperity. Memories are long, unforgiving on this kibbutz: So-and-so did such-and-such to me nineteen years ago; why should I help his daughter (cousin, uncle, grandmother)?

I don't understand why the kibbutz takes upon itself what seems to me like domestic concerns. For instance, a late middle-aged couple has grown children who have left kibbutz, have refused membership. The couple remain, as did one grandparent living in elderly housing. But the father develops scleroderma, has trouble swallowing, skin irritations. Can't work. His wife stays home to care for him. Grandmother, while living independently, wants assistance, which the kibbutz should provide.

But, the oldest daughter, who left kibbutz, unmarried, is now 34, has lost her job in Tel Aviv. She moves back to live in her parents one-bedroom apartment. She sleeps on the couch, running the TV loudly much of the day and night. She visits her grandmother daily, helps around the house. That's nice.

But the daughter's night-long TV aggravates her father.

So? Her parents approach the kibbutz. Their daughter still refuses to become a kibbutz member: why should she let the kibbutz dictate her life—like, when she could borrow a car; why should she pay her paycheck to the kibbutz (should she get a job)? All three insist that the kibbutz provide a separate apartment for their daughter.

A committee member suggests the kibbutz buy radio head phones for the young woman to wear to listen to T.V. so that father doesn't hear it. Her parents insist: why should she have to walk around with something on her head?

Oh, and the kibbutz should pay her for caring for the grandma: after all, if their daughter doesn't do this, the kibbutz would have to hire someone. Why shouldn't kibbutz pay her?

Arguments can be made on both sides (and are). But for me, I see no reason to argue. This is but one example of how too many kibbutz members are becoming leeches on the community. I know that's harsh. I do not want to support them.

So, Chen and I leave.

And the fellow, the inventor, you ask? He figures he can make a fortune leaving the kibbutz. So, he makes a deal, makes a partnership with the kibbutz, leaves the kibbutz on which he was born, raised his family. Unfortunately, he takes his buddy from kibbutz with him, makes him an officer. The fellow, more bluster than substance, sabotages the business.

So, I leave his business. I now work in a great situation. I told you that we observe and coach officers in a test field situation. We have a battle zone setup some place in the Negev. We have video cameras throughout and we have mockups of tanks, armored vehicles, antitank weapons and infantry. We ask the officers to set objectives, or we assign them objectives. Then the officers have to carry them out. Afterwards, the officers sit with us and watch a panel of digital video computer monitors to watch the battle's outcome. Often that's all that is necessary: they draw their own conclusions; other times, they ask us for advice, suggestions.

I also enjoy the drive to and from work. The Negev clears my mind, refreshes me. Sometimes I detour through the Valley Elah, where David slew Goliath. Much history here.

*   *   *

A year later, they have moved back to kibbutz with their new babies. But before we hear about that, we hear about more death.

Rabin's Murder and Death's Echo

Last time you asked me about guys I knew who died and how it affected me. In active service, since I am sitting at a desk in Tel Aviv, I really don't know anyone closely who died. But one of my officers gets killed a month after I leave my reserve duty. He was due to finish in one week. He is in a simple operation gone bad. He wasn't close to me.

But, as I think more and realize that Rabin's death plunges me downward, like the dive from the Old City of David into Ga Hinnom[23]. That makes me most sad ... I wonder if this is what happened when my mother died and it didn't affect me at all. Then. I don't know; I still don't have feelings about this, her death. But, I wonder if during Rabin's death, some feelings from then occur.

We can't sleep that night, the night before his funeral. We go to a bridge to watch the funeral procession the next day, to see them draw his casket. For one week, nobody goes out of their homes ... there were no car accidents.

It is so sad.

I liked him. The human things of him ... a shy guy, a straight arrow. You could see it in his behavior ... you can see it in Rabin ... I believed in him. I lost somebody who was probably close, like my mother. It didn't affect me then as I was now affected by Rabin. You know, when he went to meet the US president, he was told to wear a tie. And he didn't know how to tie a cravat; someone had to do it for him. He was a decent man.

(I now hear that he is also talking about the kind of man he is, his character: recalcitrant, a plain man, who shows his life in how he lives it. Rabin is his ego ideal.)

And back on Kibbutz

Now, we are back on kibbutz. We have two children and kibbutz is good for them. Also, the kibbutz will let me work outside. I pay them my whole salary, but I have a car from work; I don't have to beg for rides, sign-up for a car. We are close to Chen's family: her parents and most of her siblings love spending time with the children.

What I said to you some months ago about people here who won't pull their weight was harsh. I still believe that it is true and

---

[23]   Ga Hinnom is the valley known in Christianity as Gehenna, the model of Hell. In Ga Hinnom lived a non-Jewish tribe who engaged in savage and primitive rituals.

a problem. But I talked with a buddy here, Eitan. He was born on kibbutz, his grandfather helped found the kibbutz, his father is a Zionist firebrand, a real idealist. Eitan is very even-tempered, calm. He agreed that some of the kibbutzniks don't work as much as they could. But, he says, "They work good enough." Maybe that's it. They work good enough, and others of us pull a greater weight, because we can and want to. This tempers my discomfort. And, when I see my children playing here, and the community's way of caring for them, I am more comfortable.

Am I a soldier, a medic, a Jew?

*The first time I shoot someone was in Lebanon. Not shoot, kill.
I am the unit's only medic. Zo'ar and I were switching off rearguard.
I see him first. The sniper. Not him; a glint of light in the tree. It
is probably the sun's reflection off his sights. I signal the unit, even
as I fire, as does Zo'ar. We get him. Afterwards we are lying next to
each other, trembling, hugging in relief. I feel pumped, adrenaline:
"I got him just before he got us!"*

My officer comes to me. Dresses me down!

*"You're the medic! We count on you to keep us alive. Don't
shoot first. You shoot, you make yourself a target. You're the medic.
We'll do the shooting!"*

*I sit there, where I had been lying; can't stand up. Who am I: a
soldier, a medic, a Jew? Who am I? What order do I put these in?" Later, I
think, "I saw a person, I got him killed. Was it good, was it my duty?"*

*Later, much later, I realize that if I saw the glint from the
sniper's sight, that meant that he was aiming at me. Only later
could I realize this.*

*Years after my service, I break down, tears, at the birth of my
first child. I can not look my son in the eyes, am afraid to touch*

him. I feel that my son is pure; who am I, a soldier, to touch, to defile this baby?

Zo'ar is killed later, after my active service. To the funeral I go; see the other men from my gedud (battalion). I feel like an outsider, for I am back in officer's school and wouldn't join the unit again for several months. An outsider, I feel. Still, I cry.

I still read obituaries. Sometimes I cry.

Once done with engineering school, I am back in active service. I am 22. Most of the others in the unit are 19, 20. Now, I realize that we were endangering ourselves. Zo'ar would always be willing to cover the rear, the most dangerous position. He was special sensitive, good. That was him.

My first casualty I treat as a medic continues to invade my thoughts, nightmares. My unit was sent to Kiryat Shemona: on the far north, that geographical tip of finger between Lebanon's Benjamin hills and the Golan Heights. A belly injury, I could see immediately. He looks stable. I request transport to Haifa, perhaps a half hour flight. My commanding officer approves my decision. But the boy goes into shock, coma and dies. For a long time, I ask, "Did I do right?" O. K., I confess; I keep a photo of him. Still in my wallet. He was from Netanya. I sometimes visit his grave.

*   *   *

I am pure Israeli, although I grew up in "Little Iraq" in Petach Tikva. Not just Little Iraq—my aunts, uncles, grandmother and cousins lived with a two-block radius. Israel was a relief from the pressure cooker, the charif of my family. Charif, is hot spice we put on our food, I think makes some of our temperaments hot. Shortly after the Iraq war, a journalist asks how I feel about the liberation of Iraq. But Iraq means nothing to me. I am Israeli.

Yet, the central forces in my life came from my family. The motivating force of my life, is the drowning death of my six year old brother. I was four. I feel driven to fulfill my older brother's life.

The second major force is the hatred my parents had for each other in their arranged marriage. After a fight, Ima (mother) would turn to us after my brother, Ayal's drowning, imploring, crying, "It's not enough I have a dead child, my husband has to scream at me?" We were confused when she mentions him: all the photos of Ayal were removed; no one was to speak of him, nor his death. When I turn eighteen, before I go to army, I visit Ayal's grave for the first time. I am the first of my siblings to visit. I promise him, I will be a good soldier.

Just last year, <u>Ima</u> confides in me, after my father had complications from his hypertension, perhaps father might die soon. A divorce is out of the question, she insists; how would they divide their 1 1/2 room apartment in Petach Tikva?

My parents came with the big aliyah from Iraq in 1951. Their families had known each other. But her family had been bakers, more prominent in the Jewish community than his father's. She married "down" and reminds him of this. They all had lived in <u>Ma'aborot</u>, tents for the first years. Once they got the 1 1/2 room place, they stayed, raised five children. I remember at night my parents having sex. When I am seven, I ask <u>Ima</u> why <u>Abba</u> had been walking around naked at night. I knew that <u>something</u> good came from this; I knew that they made us from this.

From third grade, most of my life is in the youth groups, the scouts. We are in a poor working class community. By high school, a lot of my buddies in youth group are into booze and trouble. I realize I am heading in a different direction. This is part of the reason I didn't join one of the kravi (elite battle) units with them.

My parents are cousins. <u>Abba</u> (dad) is nine years older than <u>Ima</u> (mom). I have four brothers and sisters . . . had, until Ayal died.

My father is a factory manager. Later, when we were more grown, my mother cleans houses and then becomes the manager of an office building. Nothing, no work was beneath them. I think I got from both my parents this: the ability to organize well, to organize men, get a group working well. Other things I tried not to get from them, but that is more difficult.

My father is rough, beat us when we did things wrong. If we are fighting and we break something, we get the belt or his hand. You know, I don't remember the feeling of the belt. I do remember that he first warns us, "Stand up straight; take it like a man!"

But I am favored of both parents. In sixth grade, I go jogging with my dad in the evenings, just the two of us. I get good at sports and connect it to jogging with my <u>Abba</u>.

But (he sighs, he pauses) almost daily they fight. At dinner, no matter who is there, my father screams about my mother, calls her a whore. I still wonder if he knows something about her that we weren't told. I am ashamed to bring people, friends to the house. Sometimes my aunts and uncles would refuse to visit for weeks.

Then, my parents wouldn't talk with each other for weeks after some fights.

I give them pay-back before my bar mitzvah. I don't recall what the fight is about, but I have an argument with my father and I stop talking to him for weeks. My uncles come to me, implore me to talk with my father before my bar mitzvah. I agree—reluctantly.

My mother, she adores me and she would do anything to watch over me. In boot camp, I was in <u>misdar</u> (in formation, at attention). This is before we had cell phones; you have to wait for a break to get to the queue at a pay phone. Our base is secret, so no one could phone in. The officer says, "You can't believe; someone's mother just called to see how her son was." Almost every guy in the unit <u>think</u> it is their mother. But I <u>know</u> it is mine. I am right. She had used connections to find my secret camp and to get a phone call through.

As a kid, I am a <u>yoram</u> (a nerd); do well academically, the best. But I still fear my father if I do something wrong. One day, I spray pepper into my brother's face. I run into the <u>paradisim</u> (citrus orchards) surrounding the town; stay there until it got dark, cold, then return home. Nothing happens.

Funny, my reaction to doing so well academically. On parent-teacher nights, my teachers would tell me that my parents didn't have to come, because I am doing so well. I have mixed feelings; I want them to hear about how well I am performing, but I am ashamed of them.

Then my parents do something extraordinary, but quietly. I am invited to go abroad for a year in the last year of high school. But it cost $2000, an outrageous amount. I wouldn't ask my parents. Somehow they hear about my teachers' encouragement. Somehow

*they get the money. It is a wonderful six months in Toronto. My
older brother says that I was preferred, but I didn't feel that way. In
retrospect, I see that they favored me. Ironically, I always yearned
to know if they loved me.*

*I can't tell you how intense it was in Little Iraq. Sometimes I
just wanted a buffer from my family.*

*   *   *

We meet in Beersheva, at the medical school in a barren,
cinder block office with creaky metal office chairs. I have been
interviewing Bedouin children at the hospital, children with
complex, odd presentations, presentations that often veil their
families' secrets, dynamics: a girl of nine who has not spoken for
a year, whose mother, after a rape, is married off to an elderly
Bedouin, then relegated to a tent in the yard, while the child
lives with the father, whose adult children feel threatened of
their inheritance; a fourteen year old boy, "unable" to return to
school for months, whose father is listed as disabled, the family
living off the payments from the government, even as the boy
sees his father working elsewhere. The girl breaks into a smile
after she draws a picture of a house, her mother within it with
her, and her mother sees and understands the picture. They
both smile in relief as they hug each other. The boy confesses his
unbearable shame over his father's secret, only with the support
of his eldest brother who promises to protect him. All this is a
newer world for me.

But I make time for Micha and his story. He has military
bearing, even though he is in reserves, now an engineer. He is
square-jawed, moves precisely. When he turns, his torso does this
en bloc; when he greets you, his chin is tucked, military fashion.
His smile is broad. He sits so ramrod straight, so still at times, that
one doesn't hear the ancient metal chair creak beneath him.

After such an intense introduction—killing a sniper, death of
a buddy, death of a brother, the hot spice of his family in Little
Iraq—Micha turns to his transition from home to army.

AM I A SOLDIER, A MEDIC, A JEW?

It was my mother who suggests Atudah (special deferred service). It's not really deferred like in the States. If your grades are high, your Kabah high, and you study something needed in the army—engineering school in my case—they permit you to go to University, followed by army. Not really followed: I have basic training before University and army service over the summers. The first year is basic training; the second, I am a medic; in the third year, I am an officer. My Kabah as 56.

I am supposed to go to Nahal²⁴ directly from the youth movement. But I don't want to stay with my peers in the youth movement: most are drinking and preoccupied with motorcycles—shovavim (mischief-makers) they are. While we had been friends since first grade, I no longer feel I belong. Frankly, I am, more mature, more serious.

I recall tironut well. I am accustomed to doing well. When I'm drawn to something, I do it . . . usually for the better. So, they keep me as chinuch toran, kind of the lead private; usually you get that position for a week, then rotate out. They keep me there for four weeks. Fine. Well, usually in tironut the officers maintain a distance from the recruits—it is very different once you're serving actively. But I feel both comfortable and privileged having been chinuch, that when some sergeants are telling jokes to each other, I overhear them. I laugh. I get punished—20 push-ups on the spot. I feel humiliated; I burst into tears while doing push-ups. I feel that my identity is broken—the youngest one who strives hard, does well and is treated as special. I was the littlest one in third grade, but special because I tried so hard both with my buddies and teacher. But in the army, I learn; I am no different than other soldiers.

Tironut is physically challenging for me, because I had not been preparing for months, even years like my friends. When it comes to the final exercises, the long hike with a heavy pack, I make it, just make it. My parents had said that they wouldn't be able to be at the graduation ceremony; I am disappointed. But they showed—I am delighted.

---

²⁴   Nahal was established as a special unit of men and women who establish a settlement in vulnerable areas of the country, that is ultimately to become a self-functioning civilian settlement.

I change my name when I am 18 in the army. My given name is "Micha'el"—now it is Micha. Why? I decide I didn't need to an angel all the time. This is the most overt rebelliousness I have ever done. (But, my mother would consider my secret activities rebellious.)

After all the travail of tironut, *I graduate as* mitztayen, *exceptional, then am sent as a medic to Gaza to direct a group of guys from reserves. Most are in their 30's. I am in my 20's; who am I to direct them? But they hustle me into a jeep and drive me around and I feel safe. I am sorry when the tour ends.*

I have one bad scare—I scare myself—my officers never knew about this. I've never told anyone. I ride "shotgun" on the jeep; sitting high on the back, I hold the "mag" (machine gun). We ride about for three hours. You know what it's like on a jeep—down through wadis, over sand dunes, boulders; lot's of jiggling, bouncing about. I had to hold onto the machine gun handles, partly to keep from getting bounced off.

Then we get back to camp, to my horror, I see that I had released the safety catch at the beginning of the ride; the gun could have gone off at any moment. My heart sank, I frightened myself—I've had recurrent nightmares about this.

Another recurrent nightmare in the past few years. I have guns ready to fire at infiltrating terrorists; I see them approaching, getting close, see the eyes above the kaffiahs wrapped around the face; I keep missing. I have guns from World War II or M16's; neither worked. But I am not hurt—you've seen the movie the Matrix? *Probably not. Well it's like that: their bullets come in slow motion and whiz by me, like I am invulnerable.*

I am asked to join the Egoz unit. This is a real kravi *unit, but one with a history of tough guys. My friends tell me that I should refuse the assignment, should run from it like running from a forest fire. My wife doesn't want me to go. But, I have a belief that if I am asked to go do something, I do it. The commander of Egoz comes from* Shyetet *(Navy Seals); his nickname, behind his back, was "Cold Killer." He always has several special operations running simultaneously.*

But ironically, he is the one who dresses me down when I shoot the sniper. I don't know how to take what he said: either that because I am the medic, I am important enough to be protected by my unit; or, that as the medic, I am necessary to treat the unit's wounded, so I shouldn't get myself shot-up. Maybe he meant it both ways. I don't think he likes me.

Egoz is so difficult at the beginning. It isn't just my commander, "Cold Killer," seems to hate me. I can't "find" myself there. After a few months I ask to leave. My wife is pregnant, a difficult pregnancy, the first. I would get leave in at the Lebanese border around 2 or 3 a.m., catch buses or get "tremps" (hitch rides) to Beersheva. I get home around 6 a.m., have two hours then head back. It is very hard.

I am the only medic for the gedud for several months. That means that while the patrols got rotated out, I return with one and leave with another. I am exhausted.

Now, when people hear that I am in Egoz, they're impressed. Look, I know what fighting really is . . . being under fire. And I do well. I had been afraid I would panic. I don't.

The young guys motivate me. They endanger their lives for our sakes; they are special and deserved to have someone help them, help when they were injured. When I feel exhausted or physical pain, hiking with a pack for kilometers; lying on soaking ground for days, in hiding, I would think that I can't give up now; if they need me, no one else can help. I feel the adrenaline at those thoughts.

*   *   *

We have no casualties in Egoz while I am on active duty. A few months after I leave, there is an ambush; several deaths. Zo'ar. He is younger than I, but we "walk" together, do reconnaissance. We always volunteer to cover the end; I don't realize how dangerous it is at the time. Covering the end of the unit, meant that when we were firing, each of us had to cover the other; I run out of a magazine, he covers while I reload and *vice versa. We shoot terrorists. Frankly, we feel high, feel good when we get infiltrators.*

He dies. Do I go to the funeral? Yes. Many buses, lots of soldiers. (He sighs. We stop for the day.)

*   *   *

Dreams, Death and Mothers

Micha takes a detour, talking about his grandmother's death, his mother's reaction and segués to dangers he engages in outside of his army.

I don't know why I keep coming back to the dream with bullets, the Matrix-like invulnerability, my guns not working. I think this has something to do with your interview with me yesterday. I keep thinking about it.

(What keeps recurring?)

My grandmother's funeral. I keep thinking about the funeral. One picture keeps recurring: my mother lying upon my grandmother's grave, crying, strong cries—I could see her entire shoulders shake, sobbing. You know it's customary in Sephardi funerals, like my Iraqi family, that there is much shouting, crying. Ashkenazim are quiet.

But at my grandmother's funeral, I am maybe 21, everyone else is crying; my mother, quiet. She waits for everyone to leave, for them to go away; when she is alone, she lays herself quietly on my grandmother's fresh mound and these deep sobs came from deep inside her, her shoulders heaving. I thought she would never stop.

(You were still there?)

Yes. Well, I guess she waited until everyone had left, except me. She doesn't know I am still there, behind a tree, behind her. Yes, I think I waited to watch her.

She was closest to my grandmother. My mother's sister lived with her mother until she was 50; she cared for <u>savta</u>, never married, then my aunt developed pancreatic cancer. She was dedicated to her. My mother then went over every day to care for both of them.

AM I A SOLDIER, A MEDIC, A JEW?

Well, not just my mother. I am in engineering school and I move my bed to savta's house. At night, I sleep there and care for both of them. When my mother needs to got to the bathroom, I help her to walk.
(Your mother?)
I mean my grandmother. I don't know why I said mother. We're very close. Even now, if we hear a song about "mother" on the radio, I call her; she says,"I was just thinking of you." I sometimes feel as if she "knows" all my secrets, she feels them.
(Secrets?)
Well. Well, I engage in high-risk sports. I do it with some guys, younger guys, maybe five six years younger. Various things: bungee jumping, solo flights in low-flying micro-aircraft, rock-climbing with minimal equipment, also deep sea diving without equipment. Free-diving, I think Americans call it. Pearl divers are expert at this; may wear only goggles. The guys, we get together only for these activities . . . we're not friends, don't socialize outside of these activities. Often, I know only their first names. Socially, I would have nothing to do with them. Since they are younger, I look after them. We dive tandem. But, I notice that they challenge me—dive deeper, stay longer. I think the record for free-diving is 282 feet; people die doing this. I would never tell my mother; it would be too hard for her. But, don't you think that mothers know, they feel?
(Your wife, children know?)
Never the children, I would never tell the children, would frighten them. I finally told my wife, but I try not to tell her each time I do this. Then, once, at a conference in Australia, the Great Barrier Reef is too tempting. Yeah, I could have gone SCUBA, snorkeled, or in a glass-bottom boat, but there's something about the excitement, the tension, the challenge of deep dives without equipment; like an addiction. The descent, the darkness, the self-control not to ascend too rapidly, avoid the bends—these heighten being surround by the beauty buried beneath the Ocean's surface. You know about this type of diving? I started with snorkeling, then deep sea SCUBA. I love the limitless boundaries of the sea. With SCUBA I could stay beneath, lounge with the fishes. I recall a school of barracuda below me once,

bare white, silent, wavering shadows. I hover over them, unafraid. Silent death lives below the seas. Another time I saw bone fish off New Zealand: ghostly, translucent, haunting. But diving without equipment became my challenge, my dedication, my addiction. Yes, you go with buddies. I always have them in my peripheral vision, checking, are they O.K. Eilat is good: beautiful reefs, colors of fish. You practice both breath-holding and controlled surfacing: surface too quickly, then the "bends," too slowly, breathlessness and panic and fear. Use ballast to help descend. I feel closer to the fish without equipment.

When my heart pounds, I sometimes wonder if this is how my brother felt.

You know, my wife met me at the airport after Australia, takes one look at me and asks "Did you do something?" Maybe it is my guilty look. I don't know what to do about this drive to risky sports. She knows there is a bar in Tel Aviv where free-divers gather, talk about past, upcoming trips, the excitement. Again, I don't know these guys, what they do, their family names; I just dive with them. My wife doesn't feel comfortable even with my going to this bar. She worries I will drown. But, I know myself, my limits; I am careful. I ask her to accept me as I am. I don't tell anyone else, although the other officers, engineers consider me more "macho" than they are. I think it might be because of how I was in the Egoz unit: others might have been in _kravi_ units too, but Egoz had a reputation of being filled with tough knuckle heads.

One of my colleagues teased me when we were on a walk in the desert with you. Remember when Tzahi asked me to take a photograph of the two of you at the edge of Mitzpeh Ramon crater and I borrowed your camera? Tzahi started chuckling and said in Hebrew as I prepared to shoot that he saw me take the rifle stance, then take and hold a breath, as if the camera were my M16. He calls me an eternal soldier. I was not aware of it until he said that. I felt a bit embarrassed, but he was right.

The deep sea diving without equipment, and such, I am trying to sort it out. It feels exciting. But is remains my secret. I guess it's even a secret from myself.

AM I A SOLDIER, A MEDIC, A JEW?

*   *   *

We are living on a kibbutz, my wife's, where she grew up. It is wonderful for my children, for children altogether.

But there is tension in our marriage. Also, my son began having troubles when he was four. Now he's five and one half. Bites his nails, pulls his eyelashes, follows other kids around, hates his little brother. His kindergarten teacher says he needs deep massage. But on kibbutz, they sometimes have odd ideas; makes no sense to me. He may pick up the tension with my wife. It's usually around my diving, going off to Eilat with these guys, or trips to Tel Aviv.

I married Shira in part because I really wanted to be a part of her kibbutz, her community. But I have mixed feelings. At times, I feel constrained, need to get to Tel Aviv for the night life. Also, everyone knows everyone and often everyone's business. But it is not as bad as living among my relatives in Petach Tikva: not as intense, intrusive. On kibbutz, people don't just walk into your house. But, I am still adjusting.

*   *   *

I think we are finished. But, Micha is not. He continues.

Zo'ar keeps entering me thoughts. I notice when I talk to you, I keep thinking about thoughts that intrude on me, into my dreams also: Zo'ar, the boy with the belly wound, obituaries, my mother crying on my grandmother's grave. Do you think these are connected with my brother's drowning. We never talked about it. We weren't supposed to say anything. I think I remember them carrying his drowned body from the sea, his arms hung back, flopping. But no funeral; no talk.

There is a photo of him, just one, my mother keeps in a secret place. Of course, I know where it is; I look at it sometimes.

With Zo'ar, I was 25, he maybe 20; a big difference in age in the army. So, we weren't friends. But we were close. Something about doing rear guard, at night, on patrol. At his funeral, I remember thinking that he was special, sensitive, good. I just can't remove him from my thoughts.

Truth and Mercy; Redeeming one's country, one's people, oneself

In 1924 a settlement, "Har Hamidbar," is founded in the Judean Hills, land purchased by the Jewish National Fund. In the 1924 Arab riots, it is abandoned. In 1935, forty workers arrive to this rocky escarpment. In 1935, under Arab sniping and sabotage, it is abandoned. In 1943, the Jewish National Fund establishes a new kibbutz. In 1947's Arab threat, women and children are evacuated. Those remaining are surrounded by Arab irregulars, surrender—then, are slaughtered. In 1967, the sons of those killed in 1948, liberate Jerusalem, pray at the Western Wall. Job done, they hop jeeps, race to Har Hamidbar; rebuild the kibbutz of fathers they never knew. Here is the story of a kibbutznik[25], son of a 1967 paratrooper, grandson of a 1948 hero.

---

[25] "Yonah" is a pseudonym. While he has given permission for me to tell his story, I will disguise his identity in various ways for the sake of his and his family's privacy.

For this, I get myself into trouble, almost, at the end of my paratrooper training. I will tell you what I did, but even now, after ten years, I don't know that I could have done differently. And I agree with my _mefaked's_ [26] decision, for I did break a regulation.

Because of my glasses, these rimless goggles, I can't become pilot, nor sayeret matkal, special forces. I am fortunate, for they put me into _tzanchanim_, paratrooper: the training is very demanding, but you are with a buddy and your group. My father was a paratrooper. In '67, he landed to liberate Jerusalem; prayed at the Western Wall. From him, I learn that if my relationship with my officer is good, everything would work out. My officers respect me; I, them.

The last eight weeks is special training; the last week, the most memorable of my life. Usually, Central Command insists that soldiers have six hours sleep. For this segment of my training, we sleep one to three hours nightly and have nine to thirteen minutes to eat, wash dishes, change guard. The eating is hard: I like food; become very focused on my meal. You learn efficiency, you learn concentration. You learn: sleep while standing (but only if your khaver is alert). It is winter.

For the last exercise, we are paired up, told to reach a goal at night, and return with reconnaissance. It is not officially a contest, but for me, I want us to be the first pair to return.

I still regret my decision. What could I have done?

A night drop is treacherous, even from helicopters. Before you ever jump from aircraft, you train repeatedly: how to wait before opening a chute, how to kick counterclockwise as you leave an airplane to counter your spin; how to fall, especially how to fall, roll, then collect and hide the chute.

You are forbidden to go alone, always a buddy. Here's what happens.

Meir tells me later that on the last drop, his left knee hurt, throbbed, but he would tell no one for fear that he would be cut from _tzanchanim_, for our unit, from being my partner. In fact, the

---

[26] Officer's

night before, he mentions something to our officer, who asks him, "Can you bend your knee? Yes? Then you can jump." Meir thinks, a bruise, it will get better. He ices it prior evening.

The drop starts badly. I am very good on night navigation; still am. I can be anywhere and with a map and the night sky, find my way. The 'chopper drops us; we find that we are on a plateau with cliffs on three sides, sheer drops. These are the wrong landmarks; I had studied the drop site before, on day explorations; these aren't on our map. You learn the land better than the landscapes of your mind.

I check the coordinates; we are off by several kilometers. I radio the pilot. Now, this they never do, but the pilot does: he admits he's wrong. They _never_ return, I had been told. He returns: drops a ladder so that we could climb up, get dropped in the right area.

Maybe it is because of the second drop, but now, Meir is limping badly. He doesn't complain; I can see. Afterwards, we learn that he has fractured his knee; needed surgery.

For now, at night, we only know he is limping. I carry him. First, he gives me his arm, then leans on me, hobbles on one leg. When he can't do that, I store my 50 kg backpack in some rocks, and gunny-sack him on my back. But we are too slow. Meir insists I go ahead alone, do reconnaissance, collect him on return.

But we are forbidden to go alone. Alone you are much more vulnerable, especially Meir with a bad knee. He insists that if I did not go forward, he would refuse to ride on my back. He insists I leave in a crevice, continue on. What could I do?

I go ahead to the river, take notes, return for Meir. We hike back to base.

Of course, I tell my commander. I have to, since I have broken a command by leaving Meir alone. But, the commander only reprimands me; no punishment. I think that he feels guilty for sending Meir with the bum knee.

*   *   *

So, Yonah introduces himself to me, almost apologetic, almost asking me for understanding of what he considers his transgression.

We meet on his kibbutz. He has reserved a private apartment for me overnight; an austere place with a single mattress on a wooden platform, a green baize-textured couch on which he sits. If he were designed by an architect, it might be Mies van der Rohe: lean, buzz cut, clean-shaven, meticulous jeans and a gray t-shirt, sandals wire-rim glasses. He moves with almost choreographed soft articulation, hands playing clearly the notes beneath his words. His bookish look befits this high school teacher.

Kibbutz

I grew up here, on Kibbutz "Har Ha Midbar," I returned and I will stay here. Except for six months at Yamit, and my army duty, I've been here.

For kibbutz, we are a large family. I have nine brothers and sisters; well, officially eight, since we adopted Rimonim when her parents were killed. But for us, she is a sister.

My name, Yonah[27] Hassid, comes from, well, it comes from two origins. Yonah's father was Amitai. This comes from emet, truth, which is related to the word "Amen," "I believe." Israel is a country filled with stories. I can tell you a story of my name? Yonah and "truth" plays against Hassid, my last name, "mercy." God wants Yonah to go to Nineveh, the home of the Assyrians, the Israelites worst enemies, to warn them to repent their evil ways and be redeemed. Yonah refuses. Instead takes his journey, first in a boat, then in the belly of a beast, until he, still reluctant, goes to Nineveh. Yonah thought of God as a God of mercy; Yonah figured he didn't have to go to warn the Ninevens: God would not destroy them; God was merciful. God had destroyed Sodom and Gomorra, but only after Abraham negotiated and saved the few good people. God had deluged the earth, but apparently regretted this and promised, with the appearance of the rainbow, that he would not do this again. When Yonah protests God's destruction of a castor oil plant (which

---

[27] Yonah in English is Jonah.

had shaded him), God reprimands, upbraids him, "You want me to have mercy on a plant, but you ignore thousands of my children in Nineveh?" Yonah prophesizes—quite uneloquently by the way—to the Assyrians, who bide God's word, mend their ways. We could say that Yonah learns a deeper emet, truth; that God is both a God of truth and mercy. So, I am named after truth and mercy. Most people call me Yonah; my closest buddies call me Hassid, "mercy."

O.K. enough lectures.

On our kibbutz, we sleep at our parents until fourteen, when we go to the p'nimia²⁸. That was only two kibbutzim away, but I'll tell you more about how hard that was for me.

I grow up thinking of my grandparents and parents as heroic figures in heroic times, building the land. My father teaches us that we have a responsibility to redeem the land, a responsibility to the Jewish people. But he also says that our working the land redeems us. This I don't really get as a kid; I just like my garden plot.

"Redeeming," its an important Hebrew word that I think is different than the more religious meaning in English. Maybe I can give an example. When the Israelites left Egypt after 400 years of slavery, they were physically freed, but they also needed to be redeemed, to be freed-up from the mentality of slavery. How? They needed to act, to do. Over many years in the desert (not simply by the actions of Moses), they had to show themselves their freedom from the mentality of slavery. Or, when the early pioneers came to build the Jewish State, when they worked the land (not simply lived on it), they redeemed the land. Redeeming has within it the idea of taking action that results in a sense of liberation: interesting idea, that the land itself can become free by our acts. This, my father teaches me.

It is only quite later, when I am a young man at my grandfather's eightieth birthday, after my army duty, that I realize that for them, their early lives were traumatic times; they do not think of themselves as heroes.

---

²⁸ A boarding high school, with teens returning home for weekends and visits permitted by parents.

You ask about the army, but I have to tell you about my family.

Before Kibbutz, Then Building the Land

Both sets of grandparents survive the Holocaust. They arrive for the '48 War. My mother's father is captured by the Arabs from his kibbutz on the Mediterranean: he is one of the few not killed. My father's parents are on shlichut away from their kibbutz, when it is overrun by Jordanian irregulars, who kill everyone on the kibbutz: all murdered after they surrender. My father was seven. At his eightieth birthday, my grandfather speaks with guilt and tears that he was not there to fight with his khevre.

My father is a character. In the '67 war, he is one of the paratroopers to liberate Jerusalem. He and some buddies then hop into a Jeep and drive to the kibbutz that had been taken by the Jordanians in '48, now abandoned. He and his buddies plant the Israeli flag, then call for permission to take this action. Chutzpah.

As a boy, I recall my father always, always teaching, wonderful things: how to become an adult, connecting Torah to Zionism, responsibilities to the Jewish people. Even though he is not religious, he would quote Talmud to argue points of philosophy. On Purim, every Purim, you know, we are permitted, commanded to get so drunk that we cannot feel if we are Mordechai or Haman, good guy or bad. My father would pick up one of us, even two, in his arms and dance on the tables, hop from table to table in the dining hall. Only once does he stumble.

During the week, he often travels the country, to meetings, always to build the Land. But every Shabbat, while we are not religious, he insists on being home. We are not well-off, but he would return with sweets for each of us. Once perhaps a year, we go to a restaurant, a little place on a dusty road, a "pita-parlor," owned by a Moroccan family, schug[29] on every table. These are such handsome people, short-cropped thick black hair on the men and the

---

[29] A hot, spicy condiment.

women with dark eyes and hair. He insists that we order anything we want to eat; usually this is chips and pasta and burgers, not the pita and felafel.

When I am older, I hear my father congratulating a fellow kibbutz khaver on the upcoming wedding of his daughter to a Yemenite immigrant. He says that all the khaverei kibbutz envy this man because his daughter is marrying a Sephardi Jew, not one of the Anglos or European type. For my father, this girl's marriage is an embodiment of true Zionism. Still, he adores my wife and my siblings' spouses.

My mother is restrained, dedicated, always there. She never goes to parties or movies until we are much older and only returns to University when the youngest leaves to p'nimia. She is warm when we are little, plants kisses on us. When I turn six years old, she does not kiss me so readily; but I can see her pride and love in her face. While she and my father are proud of my achievements, I always feel a bit embarrassed by praise. Even now, with my son, I feel both pride and embarrassment when he is praised by his teachers.

Now, when I was in the army and needed something, no matter who answered the phone at home, I know that if I tell my mother, she would get it to me. I picture her writing a list next to the phone on the wall and sending a package to my outpost.

Yamit[30] happens when I am nine years old. Recall that after '67, we get the Sinai Peninsula from Egypt after they attacked. Among other places, the Israelis built this town of Yamit. I came with my family later, about six months before Sadat made peace with Israel and we returned all Sinai. The Israeli government has to force settlers to leave Yamit. I recall living there as exciting, fun. But I think I was in love with my counselor, maybe why. Yet, I can see that the people who had built Yamit seem wounded at being removed from their homes, from even the roofs, by their own Israeli soldiers. I see soldiers in tears. People feel like refugees. I remember.

---

[30]   Yamit was a city built in Sinai that, following the agreement with Sadat, was abandoned with great distress for both its residents and soldiers; both were in tears.

Fourteen and Leaving Home

I may have felt independent as a kibbutz kid, but my move to p'nimia is difficult for the first two weeks when I am 14. I cry (privately, not in front of my parents, friends), I feel lonely. Then, at the first parent visit, I buck-up and thereafter do well. This is my first real exposure to non-kibbutz kids, or adults for that matter. The p'nimia serves about half kibbutz students and half from the surrounding towns. It is known for its educational excellence and humaneness. Humaneness? I mean that the teachers love and respect us. No harshness, while at the same time demanding academics and respect for each other.

Meeting the non-kibbutz kids, I realized that we kibbutznikim are more green, more closed in, less open. I feel jealousy: they don't need to look tough.

*   *   *

Being Chosen; Army Bound

I told you that I feel lucky that I am chosen for sayeret tzanchanim. I want to be one of the muvkheret, "chosen." This is the same word as in the Torah about God making us the chosen people. I feel chosen, special, with special obligations, responsibilities. Yes, I want this.

The first levels of training are very, very difficult, not just physically, but also psychologically. You know I said about how important is the relationships with the immediate officers? Here is what I mean. When you suddenly get an order to drop everything and do something that seems both hard and meaningless—run full-tilt for some time, carry rocks from one place to another—if you have an officer you trust, you just do it without thinking, for you believe that he is deciding it for your sake. If you have an officer you don't trust, you wonder: is he being arbitrary, punitive?

Like what would a mefaked do? One night our mefaked is angry because some of the unit did not do a task as well as he wanted. So,

*he decides to punish our <u>whole</u> unit: we had to run the entire night
with two heavy bags on our shoulders: the whole unit. Sometimes,
if you don't do something in two minutes, you get punished.*

*My officers' motto is: "<u>You can do it if you want</u>." That is,
we can not say, "I can't do it." There is no acceptance that we are
limited. Rather, if we muster our wanting to do something, we can
do it. I find this very valuable until today. Now, I believe that I can
do anything if I want to do it.*

*My favorite training was navigation, especially night
navigation.*

*My good fortune also is that both as a soldier and later as an
officer, my soldiers <u>he'erichu li</u>—what is good English for this—not
simply "liked me," more like "had a good evaluation of me," better,
"valued me." But I decide as a soldier that I would be a <u>mefaked</u>
whom my soldiers would trust and value. I learn even from my
nasty officers.*

Crisis

*I have a personal crisis in the last week of special training. Our
unit of maybe 30 are asked to do a very grueling hike. At this point
we have three officers, <u>mefaked kitah, mefaked tzevet and mefaked
yehida</u>. It is the end of the week, winter, very cold, damp in the
Golan. We have missed Shabbat. Some of us are worried that we
would get thrown out of the unit if we are not up to snuff. We are
commanded to go on a long <u>tiyul</u>, a hike. Half the unit refuses.
Know this: perhaps the worst you could do in the army is to <u>lesarev
pe'kudah</u>, "refuse an order".*

*Our officer is smart. He cancels the <u>masa</u>, the hike. He leaves
us alone to have a group talk. It is an important moment for us
as a unit. It is a black mark against us. I'm not in the group that
refused, but I feel I shared responsibility.*

*Why you ask do I feel responsible? If feel, I believe still, that as
a valued khaver, I could have been more persuasive with my fellow
soldiers to change their minds, to take the challenge. I am one of
four whom our group look up to. Worse. Some of my buddies say*

to me, "Yonah, the others respect you. Talk with them." But, I feel stuck; I feel my words would not persuade them. I fail them, myself, my officer.

Extracting Terrorists

Our major task when we finish training is to extract terrorist suspects, live, from Arab villages. We bring them to Shabak [31] for interrogation. We enter a village at night, quietly, encircle a house and take someone. No shooting. We never get shot. I don't see suffering of the Palestinians, because we really don't spend a lot of time in Yehuda or Shomron villages. Our task is professional: enter quietly, retrieve suspects, do not engage in battle if avoidable.

We have to prepare ourselves for screaming women, crying kids. This is challenging. But I feel that because we are sayeret, because we do not have to stay in the area, we are treated like princes by other soldiers. You don't understand? Those infantry who have to patrol for hours, days, weeks, in Gaza or Yehuda or Shomron, are worn down by the experience. We, sayeret, only go into the Palestinians areas for short periods, then return. And we feel that we are just in what we do: the army would only send us in for dangerous, threatening figures.

Still, we are frightened.

I am particularly terrified in '96. We are sent deep into a dangerous area on a night operation. I am rear guard. I am quite convinced that I would be shot in the back during an ambush.

In my regular service, there is only one injury in sayeret; not in my group. But my brother's group, also sayeret, one is killed. On this operation, my brother and I go together. The army does not like this—sending two brothers on an operation. But both of us refuse to be taken off the operation. The radio carrier is a friend of my brother's from a kibbutz in the Galil. His antenna is tall; touches an overhanging electrical wire; he's electrocuted.

---

[31] Like the F.B.I.

By the end of my service, by the fourth year, I am an officer. I learn how to manage groups of men. Once, I have to organize a training in shooting and navigation of five groups of men, about 100, in different areas of the country simultaneously. And I learn how to plan a mission, prepare myself and others. These build on my kibbutz experiences. Further, learning to organize groups for a mission also helps them now as a teacher, also in our plans for enlarging the kibbutz community.

Echoing Deaths: Nasich and Yael; <u>apres</u> <u>coup</u>

But after four years, it is enough. I don't want to stay. I want to study, to make a family. You know how we have reserve duty? That's plenty enough army for me. Only once do I consider returning to the army as a career, after Nasich's death.

Nasich, I don't talk about him, not with anyone. Until now. Odd, I won't <u>feel</u> Nasich's death until after Yael's death.

Nasich I replace as an officer when he gets promoted. He decides to stay for a career. He always speaks of our commitment to the Jewish people, our responsibilities to our people. He's a distant cousin.

This is maybe too difficult to tell you. I feel a chill on my back.

It traumatizes all of us. They have just married. We are close also to Nasich's family. It is a marriage of two people and two families. His wife . . . it is almost eight years, and she is still half-dead. She will remarry soon, a friend of Nasich. It is not the same, not like before. Also, three months before, my younger sister's boyfriend is killed in action. They had recently broken-up. But, I believe that it is not a permanent break. Death makes it permanent.

How he is killed? It is very simple. He is leading a night action: point man. He is the only one killed. One shot to the head.

I cry very much; hard. But I don't realize that I won't let myself <u>feel</u> until later.

He, Nasich, is almost a complete man. Every one would follow him. Not just his men, children cluster around him, like bees around bright flowers, nourishing themselves, while pollinating the source.

He believes strongly in thinking about life, how to live a good life. He wants debates: is it better to do this thing or that, in order to do right? He would ask me what he could do to become a better officer, a better man. He asks me! Then he looks directly into my eyes, quietly, rests his chin on his right palm, and listen. Before an action, he would check if everyone understands what to do and why were doing it. During an action, few words, but the look of his eyes, his hand motions, the way he coiled his body. Like Jacob's dream, he _nitzav_, he "stands poised" for action, not just in war, but in life. I want to say he is a complete man, but I would hear him object that this is not _tz'nu'a_, not modest.

Two days after his funeral, I have to return to reserve duty. I _have_ to go. At first it is difficult, but after two days I am grateful: I am busy, not left alone with my thoughts. I must take care of my men.

After his death, I consider briefly returning to army as a career, to carry out the responsibilities that he would talk about for himself. (Never, never would he say that someone else has these responsibilities. He leads by example.) Had I returned, I would have been so unhappy, missing my family. I am glad I stayed in reserves.

I wanted to live like he lives . . . . wanted to live.

Nasich's death gives me _proportia_, proportion in life. There are problems with my students, my work, with a roadblock making me late? I have my life, my children and wife are alive. It's O.K.

My wife and I have this dark humor: if you die first, what should I do? She insists on this, as if she were preparing herself for my death. But, I do not engage in it. I see my children, I do not think about death; it is not imminent for me.

All right, I admit that when I am on reserve duty, when I am away from them, it is difficult for me. I yearn for them. In Hebrew, the words for "yearn" and "to touch" share a three letter root, NGA. I yearn to hold them, to feel their touch.

Desert Death

What was it about Yael's death that I began also to feel Nasich's?

Tzava makes me, made me into who I am today. I didn't want to stay to advance higher, for then I would have had a larger number of soldiers. I wanted to stay with 20 soldiers, which is what I have in mil'uim.

Yael means the animal ibex. You know with the big sweeping back horns. They look imposing, the horns, but they are in fact light and the yael is graceful. If you go to Ein Gedi, the kibbutz oasis north of Masada on the edge of the Dead Sea, you see the ibexes. Even in the parking lot, they are tame. Gracefully, they rear on their hind legs to eat of the trees. So, his name is fitting. I replace him in his unit when he is advanced.

He goes to Midbar Yehuda, the Judean desert, the stretch of deep, desolate looking wadis that descend from Jerusalem to the Dead Sea. Here, he will die. The prophets in the time of the kings—when they were being pursued because of prophesies that they poured upon the porches of the kings' ears—would hide in the caves of the deep wadis of the midbar. Hard to get to these caves; need to rappel down by rope. There is a priest, I think Russian Orthodox, who has lived in one of these caves; bread is lowered to him by rope and he stays within, in solitary. Also, we think that some of the terrorists escape to the midbar.

While the land looks desolately dry, you often can hear the deep rush of waters hidden in the wadis. These waters come from the rain falling on Jerusalem and surrounding hills. The water run through the wadis, percolate through the stone, are pulled by gravity to the Dead Sea, and emerge maybe 70 years later. In Ein Gedi there are streams that flow from the rocks, some streams still hot, others cold, pouring as water falls into the ponds below. You can swim in these, bathe your head in the hot springs descending, or in a frigid stream.

In the arid hills and wadis, there is a plant that emits salt from its leaves, like tears; these salt the ground around it to keep other plants from growing. Such is the midbar, a place that can keep others away. When you rappel down, you can find small pools of stagnant water hidden in crevices. Things like this you learn when you are taught how to survive alone in the desert, should you have a bad parachute drop. The desert carries secrets of death, but also of survival.

Yael is devout secular, absolutely not religious. But he loves his soldiers. When several of his religious soldiers have leave for Shabbat and are in this remote location, he offers to drive them with the Jeep to a closer tzomet, junction, so that they can get home before Shabbat starts. It is late by the time he returns, alone. His jeep goes off the road into a wadi. We suspect he fell asleep at the wheel. We used to kid him about this.

Sometimes, when I hike in the wadis, I imagine that his soul escaped, wanders there among the prophets. I talk with him.

It is the first Rosh Hashana, after my marriage. I am shocked. But the shock is much greater as I began to realize how I feel about Nasich's death. These are two great losses from my life.

*   *   *

Back to Kibbutz

You ask about why I returned, why I plan to stay on kibbutz. I know that many of my khevre have not returned, or have left, or plan to leave. Some have said that if we turn into more of a yishuv, a closed settlement with private property and wages, they want to come back.

One girl with whom I grew up even knows exactly which plot of land she will build a house, if we become a yishuv, then she'll return. I spy some old khevre who come for weekends, hang around, partly to visit their parents or friends, but I believe that they yearn for the kibbutz. Another neighbor who grew up here, moved just three or four kilometers away to a nice town. She has a bigger apartment with a red roof. Yet, she confesses to me that she misses living in a community in which she can do more for those around her. She does mitzvoth in her town; when a husband is on mil'uim, for instance, she will organize the women to bring dinners to the family, to take the children. She has her own family and a job. But she misses a community in which each person has a sense of responsibility to the others. Yes, she says she left because she had to rely on the car pool to get to work and the fellow who drove her car was a nasty fellow, would *"forget"* she was waiting, come late and such. Now she has her own car, or the bus. But she doesn't have kibbutz. She misses us.

For me, I am a <u>ben</u> <u>meshek</u>, a son of agriculture, a son of kibbutz. I have friends and family here. I take my children on <u>Shabbat</u> to our Noah's ark, you know the tiny zoo I showed you. They go after school to feed the animals, curry the pony, ride the donkey. I feel good about being here.

It's not ideology. I know ideology and I like part of it. But ideology is not most important. Most import is the <u>shituf</u>, the flowing together with each other. It's not a good translation, maybe, but it is like the word for *"fluent,"* <u>shotef</u>. Helping others is a value, so that there is balance, equality in society.

Kibbutz is not sacred. It is a framework. It is not the same kibbutz of my parents.

Private people need privacy today. They need material things. Freedom.

Now, I believe that it is important that people do work. I hear from one of my best friends that he gets irritated when people don't like to work. But, I have found that most people want to work; maybe not <u>so</u> hard, but enough. Most want to work, well . . . O.K.

In the past, you came from somewhere, Brooklyn, Johannesburg, Warsaw, Buenos Aires, and the kibbutz said to you, "Work, work in the chicken coop. After five years, you can come to talk to us about something else."

Today, people won't do that. Many want to find professional satisfaction in their jobs. Although, frankly, the fields and the chickens are quite satisfying to me. Land is simple: you care for it; it sustains you.

But, my wife for instance, wants more. She works in Tel Aviv. It's an hour by car, but to take the shared car of the kibbutz, she may have to wait another half hour before she gets picked up and then go on a circuit until the whole car is full. And then, with a shared car, you wait for your 7:15 departure, but the driver hasn't finished his corn flakes until 7:30. So, you wait. Or the fellow who used the car at 7:00 am to drive his son to the bus stop at the road outside the kibbutz, isn't back yet. You wait. Or, someone took out the car, *but forgot, maybe, to sign it out; and they aren't back; just late, or an accident, or an ambush? More waiting. Then you leave, O.K. a little late already. The driver picks up a few trempistim[32]; what can you do—drive with an empty seat? Then near Tel Aviv, besides the traffic jams, the driver takes an earlier exit to let off someone closer to their work, and in Tel Aviv, a few stops for others before you get to work. At the end of the day the repeat; and she finishes at 4:30, but has to wait until 5:00, because the driver doesn't get off until after 4:30. Before we had children, she did not complain. Now, she wants to get directly home, she wants to see the children. She wants a car; not too own, just to use.*

Also, by private car or shared, the road from kibbutz towards the Sh'veila[33] passes Tzurim, an Arab town where you can get stoned. From Tzurim came the Arabs in 1948 who killed the thirty-five Jews bringing supplies to Gush Etzion; the Jews had seen a few Arabs initially, but chose not to attack them; the Arabs returned to Tzurim and came back to kill the Jews. And the bomber of Cafe Apropos in Tel Aviv? Also a Tzurim "graduate." But the stoning from Tzurim is not as frequent as places on the West Bank. You duck.

For me, it's O.K. if she can be granted one through the kibbutz. For me, it's O.K. to get a tremp or the bus, or ride with the khevre. I too want to see the children, but I am surprised how much I can learn and accomplish in the car with other kibbutznikim.

It's like the common dining hall. Fewer use it since we started charging for meals. It's very cheap, but some people are either offended or want to have private meals at home. But, I like seeing the other kibbutz members, especially those who now work outside the kibbutz and whom I might not otherwise see as frequently. Also, I get a lot done at the dining table with kibbutz members. Sometimes, I come with the kids to buy prepared food to bring home: it's a compromise. I can see khevre, patronize the dining hall, have my kids ride on the wonderful food cart, and still bring home dinner for my wife and family.

---

[32]   Hitchhikers; often soldiers, or students waiting a bus stops.
[33]   The Sh'veila is the coastal, fertile plain.

NATHAN SZAJNBERG

Or, someone suggests that instead of our doing guard duty by kibbutz members around the clock, we should hire a private company to do it: he says it would be easier on us and would also save money (based on work time lost when you have been on guard the night before). Guard duty can be onerous: my father, in his fifties still does night guard, although we divide it up into three or four hour segments. We had a woman killed by a sniper from the Arab olive groves a few years back. But we do guard duty around the perimeter in pairs: you always go with a buddy. Now, this may mean that I get to guard with someone whom I haven't spent much time with for awhile; get to talk about matters—his kids, how's work, any problems. It gives me a greater sense of what is going on with the community. And we also feel more committed. I feel strongly that we need to continue this for the sake of our community, in spite of the economics.

Now, I am a _m'chanech_ in the high school. You know how we have at least three types of educators with the teens: the _madrich_, who is often younger and may live in the dorm, takes them on _tiyulim_, has bull sessions; the _m'chanech_, who teaches some subjects, is responsible for a core group of maybe 20, but a larger group of 40-50 and also spends time talking about the philosophy of life, of kibbutz, of upcoming army; and the _moreh_, the more traditional teacher who covers specific subjects. I have been a _moreh_, I like that, but I really like the connection I have with my teens as a _m'chanech_. I like having both the boys and the girls, but I sometimes find that when I have discussion groups with the girls, they talk more freely. This is what I want to do, to be a teacher.

But also for kibbutz, I feel responsibility to the community. I am organizing groups to refresh and discuss the meaning of kibbutz, our responsibilities to each other and to the kibbutz. Right now, for instance, we are considering requests from former kibbutz members, _b'nei meshek_, who want to move back, but don't want to be members of kibbutz. They might want just to rent here and such. They want to raise their young children here. Some nostalgia, I think, but also some memory of how good it is for children here. I don't know what the kibbutz will decide, but the process of getting people of different generations to regenerate the kibbutz, is rich for me.

We have a wonderful opportunity to build the kibbutz. I chair
the committee for new housing. We have people on the committee
who are from my father's generation, others like myself, born on the
kibbutz, others who moved to kibbutz. We are interviewing several
architects. They ask us to look at our whole kibbutz, the landscaping,
the views, not only the new homes. We are looking at our old places
also. Modesty is important on our kibbutz, modesty of material
means. For instance, a current three bedroom place is maybe 80
sq. meters, small. People who want to join our community like the
sense of modesty. Others say they would join us if we make larger
apartments, let them rent and their children use our schools. But
we are not interested in having the latter move here; we want to
maintain the cultural values of the kibbutz. One architect asks us
to look at the flow of people in the kibbutz; how to increase people's
contact during the day. What should be the center of the kibbutz?
We are trying to open up the kibbutz's view to the surrounding hills,
so we are not turned so inward. Right now, maybe you noticed,
when you enter, to the left is the industrial area, the turkey houses
(which smell badly), then you arrive to the bus circle and an open
field with some olive trees. One architect suggest we not welcome
ourselves with the view and smells of a factory and turkeys. We are
reading about landscape, architecture—Olmsted and Vaughn,
Frank Lloyd Wright, William Whyte—and we listen to each other.
We are literally building community.

It is a struggle at times, but this is the nature of a true community;
to listen to each other, respect each other, make a place for children
to love, for elders to rest. One man, born here, wants no change;
prefers that his house be a "cave," says he wants to retreat there at
the end of the day. Another wants a nice patio at the back of his
apartment. Some insist that the new homes not be bigger than ours;
others realize that most people who also want to move here, need
bigger places, since we closed the beit yeladim, their children sleep
at home. The architect I prefer, asks us to think of ourselves in the
days of Medici Florence, building a beautiful community. Well,
we are not Medicis, but I like that he pushes us to think about our
relationships and how the space around us can affect our daily. I

want people to feel welcomed within; have a sense of privacy, yet connected to each other and to the land.

I don't forget my crisis in army, when some of my unit refused to do the tiyul and I kept quiet, did not try to persuade them, because I had doubts that I could be successful. Today, I still do not think that I am eloquent, but I will no longer hesitate to fulfill my responsibilities to others.

I _had_ to return to kibbutz. My life is built around my parents, my siblings, those who built the kibbutz. My life is filled with Nasich and Yael, my children and my wife.

An Officer and a Teacher

Yedid almost didn't appear here, courtesy the Intifada. I agree to see him on his West Bank Kibbutz. We had met previously, over several visits, even attending the brit milah of his third child. But, my first three formal meetings are Intifada sideswiped.

My first visit, I arrived after midnight by cab from Jerusalem, getting lost on the way. At the start of the Intifada, I can not get a late-night Jewish cab driver on the way to his kibbutz, near the Green Line. The King David Hotel's guard/doorman hails a very young Arab driver. Through two security tunnels, we pass the roadside concrete slabs on the left, episodically protecting us from gunfire from Beit Jala on the southeast; episodic protection, as they are not complete, have gaps, like in a shooting gallery at a fair. We get a stroboscopic view of Beit Jala, its church. We approach the first roadblock. Stopped, we are pulled aside. One soldier checks the Arab's ID, looks at him carefully, as do I in the rear view mirror; I notice the fine sheen of sweat collecting on his face. The young soldier's torch makes a pendulum of light from ID, to face, and back again. A second soldier approaches from behind, then on my right. I lower the window. He checks my U. S. passport; asks what I, an American, am doing driving at midnight south of Jerusalem. We are waved on.

The driver barrels down the unlit road, misses the kibbutz turnoff, stops in an unlit Palestinian village. I know not to get out. By cell phone, I reached Meir on kibbutz; I hand the phone to the driver, and Meir guides him back, to the kibbutz electrified gate, where Meir is waiting, phone in hand. He waves us in, smiling, as if nothing has gone wrong. Only the next day does someone explain my treacherous situation.

A few months later, my second attempt. My Egged bus—faced with turkey wire to protect from rocks, with scarred bulletproof side windows—is turned back on the tunnel road: a bombing on the road ahead. We see smoke rising. I call Yedid, reschedule.

My third try, as I am ready to leave Jerusalem, Shira, his wife, calls from the kibbutz: Yedid, wounded in Jenin, is in hospital. Yedid phoned from the emergency room, to be sure I don't make the trip down. When Shira learns that I am en route, she asks if I would come for tea: Yedid, a flesh wound in the thigh, will be home in a few days and suggested to her that I meet with Shira. He knows that I have been meeting with both female and male soldiers.

Listen to the men

The children are at school. Shira is plainly dressed, brown hair long, held back with barrettes. She reassures me that Yedid will be fine. I ask if she can tell me about her background, her soldiering.

I grew up on another kibbutz and have deeply visual and warm memories: as a five year old with my class visiting my father in the fields, he perched on a tractor amid a field of sunflowers facing one direction in unison; the red tail lights of my grandparent's car as it recedes in the distance, following their visit from the city. My grandfather recently died at eighty-eight; was a businessman and proud of it. Two of his four children become socialist kibbutzniks: he is proud of them, but still believed that capitalism is a more robust system. But what I really recall of him is warmth.

She pauses after saying this, looking beyond me, tears brimming. She takes a sip of water, continues.

I meet Yedid in the army. He is really handsome, but quite shy. I know he turned the heads of other girls. I am placed in teacher corps, to teach new immigrant recruits. I especially adore working with the Ethiopian boys, new soldiers, who have never used a watch, who must learn to tell time. In weeks, an officer will command them to dash a path in four minutes, eat, wash and fall-in in fifteen minutes. I will teach them to tell time, to understand rapid-fire Hebrew, to read. And they, they are famished to learn, eager to be new Israelis. The Ethiopians are families who have maintained Jewish identity from the time of Solomon, who have been cut off from post-Biblical Judaism, are unacquainted with Talmudic and rabbinical Judaism. One soldier tells of me of his grandmother, upon receiving fresh vegetables the day they arrive to Israel, goes to wash them in the new, white porcelain, water-filled basin. A social worker enters, alarmed; this white "basin" is a toilet. From a life of Ethiopian shepherding, this generation is to become soldiers in a modern land. And they desire this.

Later, I teach young French boys who come for army duty. From these two years of my army duty, I know I will attend University to become a teacher. As I am now, teaching math in high school.

Yedid and I talk about marriage in the army. He was in for seven years; he is older than I. After army, went traveling for seven months. When we talked about marriage before he left, he decided that it would be too difficult to be a career soldier and have the kind of family we wanted to have.

Her oldest daughter, Anat arrives home with her kindergarten class and teacher to visit from school. They have cookies and juice as Anat gives them a "tour" of her house. Not all the children live on the kibbutz. It is clear that Anat would prefer not to leave with her class; to stay home.

I wish I could have her stay. I thought of asking the teacher, but then I thought that this would overstep my responsibilities and also would not be fair to the other children. Maybe I should tell Anati this.

But, you should talk with the men about army. I had a wonderful experience as did many of my girlfriends. We worried about our boyfriends, heard their stories. But this is not the same as facing death. You must listen to the stories of the men.

*   *   *

Kibbutz

My fourth visit is the charm. I arrive at his house Saturday night, after he puts his children to bed. He is in a blindingly white T-shirt, worn, but clean jeans, threadbare sandals. He finishes the dishes, wipes his hands on a waffle-weave dish towel, with a final wipe on his jeans, before he shakes hands. He has a brush cut, clean-shaven, lean, tall, tightly muscled. We sit at the kitchen/dining table in the railroad-style single family room: foyer/kitchen/salon, leading to French doors out to a small terrace. The three children sleep in one room, a second room for Yedid and his wife. Everything is meticulously in place in this 80 square meter flat.[34] Tea on the table and just-baked rugelach. Our backs are to the sleeping chambers, but periodically, Yedid checks over his left shoulder.

Our second meeting, a few months later, also on Saturday, near midnight, is in the unheated guard booth at the kibbutz's electrified gate. His rifle leans nonchalantly against the corrugated steel wall, a gun in his belt, grip only showing. He listens to the two-way security radio, answers the occasional phone call about a voltage drop in the electrified gate, monitors the cars begging entrance, and yet, stays engaged with me.

His appearance mirrors his character—minimalist exterior, belying solid infrastructure. He wastes no words. His eyes park on the darkness beyond the gate, the people waiting entrance behind the blinding headlamps. Yet, his attention is to me.

When he talks about the army, he weaves back and forth in time, from kibbutz childhood, to current fatherhood, to being an

---

[34]   About 1,000 sq. feet.

officer, to being a teacher, making a coherent fabric. In this fabric, deaths become a background pattern; life the foreground.

He begins with his childhood, giving a surprising portrait of himself as a bit rebellious, strong-minded.

You ask about growing up on kibbutz. Well it is not a big thing. I was born outside Tel Aviv. My father is from South Africa, my mother, born in Netanya. But my grandparents are Yekke, German Jews, who came here before the war. I only know my father's parents from pictures: they died when I was two or three.

My parents move us to kibbutz when I was young. Eventually there are three of us, me and my sisters, in our two-bedroom home on kibbutz. My parents had a room, we sleep in the other room. The kibbutz had closed the beit yeladim. At fourteen, I go to the beit he'neu'rim, the apartments for high school. The school itself is at a nearby kibbutz, but still, I came home only for weekends. Other kids' parents would telephone, often visit. My parents are O.K. I phone, but they never visit, except for special events. My parents don't worry about me.

What I remember best from my mother is caring and hugs. My father teaches me. He challenges me—do a hard mission, get to a goal. Teaches me karate and basketball, how to ride a bike and when I fall, kadimah! (forward). Also, he teaches do not waste: he is the one who ate the brown bananas, that we refused with "feh!" And one lesson from my father is to do what I think I should . . . even if others disagree.

I argue with them a lot then. Later, I realize that they are usually right. Once, when I am little, I state that if they did not let me have an extra piece of candy, I would run away to my khaver's house. They say, "Fine. Be home for dinner." So, I did.

But, he does spank us. And I decide I would never hit my children. I read Adler when I was in officer training. Learn from him about the needs of children; you have to find the needs to give them.

Understand their needs, then you can give them love rather than fight. With children, love and fight may be the same. But in your eyes it is different. Listen, they can drive you nuts, but they just want you . . . they don't want to drive you nuts. If you understand them, you can hug them . . . or if you need to ignore them, you tell them, let's talk in a few minutes.

My parents, basically, were busy thinking about what is right to do with my life.

Suddenly, we plunge into his first weeks of basic training in one of the "cherries" of special forces.

Seeking the Red Beret

In the <u>Bakum</u>, the huge recruitment center, they give you choices; on a paper, you give points next to the various units that you can choose from.

I list Duvdevan, the red berets as my top choice. Others, I give little weight. I had dreamt of Duvdevan, want it, worked for it, hoped for it. Got it.

Getting assigned is the first step. Then comes the <u>gibush</u>, the "crystallization" of the unit. Perhaps one quarter of the initial group makes it to the final unit.

Why Duvdevan? I don't like fighting, in fact, am happy to finish my seven years, get away a few months, start a real life. But, I am, excuse me, a patriot. Why I apologize? I think that you Americans frown on such things. Anyhow, if I have an enemy, I want to protect my people from him, directly not sitting behind a desk. Also, the red beret from Duvdevan means much; even if you wear it tucked into your left epaulet, people notice. More importantly, I demand much of myself, drive myself and feel deeply satisfied when I reach a difficult goal, a challenge that seems beyond my reach. This is Duvdevan.

I'll tell you the good feeling I have in <u>gibush</u>. The challenge becomes more mental than physical. You feel like your body has reached its limit; then, you have your sergeant, or see your buddies continuing on, and you push yourself beyond what you body permits. And you do it! It is more an internal competition, but my buddies help. For example, you are given either a heavy sack of sand or a jerry can of water on your back; commanded to run a hillside in ellipses; first down, then around a marker at the bottom, then up *and a marker, then down and so on. You can, then you tire; you see a buddy pass, maybe another, you glance at the sergeant, think he sees you passed up; run harder.*

And I am progressing.

Until my mother writes to the army. Did others tell you about only sons, or sons whose brothers or fathers died in service? A mother can request from the army that her remaining son not serve in a high risk unit. Without warning me, my mother writes; says I am her only son; asks me to be transferred out of Duvdevan.

Here, the army and I don't see eye-to-eye. They agree to her request and assign me to Nahal[35], "green berets." For me, Nahal is not combat. I tell the army "Sayeret o Nayeret," "special corps or paper pusher," I insist. I want the best or the least. I absolutely won't push papers, but I believe I can force their hand. Well, I am not at first successful. They respond, "Fine, you refuse orders; you go to jail." So, I sit in jail. Fine, I will sit in the brig.

Ultimately, I win. After some months, they compromise. Send me to Tzanchanim, paratroopers. My mother objects again; I love, adore and respect her. But I ask her to not be involved in this way again. She tries once more, later when I am assigned to Hebron patrol. I call her, tell her that if she does this, I will not tell her where I am being assigned. I try to follow the fourth commandment, honor thy father and mother, but I need to do my job. She doesn't do this again.

*   *   *

One of my closest buddies becomes a soldier in Shayetet, Navy seals. I really respect him and others in such units. Seals is

---

[35]   Nahal, is an acronym for the special units set up usually at border areas, to perform both agricultural and defensive positions, in the hope that these small settlements will become safe enough to attract civilian populations and that the soldiers who serve will remain there after army service. Many dangerous border areas in the State were established by Nahal.

perhaps the toughest unit to get into, stay in. I'll tell you a story about his character. We used to play basketball together. If you should ever get the ball away from him in a game, if you could, he would sit on your main neck vein, your jugular, until he gets the ball back. If you were to try to talk to him about his service, he would maybe tell you his first name and today's date; maybe his real first name.

* * *

My first death is a buddy on guard in Kiryat Arba, the new Jewish neighborhood next to Hebron. So quick, so simple. Natti is night guard watching through a concrete rectangular window, maybe this big (his hands spread just beyond the breath of his shoulders). *A sniper gets him; here* (points to his forehead). *But, you know, when they use high velocity bullets, the head explodes; a puff of red mist in the gun sight. This is very hard for me. The death, the funeral. I don't talk about it.*

My next death is Moshe. And his sergeant and officer. On a siyur, a reconnaissance. A fine friend. From high school on. Tzanchanim. Moshe gave us life. I am near Eilat when I hear. Take the bus to Tel Aviv all night. Go to the morgue. I need to see him just once more. Then the levayah (funeral). The day after Pesach he dies . . . is killed. Every Yom Hazikaron (Memorial Day, the day before Independence Day) *for the first few years, we buddies take long hikes to honor him, talk about him. Then we go to his grave. But, sometimes, I go alone to his grave on Har Herzl. I talk to him: what our buddies are doing, about my kids.*

This is very difficult to tell you.

He is a very missed person.

Travel and Dreams

Yedid spent seven years in the army, four additional as an officer. For now, this is all I will hear about deaths. Three more he will tell us, but later.

Now, he wants to turn to life. And life for him is kibbutz.

After my years of army, I take seven months to travel: South and Central America, southern California, where an uncle lives. I like the feel in California: how everything works, how people give such good service, everything so clean. In Disneyland they don't sell gum to prevent people spitting sticky gum on the ground.

But, I recall the flight home after seven months away. I have a humus deficiency. A hunger for real Israeli humus. Look, I tell my buddies, I am a simple fellow. When I am young, all I need to be happy is a trip to the beach with my buddies, a plate of hummus, tehini and felafel; a nargila; a sunset. It's a long drive to the beach, but _kef_ (fun). In my youth, this is enough.

But, it is no longer enough after army.

I had two dreams after army while I was traveling. Two dreams. And I begin to think about them. Previously, I thought dreams were silliness, the product of an idle mind, things to be forgotten, dismissed. Until my dream about my grandmother. Then I thought about something one of my teachers in high school quoted, I think from Rabbi Hisdai: a dream not understood is like a letter not read. My grandmother died after army and during my birthday month, September. The month I am planning to leave for my seven month _khufsha_ (vacation). My grandmother I adored. She was warm, always dedicated to me. She died after I lost Moshe, the others in army.

But, I didn't dream about her until several months into my travel. I am in Buenos Aires, having a wonderful time. Many Israelis travel through South and Central America and the Jewish community is very accepting, warm. I dream this.

> I visit my grandmother at the elderly home. She is dying right before my eyes: pale, making deep gasps, sighs, final ones. She thinks I am her son, my father, maybe my uncle, not her grandson. She motions me to come closer. A secret she wants to reveal. Then, she speaks Spanish. So you know, my grandmother was from Hungary, didn't speak Spanish. I don't understand what she is saying; I don't know Spanish. But I concentrate, move closer, listen.

On a couch perpendicular, behind me, sit four old people who start calling my name repeatedly, "Yedid, Yedid!" I turn to them, politely, mind you, and signal with my hand and say: "a moment, a moment, just a moment." (He gives the Israeli gesture; palm upturned, fingertips pulsating against each other with each syllable.) *Usually I would say to such people, "Shut up!" But, in front of my grandmother, I am always a <u>mensch</u> (gentleman). I was raised this way.*

I awaken before she dies.

I think on this dream very hard. I feel guilty for leaving on my vacation one month after grandmother dies. Yet, I enjoy the trip thoroughly; Argentina, the people are so warm. I believe that my grandmother is trying to tell me in her last breaths that I should enjoy my life. This dream permits me to continue my trip and to be a mensch.

My second dream is just before I return to <u>Aretz</u>. In the army I meet and fall in love with Shira. Other women are also pretty, are interested in me, but my thoughts return to Shira. When I leave <u>Aretz</u> for my trip, I am not sure with whom to make a life. Before I take my return flight I shave my beard of seven months. And I dream this.

I am clean shaven. A woman is caressing my cheek, like so, like in a romantic movie, gently. She says "I enjoy touching your cheek." But I cannot see her, do not to recognize her voice. Yet, I know she loves me.

The dream leaves me puzzled: who is she, why can't I recognize her voice? But I do realize that I prepare myself for something more important than humus, nargila and the beach. Preparing myself to be in deeper love. I tell my closest <u>khaver</u> about my dream. He says it reminds him of Jacob's ladder dream just as he is about to escape, just as he is about to leave his homeland for two decades, just before he meets Rachel, his beloved. He dreams of the ladder, angels ascending and descending. As if he is hoping to reach heaven, which he does

when he meets Rachel. Here I am returning home, preparing
to meet a woman who will love me and whom I can love. I like
my friend's suggestion.
    And that is what happened.

Shira I met in the army. She is a teacher in the army also. She
is from another kibbutz, but agrees to return to my kibbutz with me
after army.
    As he talks about her, he drops his eyes in shyness. Moves on.

Back to kibbutz

The kibbutz gives me a year to study what I wanted: and
I study everything—Torah and archeology, Jewish history and
literature—everything. I am famished to study. But I want
something concrete to do, something useful to kibbutz: I request to
study carpentry for a year, but also take teacher training courses.
I'm not sure then that I could be a good teacher, so kibbutz sends
me to work in the kibbutz business, manufacturing and import
of sporting goods. I do marketing, sales. From the carpentry, I
make these French doors you see, with the beveled glass inserts,
brass handles. I asked the kibbutz if it is O.K. to put them in my
flat; can be jealousy if I have something too special or decorative
facing out of my flat; inside, is O.K. Since I make it myself, they
say all right. I miss carpentry.
    Work is almost central to his identity, next to being a father
and husband, which is central. He begins with his work, before
he speaks of his children.

Being a Teacher, an officer

Now, I am the head of the high school counseling staff,
madrikhim. From the army, I learn how to work with people,
organize. Only if we are a unit, can we do things right. It's hard.
    We have a responsibility to the students. We have to invest a lot
of energy . . . tell them what is right to do . . . see if they listen. We

have to think how to interest them. Have them feel our excitement. They are studying (pedagogical subjects) too, but we want them to do other things, things that are not "learning." A few days' tiyul in the wilderness, camping, rappelling, learning to know, love and respect the land is important for us and them. I have to teach them how to climb, rock climb. We have a wall on kibbutz to practice with knobs of different shapes. The kids are belayed with a rope two of us hold. Then I take them to nature. Most important, I tell them is to hold your body to the rock, embrace it like a nursing child to its mother. At first, they hold themselves away like spiders. Gradually, they bring themselves closer to the wall of stone. Then, push with the legs, seek with the fingers. Later, when they are advanced, I blindfold them, so they really learn to trust their touch, use their fingers.

I have a special rappelling place, in a wadi, east of Jerusalem. A hole in the rock they drop through, into a cleft, then down maybe an 80 degree incline. Not too far down. The student must learn to trust his body and his buddy belaying the rope; legs extended, but knees not locked, hopping down.

At the bottom of this wadi is a special plant I show them; its leaves drip off salty water, leaving a ring of salt around it to prevent other plants from rooting. Yet, if you are a stranded soldier, if you are a pilot shot down, you learn to incise the fleshy leaves to get water. Also, under a rock shelf, shadowed from the sun, usually is a pool of water; I teach them about filtering it. I believe when they do this, they trust their bodies, their buddies, but also learn to be closer to the land. From the army I learned how to do this.

We do kumsitz,[36] *listen to lectures, have man-to-man talks to know them better, social activities.*

The kids have to feel a connection with the teachers. It is not easy when the kids have two different groups of people responsible for them—morim and madrichim. But our high school is well-organized

---

[36] Kumsitz are late night campfires, around which one sings songs, play khalil recorder, tell tales.

to make the connection. Since the high school is on my kibbutz, it is easy for my to be there evenings, see them during the day as I am walking about or taking my kids from school. I work in the morning to noon, then again at night. Everyday. It is a lot.

The connection between my work to the army is that I see being an officer as being an educator. Not everyone sees it that way. For some officers, it is a profession. I see it as something else: a responsibility, education, a commitment to my men and through them to my people, my land.

In the army, I can educate soldiers the way I wanted to: how to be a soldier, yet a Jew, a man. How to have respect for yourself and responsibility to others. They can see me as an officer and a person. I give them myself . . . intensive, a lot of hours. But they gave me the opportunity to educate them.

There are things that bother me about the army. The biggest is that I want a family. Family is my life. When I marry, I realize I could not stay in the army.

Yedid glows as he talks about his children, three, five and seven years old. Hadar, David and Jonathan. And he explains Jonathan's name.

You were at the brit. You know that my name is spelled yud dalid, yud dalid, means "dearest friend." This also spells yad-yad, or "hand in hand." My daughter is my first blessing. I wanted my two sons to walk through life as closest friends, like David and Jonathan, yad-b-yad. They should be true brothers, true friends.

Milu'im

After this interlude, he returns to milu'im, reserve duty during the Intifada. He mentions briefly his injury, apologizes for missing our appointment, but wants to dwell on living and being a soldier among the Palestinians, before he returns to death themes.

We do bad things to the Palestinians. Many of them just want to make a living, raise a family. But who is in a cage? We are in a cage, within our borders. The fences; we are encaged from all sides, guard ourselves from people who want to kill us. Gaza's fence is to protect my family. We keep the Palestinians in Gaza and we feel jailed also. Look at us. (We are at the guard post, before the electrified, fortified gate of the kibbutz at midnight. His forefinger does a 270 degree circuit into the darkness.) I am with the fence around my house, my kibbutz. Here is the fence, the gate to my jail cell.

As we talk, the government has started building the anti-terror fence at Tulqaram. Yedid becomes somber, talks about his last mil'uim, when some soldiers had signed a pledge not to serve in the land captured in 1967.

Morale

It is a big problem of morale among the soldiers. I have a soldier who said the things that we were doing were hard for him . . . doesn't agree with the policies. I tell him that we are here in the name of the law. We can do it or not . . . and then go to jail. I ask him, how can I help him. He says that he would prefer to stay on the base rather than see the Palestinians on the road and deal with them. So, I let him stay in the base; give him responsibility to stay in radio contact, coordinate our movements. Then, he says that he would stay on base, but not do radio contact: makes him uncomfortable to support our efforts in Yehuda and Shomron (the "Territories"). At this point, I say that if he can not be with us, even from the base, he should go "to the law" to arrange it, go back to Central Command. It is hard for me to talk to him like this. I am surprised. I try to respect both his wishes, but also the ethos I learned from my officers, my buddies: if you have a strong ethical position, then take it, and pay the price. He decides that while his opinions were important to him, he wants to stay in our unit, stay with my command. He agrees to coordinate radio contact. This is a very important position when we are maneuvering "blind" at night, in the field. I trust him. He will return to reserves and I will try to be sensitive to his feelings and opinions. But, what we must do, we must do. We can ask to do things in another way, but there is a mission. After the mission, we can argue all night.

OFFICER AND A TEACHER

Death, Life, the flow of our lives

Now, I can tell you more of others who died.
Ten years ago, my commander was killed. It is hard. We visit
the families. We know each other. One who is a very good friend
from high school. Still hard to talk about it. I try to take with me
the good things that I had with him. I learned a lot from him. I
remember him here, there. As I drive through the desert where we
trained, I "see" him and me doing maneuvers. He is in the wadis,
maybe, or in the tels, among the date palm oases. Sometimes, I
drive past the soldiers tremping (hitchhiking) at the bus stops; I
peer out my window, expecting him to be standing, arm extended
to me. He just needs a ride to come back. His memories strengthen
me, an anchor.

Living people are part of the flow of our lives. When someone
dies, something stays of what he was. Something solid. Young people
doing what they must in this period of their lives. My commander
knew that nothing came easy. He wasn't brilliant, wasn't advanced
quickly. But he was always doing. He is . . . was a ben adam, a
mensch (a decent fellow), who knew his soldiers. He worked hard,
listened well to his soldiers. The bus he was riding in was hit, crashed,
the driver was killed and two more in the back critically wounded.
This was before we had good ceramic protection on the buses. Maybe,
today he would have survived.

But our unit is strong; we do not fall apart when he dies.

Pini too. I don't go to the levayah[37]; when we are on duty, we take
lots on who can go, like on Purim. We visited his family later. You
know, he gives me strength still. I know that I got something from
them and helps me continue. I remember them. Why, wherefore . . .
this I do not ask. It doesn't lead me anyplace.

Moishek, a good man . . . .

---

[37]   In Judaism, funerals/burials must be held within twenty-fours hours of death, with rare religious exceptions. There is little time to make detailed preparations in an army unit.

NATHAN SZAJNBERG

I can't deal with this too much. Life is more important than death. With the families it is hard. Hard to see how their families deal.
What makes a man a good soldier?
Yishai before he dies was one. Just do it, and he just did it. He did what he needed to do and did it well. He was quiet, disciplined. We had been in basic training together and later in my unit, but not when he died. He is wounded in the head, a bombing or something. They found him. Probably an ambush. Dead. That's it. Again, we all couldn't go to the levayah, drew lots again. But it was on Friday. I go later. Every year, we go to his grave on Har Herzl and then to his house. He was dati (religious), so we learn (study Torah or Mishneh) in his memory. All kinds of topics. For instance, since I am a kibbutznik and he was also, I challenge Yishai: "Is it possible to be an ethical businessman." Then we look through Talmud to argue how one can be an ethical Jewish businessman. Every time, I am impressed. His parents are special, amazing.
We do this at Moshe's house also.
I keep thinking I can talk to you about the deaths. Then when I try, it is still hard. When we are doing azkara (remembering service) and I am with my khevre, it is easier for me. We are learning something new about how to live a good life and we do it in memory of Natti, Moshe, Yishai, Pini, Moishek.

Back to kibbutz, the future

Midnight, we finish guard duty. Yedid begins to pack up what little there is to pack. He picks up his rifle, wears it nonchalantly. I walk him up the grade, branch off the public road to the private residences. He nods towards his house and begins to talk about his children.

I do this for the sake of my children, my family. What I want my children to learn most from me is, "That you should find grace and good wisdom in the eyes of God and fellow man."

We stand at the patch of garden lined by small stones in front of the stairs going down to his basement apartment. He turns to me, concerned.

I am not much of a talker maybe. But I hope that the people who read this will understand me.

His future is clear to him. The kibbutz his parents helped build has been his refuge. <u>This</u> is is home, and his children's home. The past is the Hungary of his grandparents, the South Africa of his father. This is done. The past that counts is his life in Israel. His present is most valuable, as is his children's future on kibbutz.

What's left to say:
The author speaks

Throughout much of this book, I tried to remain in background, my voice. Like the Greek poet whose *daemon* speaks through him, I wish that my soldiers speak through me. "My soldiers," because they are colleagues with me, they bring their stories to you. If my accounts are not as poetic as they should be, the shortcoming is with my tongue, my pen. Their voices are eloquent; moreso, their lives.

Now, I offer you my thoughts, my impressions in three areas.

1) Who are these men and how did they become themselves; what kinds of persons and citizens are they in society?

2) What is the relationship between individual and society in a democratic republic refracted through this army? How does freedom bring responsibility, and how do these men meet responsibility (including over life/death) in a paradoxical setting: the autocracy of an army, yet one which sits in and serves a democratic society?

3) What does it mean—to society and the individual—to have a participatory army in a democratic state, particularly one in war or under siege and terror for over five decades?

Our first task is more straightforward—their identities—as this comes directly from the lives in this book.

Our second and third tasks—the reciprocity between individual and democratic society—is a broader task, touching on cultural anthropology, political science, sociology and psychoanalysis. I speak as a psychoanalyst—this I can do best—but I follow the trails blazed by Erik Erikson, Erich Fromm, Bruno Bettelheim and Robert Coles. Erikson's seminal early work, *Childhood and Society*, is about the relationship between early child rearing and cultural values. He creates a model of how we raise children (feed, toilet, and more), transmits cultural values. He personalizes Aristotle's suggestion in the first chapter of the *Politics* that the family is the first "state." Erikson's later *Identity, Youth and Crisis* focuses on this book's era of life and its tasks: adolescence (identity formation vs. diffusion) through young adulthood (intimacy vs. isolation). Erikson—touching on men such as Martin Luther, Freud, and later, Jesus (who in turn have touched our lives)—articulates *how a person's identity crisis* (a normative event) can be solved in a manner that *also addresses the crises of his society and era.* More modestly, we all experience this. For the men here, their normative internal "crises" revolve around finding, creating and consolidating their identities, followed by establishing intimacies: they are affected by *and* affect the crises of the democratic society within which they live, which they now also build.

Fromm's revolutionary, challenging, lapel-grasping work, *Escape from Freedom*[38] is rarely read today. Yet, it rivets, asks fundamental questions, faces basic challenges about promoting or fostering "democracy" in the world. Leo Strauss, whose students, such as Paul Wolfowitz, have hovered in recent U.S. foreign policy-making, suggested that democracy can be safer if other nations adopt democracy. This concept guides U.S. foreign policy; explains our military interventions in Afghanistan, Iraq and our political

---

[38]   Fromm, Erich. *Escape From Freedom.* New York: Farrar & Rinehart, inc., 1941.

moves elsewhere. This policy departs from both the history of U.S. isolationism, and Kissinger's Bismarckian *Realpolitik*. But, when we look at hoped-for democracies, we need to return to both Aristotle's concepts of democracy, and Fromm's elaboration of our internal need to escape from freedom, driven by our escape from internal responsibility for our decisions.

I will return to this later, when I discuss how, paradoxically, the Israeli army—by definition, not a democratic organization— prepares soldiers well for taking the responsibilities of democracy. I will refer to my work with a U.S. cohort, as well as other democratic societies that have almost universal conscription.

The third task follows from above—the army's role in a democratic state, using Israel as a unique example—and leads us to Israel's future. In 2005 Azure, an Israeli magazine, Michael Oren speculated about the impact on Israeli society of major changes in the army.

These soldiers who have spoken to you give us in democratic societies an opportunity to reflect. A recent article described how one prestigious U.S. private school kept plaques in the common hall of those students who had served in the armed forces: the names are prolific throughout the twentieth century, then drop precipitously for the Iraq desert war: upper crust Americans are not serving in the proportion they once served. A colleague in Greenwich Ct., the outer crust of upper crust, who is a strong Bush supporter, including of the Iraq war, sees his Ivy league graduating son serve in—the deserts of Washington, D.C.; wants him to avoid the danger of Iraq service. In contrast, Israel's elite are represented in the most dangerous army units. What happens to a democratic state when its leading citizens—at least as measured by their wealth and education—no longer serve?

Who are they and how did they get that way?

Recall, I study a select group. I chose to look at the best and the brightest, and those who elect not to become professional soldiers, insist on returning to civilian lives. These men had the highest recruitment scores possible. I chose mostly kibbutz youth, as I wanted to catch possibly the last cohort to come from this unique social experiment before kibbutz disappears. In part, this is a legacy from one of my teachers, Bruno Bettelheim, whose *Children of the Dream*, celebrates the success of excellent communal child-rearing, and predicted that it would disappear as mothers would insist on having their children home. (As I noted in the beginning, Bettelheim's book is often cited, less often read, and generally misinterpreted as a critique of kibbutz child rearing. It is not.) Yet another reason to study this cohort, is its disproportionate contribution to the elite corps and officers.

The nine chapters show how individual, how different these men are, as well as their major life themes. Here, I articulate their *common qualities* before they entered army, during service and today, some six to eight years after leaving regular service. *And their reserve service*—during the Intifada, particularly in Spring 2002, after the Netanya Park Hotel Passover bombing killed hundreds gathered for Seder, and all these soldiers were called up to enter Jenin and Nablus—*affected* these now-citizen soldiers most severely, albeit with variations.

Pre-Army

Before army, many of these then-teens were thinking about army and which unit to achieve. All desired combat units— small groups, facing greatest danger, for which you are selected, cannot simply volunteer. Some came with personal histories that influenced their choices: Yonah's father was in *Tzanchanim* (liberated their kibbutz, in fact), David's relatives in *Golani*, Chaim's two older brothers in *Tzanchanim*. Others were dreaming beyond their fathers' achievements, particularly Avi, who sought *Sayeret Matkal* (Special Forces) and whose father, an Argentinean immigrant was a "lowly" infantryman. None described a push from their families, neither towards army nor towards specific combat units; to the contrary, several spoke of how families considered army to be a responsibility, only a way-station to (more important) aspects of life—education, family, even studying Torah. Some parents (almost always mothers) even expressed concern, quiet reluctance, about their sons' promotion in dangerous elite units: the mothers with three sons in *Duvdevan*, simply wished that their sons were not in these units, even as they knew that their wishes were to naught.

Some, but not most, described thinking and training for army beginning around ages 15 or 16: talking with peers, or uncles about various units, getting advice from relatives about the "do's" and "don't's" and getting into shape—boulder-jogging with buddies in fields. Most didn't do this, nevertheless describing their transformation physically in the first few months of basic training.

One soldier came through the *hesder* program—Orthodox men who study in yeshiva for almost two years before entering active duty in an integrated unit. He felt relieved that he was almost 20, some two years older than most recruits, felt more secure, did not experience the complete stripping-away of identity in basic training.

Yet, I begin too late when I start with adolescence, when most men speak about conscious preparation for army. For, when they speak of their childhoods, they give "formulae" for building an Israeli soldier: militarily competent, yet tempered by a humanistic tradition. Eliaz is more conscious, at least more articulate, than the others of childhood determinants of his soldiering: from his being named after the heroic uncle who died in the '56 war, to his dressing as a soldier in kindergarten and being told by his parents that they prayed and hoped that he would only *play* soldier, never have to become one. Then he descends to deeper strata. When he describes, as a boy, discovering the hole in the fence between his yishuv and the neighboring Arab town, playing with the Arab twins, picking olives with the children, he understands why in his early twenties, he both aids an elderly Arab being harassed by his officer, and delays ordering warning fire over the heads of Nablus/Shechem Arabs, jeopardizing his men's safety. Eliaz captures the richness of childhood that made him at one moment humane, and at another an officer tethered by his memories in the face of clear and present danger.

Early responsibilities, young instructors.

Recall Peretz. At nine, his first job with a buddy was to harvest grasses for the ponies in the kibbutz children's zoo. His "instructors" in the use of sickle and scythe were two eleven year olds. While they taught him the details of technique—how to sickle near, without gouging the fence, how to load the donkey cart—they were bullies. A passing teacher intervened, although nine-year-old Peretz wanted to handle this himself. When Peretz became a "boss" at eleven, he and his buddy had decided not to bully their charges. There are many such tales on the productive and protective boundaries of the kibbutz, where each child had a "garden" to care for starting around primary school, where the kindergartners would gather outside around the pecan tree to listen to stories, then "harvest" fallen pecans. Later, as described by Avi or Aviv and others, by age 14 or 15, they would have more serious responsibilities: in the fields, running irrigation, conserving waste waters beneath household sinks to irrigate the gardens and so forth. Physical labor is highly prized, highly respected. For example, Peretz recalls his *disappointment* when his father is promoted from the fields to run the profitable swimming pool, and his mother the guest house: while he understands today how important this was for the kibbutz balance-sheet, at the time, he looked down upon them for "abandoning" agriculture. Another recalls his relief when his father finished his two-year stint as kibbutz chief administrator, so that he could return to the fields. This respect (and capacity) for physical labor prepared them for the very physical being of soldiering.

A *sense of safety* comes with the kibbutz, safety even when being bombed. Anat, a female officer, recalls the Iraqi Scud bombings of 1991. In a kibbutz near Tel Aviv, they were under serious threat. Yet, <u>she</u> recalls a festive atmosphere in the underground shelter for perhaps a week: well-lit, all the children had copies of their favorite toys from above ground. Adults were arranging games, singing, laughing. Her only memory of concern was that they could not find the family dog in time to bring it underground. Peretz describes ongoing rocket bombing of their kibbutz bordering Lebanon, and how the adults would shelter the children, act as if nothing would be wrong.[39] This reminds us of Anna Freud and Dorothy Burlingame's observation of children's reactions to V-bombing of London: the children who did best, felt best, were those whose mothers were calmest.[40] Unfortunately, good training for maintaining your nerve under fire.

Peers. Of course, the peer intimacy, including the de-sexualization (likely an extension of the sibling incest barrier) is a major experience for these children. They live closely, grow up with each other, learn how to get along, even when it may be hard to get along, because they will be together for a long time.[41] Even if we exclude the children's houses for sleeping (some grew up as these were phased out), their closeness with their peers was more concentrated than most non-kibbutz children experience. Thus, going to army, sleeping in crowded settings (including the cabin of a tank, or a tent, or a three-night stay in a covered berm) is not shocking. Pinchas one of the non-kibbutzniks, found this part of his army experience more challenging for the first few weeks.

---

[39] While superficially reminiscent of Ann Frank's far more tragic experience, in which her father tried to maintain a sense of normalcy while the family was in hiding, the stories from kibbutz are starkly different. Bettelheim ("The Forgotten Lessons of Ann Frank") pointed out that Mr. Frank did not prepare his family and children for the exigencies of their lives, did not even plan an exit. Mr. Frank tried to deny the war, it seems. These kibbutz children, while playing in bunkers, had parents who were prepared for the worst, who were actively fighting.

[40] Freud, Anna, and Dorothy Burlingame. War and Children. New York: Ernst Willard. 1943

[41] In the Finnish primary school system, the same teacher remains with the child over several years. I asked my colleague, Irma Moilanen, a mother of four, what happens if there is incompatibility between

WHAT'S LEFT TO SAY: THE AUTHOR SPEAKS

Education? Here I become educated. After I had thought I had completed Peretz's educational history, he seemed puzzled as I hadn't asked about his *hitnahagut*, a word that means something like "comporting oneself" or in French, the reflexive *se conduire*, conducting oneself. (*Hitnahagut's* English inadequate translation is "behaving oneself.") From Peretz and others, I learned that education for them, particularly on kibbutz, began with the *metapellet*, followed by *morah* (usually female in primary school), *m'chanech(et)*, and *madrich(ah)*[42]. What we consider education in the States would be the (academic) purview of *morah*. (The root of the latter is like "to see or to show.") The *metapellet* is unique to the kibbutz: the woman who cares for the infants and children in the children's house, like a second mother. As Peretz recounts, the relationship between *metapellet* and mother can be synergistic. The *madrich* (the root from the word, "path" or "road") guides the youth down the correct paths of life, how to live one's life well, properly. These are significant figures who take the youth for several days' outing, camping, learning and loving the land. The *m'chanech* is an educator. As for *hitnahagut*, which refers to comporting oneself, anyone on kibbutz can hold you to this. One kibbutz adult saw kibbutz teens at a nearby mall behaving

---

a teacher and a child. She explained that both teacher and parents, "wedded" to each other for some years, were invested in this not happening. The teachers become emotionally important to the child, use the ingredient of learning for love in order to develop a love for learning (as Rudolf Ekstein expressed in the title of one of his books). At high school graduation, a rather grand, formal event for the entire city, I met many of the primary teachers attending.

[42] For brevity, I use the feminine version for the metapellet, morah as they tend to be women in the early years. I use both masculine and feminine versions for m'chanech/et and madrich/ah in later grades, who tend to be men or women.

loudly, impolitely. He took them to task: pointed out that they were wearing the kibbutz outfit of blue shirts/rolled sleeves, and bringing shame to the kibbutz.

These attitudes captured by *hitnahagut* and *hadrakha* transport themselves well into army. Recall Yonah's disappointment *in himself* when he did not try to convince his unit to behave better, come up with a better solution. These boys have internalized a way of thinking that includes being responsible, taking initiative, showing regard for your peers and others, behaving well. Psychoanalytically this combination of *strong superego values balanced by an ego ideal*, softens the harshness of the superego; *executive and self-monitoring ego functions* the boy/soldier uses like ongoing radar, to observe how he is acting, helps him carry out his best.

And these boys had important experiences that temper harsh superego; they feel valued, cared for and hopeful about their abilities. Peretz recalls himself as a troublemaker—caught smoking in the bushes outside grade school, being mean to some kids, not paying attention in school. Someone suggested putting him on medication: nixed by *both* his mother and his teacher. With their support he did well. He recalls their faith in him and themselves.

Yonah recalls feeling parochial, a bit naive, when he attended a regional high school with both kibbutz and non-kibbutz teens. The kibbutz schools are known for their fine education; non-kibbutz parents seek out these schools for their children. Yonah found that the non-kibbutz teens were more worldly than he, an adjustment he made before the army.

One final ingredient—the spice added to the prospective soldier's personality before he leaves kibbutz—is humility. Be humble about your efforts. Remove your medals before returning to kibbutz for weekend leave; *show* abilities, don't trumpet them.

With this childhood, you begin to build a unique soldier, an Israeli soldier.

A few good words about kibbutz, perhaps a Requiem. I kept hearing about how the kibbutz, as an ideological community and economically in some cases, is dying (or dead). This unique social experiment, perhaps the most successful attempt at socialist

᠆214᠆   WHAT'S LEFT TO SAY: THE AUTHOR SPEAKS

communal living in the twentieth century, may be disappearing. In its time, starting in the early twentieth century, it safeguarded the borders of the county, fed the country and provided food export. But, as a psychoanalyst, one of its most important "products" is the young people it raised, boys and girls, many of whom became national leaders, army officers, model citizens. Bettelheim, in *Children of the Dream*, demonstrated that kibbutz communal child rearing produced a new kind of personality, healthy, but different than someone arising from a middle class, nuclear family structure. These fruits of the kibbutz were close to their peers, attached to the land, hardworking, valued action, not just words. Bettelheim predicted that as the newer generations of mothers became more middle-class, more petit bourgeois, they would not tolerate having their children raised outside their homes, in communal children's homes. He was correct. Yet, we should not forget that one of the major lessons from the kibbutz is that it could raise not only crops, but also fine citizens, who make fine soldiers and officers.

During Army: That Makes the Man (What Kind of Man We Talking About)

Giyus, call-up, is described the way Erving Goffman[43] writes about total institutions—whether army or mental hospital: stripping down individuality, losing personal external identity, and shifting to group identification including uniforms, haircuts, shared meals and sleep arrangements. And, for this tiny country with massive immigration, many describe a shocking introduction to boys of varying backgrounds, ethnically, educationally, socially. Pinchas is so stunned, that for some days he couldn't get to the food, didn't eat: he was accustomed as the youngest at home to wait until the others were served, even waiting to begin eating until others did. By day three, he was bustling in the cafeteria line like the others. Personal items stolen, he got a lock for his locker. He describes

---

[43] Goffman, Erving. *Asylums*, New York: Anchor, 1961.

this as if being thrust into an ice cold shower: first shock, then tolerance, then bracing, then not bothered. One woman, Ester, taught Ethiopian boys who had never seen nor read a clock, how to tell time; no small task when your commander gives you a command to be done in ten minutes, or seven.

Unit selection was smooth for most: they accepted their placements, generally with a quiet pride. (Humility includes no braggadocio, no machismo about killing.)

Avi's journey is a tortured exception: accepted into his highly desired *Sayeret Matkal*, he completes the full course until the painful multi-kilometer hike bearing a stretcher, then insists on transfer out. His officer tries to dissuade him, values him, encourages him to try the experience further. But Avi insists; at some level knows that he prefers a tank unit, so that he would be enclosed with at least three buddies. He experienced feeling alone on *Sayeret Matkal* (often silent) maneuvers, despite knowing that guys were buddied-up. He enjoyed navigating, because he could concentrate on the demands of the outside world and knew that his buddies depended on his focus: to be alone with his thoughts was too difficult for him, far more difficult than long hikes. Avi knew that he could not be alone with himself, his thoughts, the feelings that invaded those thoughts.

Aviv is another exception to smooth placement. Assigned highly desired pilot training, he is transferred out when they find an XRay bony anomaly that they told him would preclude him from parachuting. (He later learned that this "anomaly" was a variant of normal; was parachuting freely.) Placed in a high level desk job, he does good work, but misses the action with his buddies. Only in reserves, when he connects with a fellow kibbutznik, his officer in tank corps, does he <u>feel</u> he fits. He becomes a commander in reserves. (Being a commander in reserves is not the same as it was in the U.S. (before Iraq II). Ariel Sharon was in the reserves when he led the lightening tank attack in '73 that crossed the Suez, encircled the Egyptian army and poised for Cairo.)

These men are willing, even intent to talk about their army service. But they focused on its effect on them, about their unit,

216   WHAT'S LEFT TO SAY: THE AUTHOR SPEAKS

their buddies, and especially those who were killed. What makes this book and study different than most accounts of military service? Many other books, often by journalists, are active, lively, engaging accounts of battles and their danger—their titles capture the cutting excitement, such as *Masters of Chaos*[44], *Generation Kill*[45]—revealing little about the individual within the soldier. Some first person accounts (such as *Jarhead*, recently a leading motion picture) give some bare hints of inner life, but, not always in a convincing manner, nor thorough, some even self-serving. From my soldiers, I rarely heard details, blow-by-blow accounts of battles, and certainly not with any sense of great victory or relish for killing. I wondered if this was because as an analyst, I tend to be more interested in inner experiences. I tried to correct for this, asked about battle experiences. Yet, while there were seminal, critical battles, these men want to talk about their reactions, feelings, thoughts, memories of their buddies; they did not choose to regal me with exploits. When Micha tells of his first kill—a sniper aiming for him—he speaks more about his mix of excitement, fear (almost being the shot), followed by confusion of identity: am I a soldier, medic, a Jew? Soon, you will hear more from Naftali of *Duvdevan*, who describes killing a major Hezbollah "engineer," a bomb maker and planner. He starts by confessing that his sister missed the school bus in "Aifoh" that was bombed by this man, this murderer of dozens. He continues with how Naftali's unit entered, killed the bomber as he ran downstairs, guns blazing, then warned the gun-toting wife following her husband (and her children behind her, clutching her nightgown at the top of the stairs) to drop her guns. Then, his unit left.

---

[44]   Robinson, Linda. *Masters of Chaos: The Secret History of the Special Forces*. New York: PublicAffairs, 2004.

[45]   Wright, Evan. *Generation Kill: Devil Dogs, Iceman, Captain America, and the New Face of American War*. New York: Putnum Adult, 2004.

A most compelling part of their experience is death. Each man here, by his mid-twenties, each one, had at least one friend, relative, *khaver*, killed in combat or terrorist attack. This experience is seminal; anneals their personality. Annealing strengthens steel or glass by heat, followed by slow cooling. So too, episodes of white-hot soldiering are followed by long periods of slow cooling, for uncertain periods of time. While you have heard how strong these men's characters are, I will speak about how some aspects of this hardening results in a more sober, even somber,[46] more serious stance towards life by their late 20's. In our U.S. study, none of the 76 participants who grew up in New York City experienced the murder of a *close* friend or relative—not one.[47] We will return to death.

Concrete matters these men learned from army: be selfless; be honest; be modest; be like anyone else, not special; improvise, innovate; be independent, yet rely on your buddies; know goals, yet revise them as needed; make do with few resources; train and practice navigation in your free time; officers may come or go, sergeants stay—stay close to your sergeant; clean your weapon and keep it pure; make sure your dog tags are on tight; your *khevreh*, your closest friends in the army may be the closest you will ever have. As an officer, protect your men, lead them in attack, and guard them on withdrawal or retreat. As Avi said—now that he is an "elder" in reserves (all 30 years of him)—his responsibility on *milu'im* is: return sons to their families, fathers to their children and wives, alive, intact.

---

[46] Amia Lieblich articulates this in her compelling book, *Tin Soldiers on Jerusalem Beach*, as does Reuven Gal in his survey study, *The Israeli Soldier*.

Lieblich, Amia. *Tin Soldiers on Jerusalem Beach*. New York: Pantheon Books, 1978.

Gal, Reuven. *A Portait of the Israeli Soldier*. Westport: Greenwood Press, 1986.

[47] *Lives Across Time*, op. cit.

But, these men also need to believe that what they are doing is right. A few of these soldiers resigned or refused their positions as officer and an army career, because they began to question their roles (but they never refused orders): several described their own discomfort when they felt more concerned about protecting their men than protecting, for instance, provocative settlers in the West Bank or Gaza. Matters are not simply black or white. These soldiers did not make abstract, ideological "political" decisions: they describe specific episodes, for instance, in which some settlers put their children at danger, or provoked arguments and retaliation from Arabs, then called the soldiers to rescue them. Some soldiers are candid: while they felt sorry for some of the Palestinians, they did not think very much of the Palestinian provocateurs, who would notify news organizations when and where to appear, before they provoked a battle with Israeli soldiers. That is, some of these men began to think (like Mercutio as he lay dying), "a pox on *both* their houses!" All continued to serve in reserves, but as Peretz says, he would split himself in two: Peretz the "sergeant" and Peretz the young man.

There is 20-year-old Anat. As we stroll around her kibbutz *bustanim* (fragrant gardens), after two years in the army Intelligence, after teaching me about the advantages and disadvantages of the M16 over the Uzi, turns to me and says, "Every week, at least once weekly, I realize that I am doing something to protect my country, my family, my people." *In sum, all of these soldiers have strong internal moral compasses and also demanding more of themselves than they would ever demand of their men.* Of course, their men felt the same—demanding more of themselves than they would of their officers.

The word *"kadimah,"* literally "forward," means for many of these men, figuratively, to move forward into life in the face of tragedy. This word Avi recalls spoken by his best friend, before the *khaver* was sniper-shot dead. Move forward, into life, fulfill your obligations. This country and army are so small, I heard this same officer described by three different men as exemplary, as one said, "an almost perfect man." *Kadimah* kept Avi going, even if on autopilot, through university, marriage, and career.

But *kadimah* can truncate or delay mourning, putting someone to rest (and oneself, at rest).

Combine *khaverut, kadimah,* and too many deaths: we get a personality that is *mature before its time.* (It focuses the mind, it's bracing, when, around midnight, as your unit is preparing for a serious, dangerous action, your captain ends the strategy session, by asking what each person will do should he get shot.) In Erikson's terms, these fellows get a concentrated course in the value of intimacy, as well as a demand for solid industry—tasks of adolescence and young adulthood (and an earlier development phase). Their peer relations in their units (with which many are likely to remain until retirement at age 50) are close, tight, perhaps the strongest in their lives. Death adds poignancy to closeness. (The Hebrew for "close" shares a root with "relatives."[48]) All had important rituals for those who died: meeting with buddies to reminisce, or selecting a part of Talmud to study, one that fits with the deceased's values or ideas or interests; some go as far as to try to *live out both their lives and how they imagine the deceased would have lived.* The latter is perhaps a sublimated version of "Levirate" marriage: in Canaanite times, if a brother dies leaving a childless wife, you are obligated to have children with his wife, in his name. These men do not take on their "brothers" wives, but they take on their memories, imagine their lives. Nevertheless, one kibbutznik woman whose husband was killed in battle, finally agreed to marry after several years, but to her husband's closest buddy: she knew that he would know what her husband believed and valued; her children would be comfortable with him, as they appeared to be.

Courage

More than a few words about courage. Aristotle regarded courage one of the highest virtues; he emphasized courage at

---

[48]   Ironically, switching one letter of the root, "KRV"—"a relative/ close"—to "KVR," radically changes meaning to "tomb".

war. Our English *courage* comes from *couer*, French for heart. I want to thank my Argentine colleague David Rosenfeld for this connection. Listen to the words we use: they reflect how we think, even feel. In Hebrew, the word for courage is *ometz*; when Moshe is preparing Joshua to take over leadership of the Israelites heading into Canaan, he tells him, *khazak v'amatz*, be strong and courageous. They are entering the land that one of Moshe's spies proclaimed, "eats its inhabitants." A Hebrew phrase brings *ometz's* usage closer to the English: *l'ametz libekha*, bring (something) close to, or *strengthen your heart*. An adoptive parent is a *ma'ametz*, truly someone who both brings a child close to her heart, and with some courage, strength.

Here, listen to the stories of three men who "bookend" a soldier's life span: "Yossi," a twenty-one year old who captures terrorists, is nearing the end of his army service; "Naftali," a twenty-two year old, six weeks after finishing his regular service in *Duvdevan*; Nehamia, a retired general and a father and grandfather. They never once use the word "courage" describing their own service—too humble they are. Yet, I present them as models of courage, *l'ametz libekha* in this Israeli army. Their stories give life to this matter of the heart and refine Aristotle's concept.

*   *   *

Yossi's elite unit jumps in to protect the Jewish people where others might hestitate. I begin with him so that the reader can feel, in the moment of battle, how difficult is the tension between being a fine soldier and being a fine man. Listen and place yourself in this boy's post-midnight position.

We have met many times during the Intifada, when he has a free weekend, or recuperating after injuries in action. One of six children, he has a rapid-fire delivery, especially of jokes, and can recite film dialogue by heart in two languages: he does Topol and Marx Brothers. His smile is winning.

This conversation takes place from midnight to three a.m. before he has to return to three-week duty, and just before a national crisis: an Israeli soldier, Gilad Shalit, is kidnapped; the army re-enters Gaza, re-enters Lebanon. A I write this, I am worried about Yossi, as he is the type of soldier who will be the first to jump in to save a life. His story tells of courage that Aristotle did not describe.

We meet at midnight, as my schedule did not permit us to meet the one day he was home, and he politely offers to meet with me instead of sleeping his last night at home. He has until six a.m. before returning to base. At three a.m., after three hours walking, I am tired; he offers that he is free until six, but looks at me, and says that perhaps he should get the three hours of sleep. My sense is that he could have continued for the next three hours.

He begins with a question. As is often true, the first question leads to more central, troubling questions, in this case about his rapid, momentary decision to capture a terrorist alive whom they had been sent to kill, putting Yossi and his unit at greater risk. He once told me how upset he was that in order to capture a suspect alive, Yossi has to kill an attacking guard dog in midair; uses a silencer. That week, he returns home with a puppy for his family to raise.

Tonight, he begins tonight with his concern about one his trainees, who has done well until being sent to the field. Now, the fellow finds excuses to get a desk job—what is demeaningly called a "jobnik"—so that he can go home every night. Yossi is worried that this fellow will experience this drop-out as a failure, the first of many in his life. Yossi wants to know how to help him. As I listen more, I suggest that this boy is needing to return home nightly because of family problems that he feels obligated to solve. Yossi decides to try to get the army social worker involved and visit the home.

Then we move to another level, one that troubles him.

We had a forty-two hour action without sleep. Very tough for us, for me. Funny that what bothered us most at the end of the tour was who was going to get to shower first, having not changed clothes all this time.

But very difficult after what happened a few weeks before. One of my buddies got grazed by a bullet on the neck, starting spurting blood. We were taught about pressure points, so I punch my fist into his neck where I had been taught.

The helicopter got us and radioed the hospital; they tell me not to release. My fist turns blue, really hurts. When we get to the emergency room, I release after the doctors are ready. Then, blood sprays all over before they get on a pressure bandage. I look at myself, my uniform, my hand, covered with blood, not mine. He's O.K. now. I have a rare blood type and tell the doctors. They take a donation, leave me feeling like a raisin.

But on this 42-hour action we start with a jump just a meter or so from the helicopter. I'm the second guy to jump out, but the guy who jumps first gets three bullets into his chest. I yank him back and we lift off. There's a doctor on board. We strip the bullet proof vest off and blood is all over. The vest slows and deflects the bullets slightly, almost enough. One enters his left lung; one is in his sternum, the other breaks a rib and his heart beat, when we restart it, brushes against the bullet. We restart it. The doctor right away puts a breathing tube through his throat. Here (He points to his cricoid.). Then tells me to shock him with the paddles to restart his heart. I say, "I don't know how!" He just shouts, "Like this!" I do it and I can see the machine showing his heart starting again.

We get to the E.R. and my buddy is alert: shouts at the doctors, "Save the bullets, save the bullets!" I tell him, they've got to save his life. After four months of rehab and a desk job, he's back in our unit. And he has the three bullets mounted in his room at home.

But, we don't stop there. We are to get to a known terrorist planner; kill him. We set off to the house; he's is not there. While we are in the house, we get radioed information to find him in another house.

We get to the house. We take out the three guards with silencers. We enter his bedroom. He is sleeping. Next to his wife. This bothers me. We have this sleeping gas for the wife should she wake up. But, I can't kill him. Sleeping next to his wife. I inject him so he stays asleep: he shakes briefly, then goes limp. We roll him out of bed, his wife still sleeping. I carry him on my back downstairs and we are off. Deliver him to Shabak for questioning. I think this is good, since I think that they got alot of information from him.

(There is a touch of uncertainty in his voice as he talks about not killing this man.)

Yossi continues with how exhausted he and the others were. Talk about how he was changing his mind about a career in the army. Thinks of medical school. Likes the idea of saving lives, working under pressure, working with a group. He feels a bit uncertain about whether he is good enough. I comment that the very systematic manner in which he trains his men to do a mission, stay alive, fits with the systematic thinking and action as a physican.

But, I ask that we think of his dilemma, his sleepless decision not to kill a known killer. I ask that we think about this as a form of courage, one with an informed heart.

* * *

I look forward to meeting "Naftali" who had but six weeks earlier finished his four-year tour with Duvdevan. The Duvedan's ("Cherry") job description: speaking fluent Palestinian Arabic, live in Arab areas disguised, gather information, arrest terrorists. In one, you will hear, this went beyond arrest.

Back on Kibbutz "Mishmar," he lives in the young adult dorms, but enjoys visiting his parents and two brothers' house before dinner in the Kibbutz dining hall. The young man I meet for almost two hours in his parents' kitchen is thoughtful; he shifts from initially laconic to quietly voluble and direct. Later, I see him in the dining hall at his friends' table, now animated and laughing. He is but two tables distant from his parents, balancing his desire to be with his friends, yet in touch with his parents.

Respectful, he told his mother he would talk with me for twenty minutes: no more. This lengthens to an hour, then almost two hours before, famished, we agree to go for dinner.

I learned in the army that the hardest substance in the world is water: it will get through all obstructions, even stone. Either it will erode stone drop by drop, or it will flow around it. Water prevails.

So too, a good soldier: patiently erode your enemy or evade him, make a new path.

My father is an immigrant, so I am the first to enter the army. We came to Kibbutz when I was twelve, after my father did all his training in England. I was proud to be picked for Duvdevan, but it doesn't matter who you are, where you are from. In the army, like kibbutz, it matters what you do and how well you do it.

About 120 guys are picked for my unit. After four months special training, thirty of us remained.

Well, O.K., you keep asking about kibbutznikim. So, sixteen of us were from Kibbutz. But it really doesn't matter in Duvdevan where you're from.

But, we share a secret. You see this brand of cigarettes? These are kibbutzniki cigarettes. When you see someone smoking these, in the army, you know he's a kibbutznik. Sometimes we just have a cigarette together.

We are a small unit. We work tightly together. We breathe together. Our commander insists that each of us should be prepared to take command in the field; should he be killed. Before every action, each action, in addition to going over the details, he would ask, "And if I go down, what do you do next?"

*   *   *

I try not to think about some of the things I had to do. I try not to think about them. But you ask the action of which I am most proud? This I can tell you now.

This was ordered after the bombing of the bus with school children in "Aifoh," down the valley from my kibbutz. The bombing was "engineered" by a master bomber who lived in another country. You might know where, since it was in the papers after we were done. Let's just say, an island. The host government knows who he is: guards him; pretends to be blind to his activities. We were not blind.

(Naftali shifts towards me, tensely poised within inches of my face. I feel his breath.)

My sister usually takes that bus to school, but she was late that day. Dozens of kids were killed, injured, maimed. I saw the photo:

the top of the bus was rolled-off, like a sardine can. The driver's head was blown off, his hands still gripping the steering wheel. I can't talk about this more.

We are assigned to kill him. We do it.

We land in rubber speed craft before dawn. Land in small groups a various locales on the beach; assemble in town. We had memorized not only his address, but the interior architecture of his home, his bedroom. We know that he sleeps with pistols under his pillow; know they are Glocks. A high stone fence surrounds the house, guards.

You do this quickly.

We are instructed clearly: don't harm wife or children.

We have night vision goggles, but one must concentrate, focus. Night goggles are monocular, no depth perception, give a greenish glow, and if lights are switched on, you are temporarily blinded.

We enter. He awakens. We shoot him as he is running down the terrazzo stairs, firing with both guns.

His wife follows. From the top of the stairs; she is armed. I could see the children huddle behind her, maybe 5 or 7 years old. We command in Arabic: "Don't shoot! Drop the guns! We are done! We are leaving!"

(Naftali leans back from his tense poise; falls silent.)

Of this I believe that we were justified (tzodek, Hebrew for "right," even "righteous"). I did think of my sister.

*   *   *

I didn't want to stay in the army, other than milu'im. I wanted to return to kibbutz.

The kibbutz wants me to work in the kindergarten. They know that I am good with children. But, I just want a mindless job. So, I ask to work in the factory. They compromise: half-time in the gan (kindergarten); half time in the factory. I do love the children. They climb all over me like those colorful Mexican grandmother vessels with the children clambering over her body. But, it is a relief: push a button in the factory; the drill press descends, makes a part; you spray with an air gun to clean off the metal shavings, grab the glistening, hefty metal part, toss it into the oily barrel drum. They land with a slight thump, a solid sound. Then push button again. Thump. I don't think about what I will do next. I could do a year's National service, or like my friends go abroad—Nepal, India. Right now I don't want to think.

* * *

I know how my mother feels about my being in Duvdevan. My brother is in training for Duvdevan. She begs me to convince him to ask for transfer out. He is a fine kid; I like him. He was proud to get into my unit. But, I agree with her for different reasons: he is not hardheaded enough.

My will is hard. You see that wall (a soccer head-feint to the structural wall between us and the family room). If I decided to, I could put my head through that wall. My brother can't. (His brother later requests a transfer to another combat unit.)

* * *

As we walk to the dining room, an elderly fellow, perhaps in his 80's, Chaim, a kibbutz founder, stops Naftali. He kids him: Chaim has bottled the essence of mandrakes. (In Hebrew, mandrakes is "Du'da'im," Chaim's word play on "Duv'devanim.") Chaim reminds Naftali that Rachel and Leah both coveted Du'da'im as an aphrodisiac to bed Jacob. Chaim jokes that he will sell this to men as an aphrodisiac, but adds—Chaim's emphatic finger pumping in the air—that Naftali does not need this.

The dining room is a social center. For the older and elderly there are rolling tray carts, cleverly designed: you put the tray on top and roll along the cafeteria line. But one grandfather has a grandson riding inside the cart, his head poking up through, as his grandfather gives him a ride. The boy holds the tray, arms extended, like a diminutive butler. Then a younger brother hops onto the front bumper for a tandem ride.

Naftali Introduces me to his friends, including his girlfriend, then I join his parents at a nearby table. We enjoy the pleasure that Naftali has with his friends, a sense of freedom and laughter.

Courage. Not an abstract word for Naftali. He does not pursue abstract ideologies. Courage is connected with what is *tzodek*, "right" or even "righteous". But it is more connected with a bombed school bus, with his sister.

Nehamia: A Father Speaks

I start with the end of his interview. Reluctantly, at my request, Nehamia now 64, tells me about saving David thirty-some years earlier.

Nehamia was the first commander for the CH-53 transport gun ship helicopters, Sikorsky-made, on the Connecticut River, just before the River slides into Long Island Sound, beneath a slippery, corrugated metal bridge, icey in winter.

In 1963, 18 years after Auschwitz, I helicopter-trained in Germany, at Goering's former air base, flying over Bergen Belsen concentration camp instructed by ex Messerschmidt Nazi pilots. Eighteen years after gassing Jews, German soldiers salute a Jewish officer.

By the time of the War of Attrition (69-73), I am a Major, commanding the flying Rescue and Air Assault squadron. Before night vision glasses are available, we train by moonlight. After several nights and days of continuous training over Jordan, Egypt, Syria, I take my squadron for twenty-four hours leave at the beach. My soldiers are more exhausted after their R & R.

Then I get the call at home. Two F4 Phantoms with four pilots have been shot down over Egypt: three men captured, one escaped. "Assemble a team, rescue him," Central Command said. "Within 6 hours. Take several 'choppers and we will give you ten sayeret matkal (the most elite special forces) and a medical evacuation team of two to accompany."

An hour later, revised orders. "Instead of sayeret matkal, we will give you ten regular infantry." An hour later, it was three infantry and in another hour it was no medical officers.

I decide to go alone with a copilot and one other "bird." This is a suicide mission. I can not send other men; I would captain this mission along with my copilot, technician and 3 infantry.

In the Sinai, our 'chopper stops for refueling. I have last radio contact from Central Command: confirm the names and ID's of the crew on-board. That was enough; they might just as well have asked for our epitaphs. I ignore them, take off.

The CH53 is 50,000 pounds. To avoid detection, we fly at fifteen feet, running without lights. We see only the ground beneath; nothing in front. We fly blind.

We cross the Canal. I hear David's weak signal. We triangulate, fly towards it; once we hear it behind us, we turn back. We switch on the landing lights, to be sure that David hadn't been captured; that we aren't being lured by the Egyptians. I circle ten minutes to find him; then, again, we hear his voice. Faintly. My fellow pilot says, "Turn right."

And he is there.

His first words as he clambers in, "I <u>knew</u> you would come to get me."

The rain of fire starts then, as I have never seen, like flying into a fatal Aurora Borealis. First, we fly zig zag evasively, but this lengthens our flight path. I decide to scoot straight for the Canal, our trail lit up by antiaircraft fire.

This touches me: waiting at the air base is David's mother, his eight-month pregnant wife.

I check the aircraft; we have no hits.

. . . .

Ten years later, my son, now a pilot, flies the airlifts to rescue secretly the thousands of refugee Ethiopian Jews, who had hiked months through Ethiopia, languished in parched, earth-cracked Sudan, for us to rescue them.

What I tell people about the Jewish State? I was there to rescue David, my son to rescue Ethiopian Jews. No one was there to rescue Jews in 1939.

This general insists I call him Nehamia. Bald, with remaining hair shaven, he wears a gray T, jeans and threadbare Teva sandals. His small corner office has shades pulled against the late morning summer sun. His desk is covered with pictures by his granddaughter, his book cases chock-a-block with books, folders. A small, worn Tanach sits among the books in this devoutly secular man's library. On the floor behind me, he gestures to two photographs, one leaning partly overlapping the other. A faded black and white overhead shot captures CH53 helicopters in tight triangle formation, like migrating, but powerful geese, following the leader.

With the same pride, he points to the color photo overlapping the helicopter formations. Here too are soldiers in uniform, also in formation. But their instruments are not M16's, nor Uzis, but violins, violas, cellos, woodwinds. This is his creation as the IDF's Education officer, the first IDF Chamber Music Orchestra.

I come to Nehamia to learn if my thinking about "my" soldiers is on target.

This pilot, who in 1977 became the father of the helicopter gun ships strike force, settles in quickly. I hear the rip of Velcro as he removes his Tevas, extends his legs so that his bare toes peak from under the desk's edge.

Stories of how the IDF affects youth, you want to know?

I'll start with when my daughter was six years old, we lived on a military base. Before the Six Day War, the next door neighbor was killed in a skyhook accident. He left three children, two, three and six year olds. My daughter said to my wife: 'You take care of the little ones and the momma and I will take care of the six year old.'

When she is seven, my daughter hears a pilot-less drone above—it sounds like a huge, broken lawn mower. She points to it and tells her mother, 'That's a wonderful plane; it has no pilot.'

And my son said this at his sister's sixteenth birthday party. My friends took turns telling stories about me, war stories, but teasing, not gory. After each, I got a turn to tell the story from my perspective. At the end, my son told this story that left my wife and I in tears.

The kids from the base took the same school bus. Every day, each day on their return; as they approached the bus station, they would gawk, look if there were two officers waiting at the bus stop. The children knew that if there were two officers at the bus stop, one child would be taken aside to be told that his or her father had been killed. And every time, my son said, every day, as they approached the stop, he worried it would be him and his sister who would be selected.

My wife and I had never known this.

So you see, children think about army here from early. You ask a teen, "So, what do you aspire to be?" The usual response, "Wait, let's see; after the army." Army is an awareness, beginning in childhood.

Why I became a Chief of Education for the IDF? I wanted to see the army through my soldiers' eyes. Look, it was unusual for someone like me to become head of education. I was a general, a pilot. Generals are not known for being geniuses. To become a general you have to be a little bit of an opportunist and a schmuck. Anyhow, too many geniuses in the army is a disaster. The army is about following orders: you do, not think. Having soldiers think about orders, deciding what to follow, what not, would be chaos in battle. Maybe what I say is too extreme; we Israeli soldiers are also known for thinking autonomously in the field. Perhaps there is a balance: following orders, but always thinking critically.

So, in general, I would not suggest appointing a general to be chief of education for the army: we're not so educated, maybe not so smart.

But I had at least two reasons to do this, one personal, the other . . . well, personal, but closer to my soldiers than my family.

The personal. When my son, my only son, whom I love, became seventeen, one year before army, my wife and I decided we would treat him like a prince: no responsibilities, no criticism, we catered to him.

On his eighteenth birthday, I drive him in the car to the recruitment center. I saw maybe 200 to 400 other boys there, also princes in the eyes of their families. I wait. Suddenly I hear this voice hollering, commanding them, not like they were princes, but like boys who would risk their lives at the officer's command, for the sake of their land, their people. These boys would descend into this life at least three years. The army is not natural; civilian life is.

Israel is a militarized society, but not militant.

The second reason to become education officer was to see the army through my soldiers' eyes.

Look, when I was a general, I insist to meet each soldier assigned to my unit. I talked with the group not about strategy, tactics, but about the ideology of Zionism: the why of their being soldiers. I give only two orders when they meet me individually. First, to call me "Nehamia," not general. Second, not to salute me, but to say 'Shalom' and make eye contact. Now, this I notice. If they say 'Shalom' it is with a smile or not. And if with a smile, I look at their eyes to see if they were sincere; eyes don't lie about smiles. If they don't smile, I ask what's wrong.

This I learn. At the beginning of their three year service with me, I could not predict their post-army life trajectory; after three years, I could. I asked myself," What happens in these three years?" How does our work in the army fit with their parents' work in raising them?

Here is how I understand the army's influence. The army is like a pottery kiln. The boy comes formed of soft, moist clay, glazed in certain patterns. If the kiln is not turned on, the clay leaves the kiln as it arrived and is easily smashed. If the kiln is too hot, the vessel may become brittle, or the glaze charred. Now, to some extent, for each vessel you fire at different temperatures, even different times, to some extent, but only to some extent.

I don't believe everyone should serve. I've seen some boys leave the army broken people. And, I began the IDF orchestra, because I thought: to take a boy or girl who has held a violin or cello in their hands since age six, and to exchange this for an Uzi, and M-16, or a Tank at eighteen, is almost criminal.

*   *   *

We are different than, for instance, the U.S.: we fight for our homes.

But I am worried about two trends I see in army and society. First, a soldier told me recently that our soldiers today may not risk a rescue as I did of David. Yusuf Madhat, bled to death at yosef's Tomb in Schechem. He was an Israeli Druze soldier from Beit Jann in the Galilee; he died because the palestinians harassed rescuers tring to evacuate the dying Yusuf; the Israeli high command would not force a confrontation, despite calls for help from the commanding officer at joseph's tomb, Ismail Sawad, an Israeli Bedouin officer from the village of salama. The Arabs mobbed Yusuf and any soldier who tried to rescue him. And the Israeli soldiers stopped trying; Mathout died. I repeat their names for you and their families, so that they will be remembered, as we say in Hebrew, "remember and be a blessing".

Second, I worry about a trend towards greater violence in society since at least the first Intifada. I think this increase is related what our boys are doing with the Palestinian population. For example a civilian bulldozer is sent to Hadera to knock down a house for chronic refusal to pay taxes. The driver approaches a house where the owner runs out, protesting that the driver has the wrong house. The driver refuses to listen; knocks down the house . . . the wrong house.

* * *

Army is more demanding today. When I started flying, it was simple—stick and throttle, 1 1/2 years training. Now it is three years training and with computers and such.

After I did my regular service, I stayed for career, then left for three and one-half years. I left because in the light rescue airplanes squadron I served of that time I felt I a was wasting my time. You know, we have wars about every 5-7 years, of course with an ostinato of infiltrators, wars of attrition, Intifadas, that raise the base level of non-peace. Today, I don't believe that the average soldier wastes time.

My view of army's influence on our boys? Yes, they're probably more mature, more somber when they leave at 21, 22. But we are simply cutting off their childhood. What is the big deal about becoming an adult faster? Why rush adulthood? You know, from birth to thirty is the first period of life with the last ten years of greater awareness. Then from thirty to seventy, you have adult responsibility. *If I had my choice, I would prefer our youth enjoy their youth longer.*

The army is but an evil necessity. We should make it as constructive as possible for our youth; they should not be smashed or brittle at the end; they should be a solid vessel, strengthened by their experience.

Until we can eliminate the army.

* * *

Courage? From these men, one twenty-two, the other nearing his 70's, we learn to flesh-out Aristotle's definition of courage. None use the word, would shy away from it; their actions speak. For Yossi, he saves a soldier because he must; he doesn't kill a terrorist sleeping next to his wife, because he can't. (Perhaps because the terrorist might give important information, he thinks after the fact.) For Naftali, courage, this thing that is "of the heart," means doing something that he dislikes, yet knows he must do, and restraining himself from hurting even an armed woman, certainly not her children. He enters the house, confronts and kills the murderer, with the image of this murderer's handiwork—school bus with charred bodies, roof arip, headless driver grasping wheel—in his head. For Nehamia, he considers what his son did—secretly airlifting thousands of Ethiopian Jews yearning to return to their Jewish home—as more "courageous," than Nehamia's act of bravery. In fact, only at the end of the interview would he tell me about this story, and only at my urging. Nehamia is more invested in his "unit" of musicians than stories of his actions. Such men teach us what true courage is—something that beats from the heart.

After Standard Army Service; Coming Home

We have looked at how a soldier is formed before army; how he is formed by the army. Let us turn to the early adult years upon choosing to leave regular army service, facing a life.

Intimacy. Upon leaving army, these men are ready for marriage and family. And, family for all of them is built on a core of marriage, a full life. Those two not yet married, strengthen this view: like Plato's original beings torn asunder, they feel incomplete. These men differ from our U.S. cohort,[49] even our highest functioning group, in which marriage and certainly children were delayed. Of 76, for instance, less than one third were married (although others had "significant others") and only six had children by age thirty. Our Israelis' remarks demonstrate family's centrality and how army (and deaths) move them towards this. One man at 30 is a graduate student in an esoteric field, awarded a prestigious fellowship to study at major U.S. university. Recently married, he considers his fellow graduate students, who are younger—24 to 26 years old—more qualified, at least better read in his field. He respects their knowledge, feels that he has to work hard to catch up. But, he continues, parenthetically, that he feels at times that he is in a group far younger than he, more like adolescents. He will finish his Ph.D. in four years; plans to have a family soon; no time for beer parties, bull sessions. Bright as he is, he doesn't really "get" the extended adolescence that pervades his peer graduate students. After hearing the stories of our soldiers herein, we can see his perspective more clearly: life is precious; relationships leaven life; family is life's yeast.

Work. To love and to work, Freud asks of us for a full life. And these are the two tasks that Erikson says we elaborate in adolescence and young adulthood (identity leading to intimacy and the capacity for generativity in family and work). How do these soldiers do with work? Not only how do they *do*, but moreso, what is their *attitude, approach?*

Of the practical matters they learned in the army—such as focus, goals, organization, improvisation, independence balanced with *akhva* ("mutual reliance" or "brotherhood") make do with minimal resources—these men apply to their vocational lives.

---

[49] *Lives Across Time,* op. cit.

Several found work, business, career were relatively easy following the challenges, and the legacy of army. As one said, making money is both not very meaningful nor very difficult after the army. Pinchas, referring to his (high-powered) post-doc in the States, feels as if he is on *"pension"* (retirement). There is a quality of *efficace*, a certain straightforward approach to the problems of making a living for these guys: you do your job, you take care of your family, you don't overemphasize work or income.

Another describes how his fellow Israelis in the States are perceived a bit aggressive: they work as if there might be no tomorrow, he remarks. Then he adds, "They feel like there may not be." Yet, they are highly valued employees or entrepreneurs; take quiet pride in their vocations.

And the distinction between attitudes towards family and work is not so clearly defined in their minds at times. An Israeli department chair, while recruiting a colleague from the U.S., is concerned more than his foreign colleague about the position being on "soft money." He continues, "I have to plan for your security, your future should something happen to me." This healthy middle-aged Israeli injects his sense of (his) life's impermanence and his concern for his colleagues well-being.

Overall, in Erikson's terms on the voyage from adolescence into young adulthood, these men have a solid personality, establish identity, value intimacy; balance intimacy and work.

But, looking at their lives pre-army, during army and afterwards, a thread runs through these men's lives: the history of this army and this State. Like the single almost incandescent blue thread of *techellet* that wends through the ritual fringes of the Jewish *tallit*, this strand of history colors these men's inner lives.

What Kind of Army Makes These Men? To state that army makes the man, tells only part of the tale. Their life stories tell only part of the tale. What is this army? When several began to tell me the history of the Israeli army, I realize how imbued both the society and they were by the development of the army in a country annealed by war, surrounded and infused by enemies.

Listen how personal this history becomes.

Moshe's unit lives among the Palestinians and brings in high-level terrorist suspects live for questioning. He is chosen for officer training. First, he complains: officer's training involves too much class work, too much homework. He, a top-tier student in high school, has enjoyed the break from cracking books. Yet, when I ask what he is studying, he comes alive with battles in the 1956 War, their tactics, the names of *privates* (not only officers) who broke the Egyptian battle lines in the Sinai passes. His finger traces on the stone coffee table the route of the jeep driver: alone, he enters the Mitla pass three times, intends to draw fire, identifies Egyptian positions, until he returns mortally wounded. History is alive for Moshe.

As I put together the various strands of history that I heard from various soldiers (Aviv's excited dissertation on the history of tank warfare, or David's account of triangulating a target), I recognize I must summarize this history. Then, you will learn how these boys are formed by the history of battles.

Bear with me as I try to keep this as focused, as incisive, and frankly, as interesting as this history was related to me.

A History of the (Modern) Israeli Army[50]

An army's fundamental structures have remained the same since the Romans; certainly its goals—to attack or defend and defeat enemies. Yet armies are affected by culture, even history.

History permeates Israel; it is in the dust you inhale in Jerusalem's hills. And stories flow from people's lips in Israel, like rivers seeking their destination, a listener's ears. So too stories flow from the history of the Jewish army, each war helping to refine the army, even as fundamental traits have endured in the modern (post-biblical) army since the 1930's. The Israeli Army is suffused by history. This Israeli Army infuses the State.

---

[50]   A more detailed history is in Reuvan Gal's A *Portait of the Israeli Soldier*. op. cit.

To begin a history of the Jewish army means several beginnings; there is a surfeit of history in the Middle East. Do we begin 2,000 years ago, during the last independent Jewish nation? Perhaps 3,000 years ago as Abraham recruits an *ad hoc* force. Do we begin with the most recent establishment of the Israel Defense Forces on May 26, 1948, twelve days after the Jewish state was formed? Or do we start before the State, in September 1907, when ten Russian immigrants to Ottoman Turkish-ruled Palestine established a clandestine group to guard settlements and named their group after Bar-Giora, who fought the Romans in 70 A.D.? These boys in this book will as easily slip into a description of Bar Kochba's guerilla tactics in an Edomite town—luring armor-clad Roman soldiers into underground tunnels, to become wedged by their own armor—as they will refer to Arik Sharon's tank tactics in '56, or Ehud Barak's disguise as a woman, pursuing a terrorists in Beirut. Modern, yet ancient, this army still gives biblical titles to its senior officers: *Aluf* ("champion," major general), *Tat Aluf* (brigadier general) and *Aluf Mishne* (colonel).

But, for this conclusion, for brevity, I hew to recent history.

Military strategy and tactics in this Jewish Army are embedded in a matrix of ideology. Before W.W.I Palestine, a group calling themselves *Hashomer*, the Watchman, is formed with three goals: *self-defense*, promotion of *Zionism* and *socialism*. During W.W.I, the Jewish Legion is formed as part of the British Army, thereby allying themselves against the Turkish occupiers. The Legion is disbanded after the War. But, murderous Arab attacks on Jewish communities, particularly during 1920-1 and in 1929—coupled with British ambivalent passivity—demands the formation of a self-defense group. This group was the *Haganah*, "The Defense." Again clandestine, its responsibilities include ideological principles of justice, righteousness, social solidarity and "a new society of farmers and workers who would subdue the land by the sweat of their brow."[51] A major principle: use arms defensively; in the present army this means *'tohar haneshek'*: purity of arms.

---

[51]   From Reuvan Gal, A Portrait of the Israeli Soldier. op. cit.

Not your typical army.

In the 1930's, the British appoint Captain Orde Wingate to protect the oil pipelines to Haifa from Arab guerrillas. He forms a Jewish and English unit, but goes further: he develops an underground Jewish army; moves towards more active defense. And Wingate (going beyond his British charge) teaches his fighters (who included Yigal Allon, later a Palmach commander) principles of leadership that characterize the Israeli Army to the present: _Lead_ by example; _discipline_ meaningfully, meticulously; _plan_ carefully involving all men before operations; _delegate_ authority and encourage improvisation in the heat of battle; _concentrate_ forces on central objectives, yet scatter forces as needed; _surprise, mobility and night actions_; _ideological_ bases for military actions.[52] [53]

A second major contribution that endures came from Yitzhak Sadeh, the first commander of the Palmach, a core of the Haganah that developed unconventional techniques: _individual responsibility, leaders' independent action including encouraging squad leaders to work as independent commanders; "group morale and cohesion, inventive tactics and daring leadership."_[54]

Further, because there were so few "soldiers," the Palmach lived among the kibbutzim, working the land and training militarily. This becomes a model for the later "Nahal" units.

Today's IDF's tactics and attitudes are constructed from Wingate's and Sadeh's 1930's principles: lead by example, improvise, use the night, emphasize the group and ideology—know why you fight.

Under severe Arab attacks, a smaller, alternative clandestine army, Irgun Tzvai Leumi (Organization of Nation's Soldiers) is formed, headed by Menachem Begin (in 1939, split into the more

---

[52] From Reuvan Gal, A Portrait of the Israeli Soldier. p. 5. op. cit.

[53] To "reward" Wingate for overstepping his bounds, the British post him to Burma; he dies in a plane crash _en route_.

[54] From Reuvan Gal, A Portrait of the Israeli Soldier. p. 7. op. cit.

radical Stern gang). It demands more aggressive responses to Arab riots (and British army), less socialist ideology.

Once the State is established, history's and ideology's influences on the Army and the State become compressed.

Each major war marks the IDF, affects its character, not least because of the phenomenal toll on men.

The 1948 War of Independence killed one percent of Jewish population, over 6,000. On May 14, 1948, some 24,500 Arab armies invade Palestine from Egypt, Jordan, Syria, Iraq, Lebanon, as well as Saudi Arabia, Yemen and Morocco.

The four characteristics of the army galvanize in 1948—*dedication, motivation, intelligence and improvisation.* They recur throughout the life stories in this book, including both the obvious advantages, but also their disadvantages. Dedicated men must believe in what they are dedicated, will be motivated by their ideology (but often by their relationships to their peers); should ideology wane or change, dedication may shift (as we heard with Avi, or Peretz). Intelligent men fight well, but question more. Improvising men make do when resources are short, but can develop a state of mind in which repairs are "make-do," on the run, never completely satisfactory.

Ben Gurion, the first prime minister, establishes six strategic military premises based on the imminent threat of surrounding Arabs: 1. aggressive deterrence; 2. accurate intelligence; 3. first attack; 4. combat-ready reserve and Air Force superiority; 5. short wars; and 6. soldiers as part nation-builders—farmers and guards.

Such "nation building" means establishing a sense of national integration, cohesion, movement into adulthood, dedication to the land. "Land dedication" becomes a compelling example of competing advantages/disadvantages: most soldiers think in terms of loving *a* place—a spot on kibbutz; the night sky in the desert; a hike in the Gallil—rather than global, "Land." Yet, some battling in Israel is over what is the land over which one should battle. In their character formation, they have connections to both specific places in their lives—a hiking path, special beach—and for some, to the millenia-old sites—where Moses and the tribes stood on

Qadesh Barnea, one kilometer above the barren Negev, where David smote Goliath. In this book this theme of building a nation is central and connected to building oneself as a person: we extend Aristotle's idea of the family as the first state and Erikson's ideas of early child rearing as a means of transmitting societal values, to the function of an army in transmitting and forming the character of its nation's citizens.

In 1953, Moshe Dayan as a 38 year-old Chief of Staff establishes a 101 men paratrooper unit that becomes a vanguard for the IDF, including using night attacks in retaliation for *fedayeen* ("self-sacrificers) attacks against civilians. He insists that officers lead into battle and retires career officers in their forties.

The 1956 Sinai campaign—coordinated with the British and French—is aimed at the Soviet-supplied arsenal along the Canal. The French and British abandon their promised intervention. The IDF reaches the Suez within one hundred hours and conquers Sinai in four days. 170 Israeli soldiers die[55]. A brilliant military victory, the war is considered a political failure, as both Eisenhower and the USSR—put-out that the British and French did not get their approval—insist on complete pullback. The effect on the military? The IDF strengthens the armored corps, establishes closer collaboration between armored corps and Air Force and tightens Central Command.

The Six Day War (May, 1967) arises when Nasser mobilizes some 95,000 soldiers and closes the Straits of Tiran to Israeli ships. Jordan and Syria also mobilize: all told, some 330,000 Arab troops, 2,300 tanks, 680 aircraft. Despite Israel's clear-cut defeat

---

[55] Moshik, a hero of the Mitla Pass battle is one of the paratroopers used for the first and only time in the all Israeli wars to drop behind enemy lines. I told him that I had heard how much he was respected for his courage. He demurred: hearing bullets whizzing past his head, he wanted to bury himself in the Sinai's sands. But, looking to his left and right and seeing his buddies advancing, he felt he could not let them down; kept running into possible death. He recalls most losing some 35 buddies in the Mitla Pass.

of the Arab armies, their Khartoum conference in August 1967 pronounced the infamous three "No's": no peace, no recognition, no negotiation. By October, Egypt sinks an Israeli destroyer in international waters.

A devastating War of Attrition along three frontiers: the Suez, the Golan and the Jordan River. International airplane hijackings begin, forerunner of today's "shoe bombers" and such. Conscription increases from 30 months to three years, more women are inducted and there is greater reliance on reserve units and officers. After some sixty Soviet-made MiG's are shot down (against two Israeli jets), among other considerations, the Soviets and U.S. impose a cease-fire. The Israelis lose some 600 men, 2,000 wounded.

The next three wars profoundly influence the Army and Israeli society: the *Yom Kippur War* (1973), when Israeli is almost overrun; the *Lebanese War*, with both perceived high mortality rates (and high post traumatic stress disorders) in a war fought on non-historically Jewish land; and the two *Intifadas*, in which the Palestinians elaborate 1950's "fedayeen" tactics to attack Israeli citizens and cities.

The Yom Kippur War can not be done justice here in its jeopardy to the Jewish State's existence. Numbers do only partial justice: Israel loses thirty times more men than did the US in W.W.II (per population); 2.680 men are killed (1300 officers), 7,000 wounded. This is not the place to articulate the strategic errors leading to an almost overrun of the Jewish State. A deeply personal account by Kahalani,[56] the tank commander who held back the Syrian army against extraordinary odds, is a place to begin for the reader.

The State and the Army recognize that the qualities developed since the 1930's—dedication, motivation, intelligence and improvisation—could not in themselves withstand superiority of numbers, sparse borders, and surprise. The Army expands to almost 500,000, at that time one sixth of the Jewish State; the career IDF is increased by some 70%; recruits came from less-educated;

---

[56] Kahalani, Avigdor. *The Heights of Courage: A Tank Leader's War On the Golan*. New York: Praeger, 1992.

women filled support roles. In turn, the Army became more bureaucratized, dependent on technical innovation.

Sadat's peace treaty (after Nov. 1977) cools the Egyptian border. But, the Palestinians open border-less attack on civilians, exemplified by the Entebbe highjacking, reversed by Israel's heroic rescue in Uganda of 105 passengers with the death of one Israeli commando, Jonathan Netanyahu.[57]

The Lebanon invasion in 1982 arises from a cascade of events, perhaps beginning with the Black September of 1970, when Jordan aggressively attacks the Palestinians, expelling Arafat and his cohort, who wander through Morocco, ultimately settling in Lebanon, once a thriving democracy that tenuously balanced Christian and Moslem communities. On the night of June 2, 1982, three Abu Nidal men shoot Israeli Ambassador Shlomo Argov through the head in London. Argov, in coma for several months, requires intensive care for the next twenty years. However, when PLO artillery attack over thirty Galilee settlements (despite U.N. presence), the IDF enters Lebanon in 1982, attacking both PLO and Syrian forces. In addition to these precipitating factors, the Lebanese invasion may also have been an adverse (over) response to the 1973 War. Golda Meir's government falls (along with Moshe Dayan); for the first time in Israel's history, the rightist Likud government under Menachem Begin takes reign. The Lebanon war can be seen as a reaction to the unprepared State of 1973, and an (over?) extension of the Ben Gurion's strategy of preventive attack. Israel loses some 340 men and 2,000 wounded; this is a politically unpopular war in Israel. There is an increased incidence of PTSD in returning soldiers.[58] [59]

---

[57] Brother of the future Prime Minister, Benjamin Netanyahu.

[58] Benson Ginsburg, personal communication.

[59] The interaction of battle in civilian settings, in a land not historically of the Jewish people and of disaffection of some of the populace towards the War in this citizen army likely is associated with the rise in PTSD, a phenomenon familiar to U.S. readers from the Viet Nam experience.

Ehud Barak's unilateral withdrawal of Israeli forces is a significant move, echoed more recently by Sharon's decision to withdraw Jewish settlers (and Army) unilaterally from the Gaza strip. Tragically, Southern Lebanon (and, in fact the entire country) becomes a vassal of Syria (and Hezbollah guerrillas), at least until U.S. and U.N. protest in 2005. Yet, Israel has been able to contain attacks against its citizens.

The first and second Intifadas, particularly the second, refines Arab war against civilians, more systematic and more traumatic than the earlier *fedayeen* attacks. In the second Intifada, PLO and other factions systematically choose to target Israeli citizens—public buses packed with children and women, restaurants, hotels, malls. This approach—particularly using suicide bombers and their mothers who pray that their younger sons will join the older—pits a culture committed to the primacy of life against a Jihad culture,[60] which in Medieval times, introduced the "Assassin," one who would value his own death over life.

Second Intifada: No longer history, no longer past. The Second Intifada marked these men, their society and this study. For the men of this book, history becomes personal: they become history builders. All serve in reserves during the Intifada, particularly after the terrorist bombing of the Park Hotel in Netanya. Eliaz recalls watching friends on his kibbutz leaving, first singly, then in groups: he recalls the jumpiness in his belly, waiting for his call to come, as it does, while he is cleaning latrines.

How did it affect these men, their *khevre*?

Soldiers are transformed. First, all lived with concern for the well-being of their relatives and friends from terror attacks: civilians were being murdered in buses, at bus-stops, in shopping malls, in restaurants. Second, some described initial polarization of political views: leftist became moreso, rightists, moreso; the former wanting the State out of Judah and Shomron. This is followed by

---

60 Bat-Ye'or. *Eurabia: Land of Dhimmitude.* Teaneck: Farleigh Dickinson Press, 2005.

a slow, but seismic shift occurred in the tectonic plates of ideology. Those who once were in the "Peace Now" camp, drifted, became either disillusioned with the Palestinians, or simply hopeless about coexistence. Like the tectonic plates beneath the ocean, such slow drifts cause huge upheavals, but within. A "wall" went up in these men's minds, long before the security fence was erected. At first, some faulted only Palestinian leadership as corrupt. Then, these soldiers saw video of Palestinian citizens washing their hands in the blood of Israeli soldiers, of Palestinian mothers—whose sons had just blown up themselves to kill others—cry and pray with joy that their younger sons will also be *shaheeds*: these Israelis became more sanguine about Palestinian society. Israeli soldiers simply didn't get how another would pray that her sons kill themselves (let alone kill others). Israeli's couldn't wrap their minds around this. The initial right/left polarization becomes internal polarization for many former liberal leftists. And those terms—liberal, left, even right—began to lose the form of their earlier meanings, became like worn coins, forme fruste images, only hinting of their former "value."

The men of this book struggle to maintain an internal humanity. Eliaz upbraids his C.O. for pulling a chair out from under an elderly Arab; Eliaz then chides himself for jeopardizing his unit because he cannot give the order to fire above the heads of Arabs busily smuggling arms. Yossi cannot kill a terrorist in bed.

As ideology seems to erode, most fight for family and *khevre*. One, unable to face this, leaves the country and yearns for his kibbutz.

Parents are transformed. Poignantly. One colleagues seats herself at a celebratory dinner in a lovely restaurant; plants two cell phones before her plate. She catches herself, apologizes, explains: one is for patients; the other is only and directly to her son in a combat unit. She trembles within when the second rings, she confesses as she fingers it. One soldier confesses that when posted for several weeks in disguise among the Palestinians, he tells his mother that he is in special training camp in the Negev; can't be reached by phone; wants her to be able to sleep at night. I sit with another colleague with three younger children in Jerusalem;

around 3 p.m., she fidgets: She explains. She listens with a third ear: each child must phone when safely home.

I listen and watch how these parents continue daily life— working, eating, talking, loving—even as a second tableaux takes place on a scrim in the forefront of their eyes. I recall Lenore Terr's[61] compelling stories of how trauma can become incorporated into a family's life, myth: color the family's view of life and the future; if there should be one. I recall Eli Wiesel, Primo Levi and Paul Celan attempting to convert the horror (the true horror, not Conrad's fantasy of deepest, darkest Africa) of their lives into an art that would both reach the living, while respect the dead. Levi and Celan both suicided; one of Celan's last remarks to his fellow writer Aaron Appelfeld—referring to Appelfeld's writing in Hebrew and rejecting German, literally his Nazi-murdered mother's tongue—that he envied Appelfeld's ability to write in his *truly* native tongue. Celan was unable to survive the murder of his parents. Levi despaired that Holocaust revisionists were making meaningless his life's writings. How can we protect a society, a family from incorporating terror and trauma into its present and future life?

Israeli Arabs are transformed, a worrisome polarization away from the State of Israel, towards those swearing to destroy the State. An Israeli Arab professor confides before we talk, that he yearns for a pork dinner: knows some digs far from the inquiring eyes of the local Imam and neighbors. We head there. As I have felafel, he tucks into a pork loin, then locks onto my eyes: explains that all Israeli Arabs, all Bedouins are really Palestinians. He continues. Since the first Intifada, he has revised his opinions. His people are more indigenous that the returning Jews, who displace palestinians, especially Bedouins from their nomadic lives, force them to live in houses with plumbing and electricity. He argues, quietly, forcefully, eloquently, that the good days of the Bedouin

---

[61]   Terr, Lenore. *Unchained Memories: True Stories of Traumatic Memories, Lost and Found.* New York: Basic Books, 1995.

are behind them—under the Ottoman Turks, the British, Bedouins were left alone, smuggled, made a good living. He marks me as a colleague (tries to recruit me to work with his Northern village), an American with liberal leanings. He continues. He hopes to work with Palestinians to regain Bedouin land. But, he will work from within the academic structure: he has already raised funds from American Jews to start Arab or Bedouin awareness, empowerment and educational programs. He hosts a gathering of Native American Indians, has sweat lodge ceremonies to enlist them in his common cause against "Israeli hegemony." He confides, conspiratorially, proudly that he starts his talks to rich American Jews by saying that they are nomads like Bedouins, moving from city to city, state to state American Jews are a minority, like Bedouins; have more in common with Bedouins than Israelis. Confesses that he resented his father sending him to boarding school, as his father—admiring the good education of his Jewish boss's children—wanted the same for his Bedouin son; a son, who simply wanted to live at home. He too seems polarized by the Intifada.

And, when Ariel Sharon, the Israeli prime minister is reported to have had a stroke, *Israeli Arabs* are filmed in the streets, celebrating by shooting weapons, showering Kalishnakov-wielding marchers with sweet *knupfe, halvah*.

Erikson warned us that pseudo-speciation—considering other humans as a different and "lower" species than ourselves—may be inherent in our being human. How to prevent societies from this pseudo-speciation—the need to degrade the "other," is a question and challenge that I can only raise; goes beyond this book about soldiers. But, Bettelheim cautioned in his last words of his last book: our challenge is to find the common humanity that can bind us together. The tension between universalism and particularism is felt more acutely in this past century. The dangers of narrow nationalism of 1848 Europe may be returning to our humankind. These matters bathe our soldiers lives, inner and outer.

While these soldiers tutored me about recent military and Israeli history, they also impressed upon me the deeply personal biblical and post-biblical geography of this land's "spine" as we drove its length and breadth.

Territories or Judah and Samaria: the Historical Spine of Judaism.

From a distance, as an American, this territory stuff seemed removed to me, much ado about almost nothing, this barren looking land. But, several of my soldiers lived across the Green Line[62], the land won in the '67 war; all of them served in this area. They ferried me on trips, tours to see this desolate scrub of land over which was much battling.

The names of the towns, except for Jerusalem, mean little to me, until my men "march" me through, north to south: Shechem (now Nablus), where, nearby, Joseph was sold into slavery by his brothers; Jerusalem, David's capital; Efrat, near Rachel's burial beneath a terebinth tree; Hebron, Abraham's' first home and where the cave of Machpela, the cave of couples, holds the forefathers and foremothers; Beersheva, where Abraham dug his first wells, later usurped from his son by envious neighbors. These are hill towns, until we reach the shallow basin of Beersheva. They are the vertebra of the historical spine of Judaism. Just as they are the rain's watershed from the Mediterranean, they are history's watershed for Judaism.

From afar, I barely knew a Shechem from a Nablus (turns out, the same city, renamed by the Arabs); figured, just leave the forsaken area to the Palestinians. I confess to a certain American impatience with all this contentious history; was reminded of Kissinger's aide, once ambassador to former Yugoslavia, who finally told his Serbian and Croation interlocutors, that he had enough of how the history of a battle in seven-hundred-something "explained" their twentieth century grievances.

However, as a psychoanalytic listener, as a researcher listening to soldiers, I hold back my opinions to receive theirs. This is easier

---

[62]   The political line delimiting pre-1967 Israel.

to achieve—holding back my thoughts—as I hear how reflective, how nuanced are these men's feeling-infused thoughts. They think in terms of both land and lives, with both mind and heart.

Many, even those who shrugged resignedly that Israel may need to forsake this turf, feel both a connection with the history and a sense of irony that those who usurped these towns from the exiled Jews—descendants of conquerers, whether Canaanite, Babylonian, Persian, Roman, early Christian, Islam, Christian Crusaders, Ottoman Turks, British—would prevail in inheriting this Jewish spine-land.

Struggling to make sense of this, I reread Saul Bellow's To Jerusalem and Back, his 1975 account of his stay at the understated elegance of Mishkenot Shananim facing the Old City and David's Citadel, and his developing love affair with the people in this country, its people. He writes about how much this country has achieved in too short a time, trying to *be* everything, *do* everything for its people: growing from 600,000 to some 5.5. million today; taking any Jewish refugee, regardless of ethnicity, of resources; forming a democracy; making everything from hinges to software, from plumbing to tanks; harvesting Nobel prizes and Jaffa oranges. He continues:

> It is both a garrison state and a cultivated society, both Spartan and Athenian . . . all resources are strained . . . I don't see how they bear it . . . . People think so hard.[63]

These Jews did something realtors warn against: built the best house in a lousy neighborhood. A first-world (Socialist-tinged) economy, education and expectations is surrounded by medieval neighbors, yearning for the golden era of Moslem conquest. This miniscule democracy (the size of the "N" in New York Times, compared to the entire front page equaling the Arab lands) is

---

[63] Bellow, Saul. *To Jerusalem and Back*. New York: Penguin Classics, 1975. p. 46, 57.

surrounded by neighbors ruled by French or British-appointed "kings"—tribal chieftains (Jordan, Saudi Arabia) or simply dictatorships (Syria, former Iraq), or pseudo-democracies (Egypt, Iran) or a tragically failed democracy (Lebanon); some are wealthy, some not so. Here is a recipe for Envy, one of Augustine's Seven Deadly Sins. Another sin, Sloth, can feed Anger in the envious, and is fostered in countries with little hope, such as in Syria or Egypt. Tyrants know: one way to keep the downtrodden subjugated is to create paranoia, fear of an external evil—Israel, Jews, the U.S.

Erikson insists that we attend to the social milieu within which these young men come into adulthood. Their life crises—their struggles between identity and identity diffusion, between intimacy versus isolation—are influenced by the social brew within which they are immersed. This Israeli brew, in turn, is deeply affected by what is brewing in the nation-states trying to demonize, eliminate it. This Israel is despised.

Between Freedom and Responsibility: The Israel Army as Training Grounds for Responsible Democracy

Let's shift to a larger focus, as if we were on a conceptual Google Earth. Let us pull back from these soldiers' inner lives, from their army units, from Intifada and the gemisch of Israel and Arabs. Imagine pulling back to look at the "globe" of democracy.

Doing so, we will begin to address our third task. What does a participatory (universally conscripting) army mean for a democratic society and its citizens? What is this army's *value for democracy*.

To begin, step back also in time: imagine looking through the eyes and thoughts of refugees from Fascism landing in the foreign, welcome arms of American democracy. Shift back to the cohort of Jewish refugees from Nazi Germany to the U.S. (and Britain).

Even a small selection of the German-Jewish brilliants, escapees who wrote about democracy impresses us: Erich Fromm, psychoanalyst; Erik Erikson, psychoanalyst (with no academic degrees); Bruno Bettelheim, doctorate in aesthetics; Theodore Adorno, music theorist; Thomas Szasz, psychoanalyst; Rudolf

WHAT'S LEFT TO SAY: THE AUTHOR SPEAKS

Ekstein, doctorate in linguists and psychoanalyst; Fritz Redl, psychoanalyst. Whatever their original disciplines, once in a free land, they turned at least once in their lives to write about the fragility of democracy and its preciousness: Adorno, *The Authoritarian Personality*; Erikson, *Childhood and Society*; Bettelheim, *Social Prejudice*[64] (among other works); Szasz's multiple books about the dangerous usurpation of freedom by government; Ekstein and Redl, on the curative potential of total institutions, a counterbalance to Erving Goffman's cautionary study, *Asylums*[65].

In my Introduction, I mention Fromm's *Escape from Freedom*[66]. Here, I can only reintroduce Fromm's ironically titled book, which outlines our *inner threats* to political freedom and democracy. Fromm's book is a major extension of Aristotle's and eighteenth century political philosophers' ideas about democracy. Fromm writes this book out of love and concern for his newfound American refuge and the the odd, ironic paradox he discovers here: in a land of such extensive external freedom, many run away from the freedom's responsibilities.

Aristotle gave a fairly specific definition of democracy not entirely consistent with our views today. For instance, he considered the optimal size of the democratic city-state to be a few thousand; larger made it too difficult to citizens to feel in touch with each other; smaller made it less feasible to function as a significant power.[67] Aristotle also insisted that citizens be landowners, have a vested, concrete interest in territory. This left out women and slaves. (In Jewish history, all voters had to pay a half-shekel to vote, a minimal sum, but one that also spoke of investment in their citizenship.) What we consider democracy today—millions

---

[64] With his co-author, Morris Janowitz, a man with whom, Bellow wrote, you could not daydream when he was speaking.
[65] Gofffman, Erving. *Asylums.* op. cit.
[66] Fromm, Erich. *Escape from Freedom.* op. cit.
[67] Smaller also makes the community vulnerable to the primitiveness of small groups articulated by Otto Kernberg.

voting regardless of investment in their country—Aristotle might have called "mobocracy" had he had the term. In fact, widespread "mobo-cratic" voting can bring about abridgment of freedom, even tyrannies as we learned in Hitler's Germany, or recently in Iran.

The why of mobocracy is articulated psychologically, eloquently by Wilhelm Reich's classic work on the *Rise of Fascism*[68].

But, let us focus on, return to Fromm. This psychoanalyst attempted to reconcile psychoanalysis with Marxism, ultimately a futile endeavor.[69] Fromm worked in larger social context, including, late in life, anthropological field work in a Mexican village.

Escape from Freedom is a *cri de coeur* to his new (but somnolent) love, America. Why do many citizens shirk, shrink from political freedom?

Political freedom arose in the ancient Greek demos. Freedom faded following what Thucydides describes as the Greek "suicide." Political freedom fell dormant until revived in the Enlightenment writings of Locke, Voltaire and others. But, Fromm clarifies that *political freedom is an external untethering* of restraints: the Church, Royalties, even governments are checked from impinging upon the well-being of the citizen. In fact, the government should be created, sustained, run by the citizen.

Here, Fromm fingers our dilemma, gets our uneasy pulse. Americans, proffered political freedom, turn away. They ask ward heelers in Chicago—or, more worrisome—religious leaders how to vote, for whom. Reverends, rabbis, imams, while proscribed from electioneering from the pulpit, hint, use buzzwords, for the "right" party, candidate. This occurs on "left" and "right": in the Civil Rights Era, Black Reverends worked their pulpits, just as today, Conservative Reverends have adopted the Civil Rights

---

68   Reich, Wilhelm. *The Mass Psychology of Fascism*. New York: Farrar, Straus and Giroux, 1980.

69   His ex-wife, Frieda Fromm-Reichmann became the talented, dedicated therapist portrayed in Hanna Green's *I Never Promised You a Rose Garden*. New York: Holt Rinehart, 1964

WHAT'S LEFT TO SAY: THE AUTHOR SPEAKS

tactics, even terminology, to persuade worshipers. In general, we see a shift from the more temperate, more measured, more tolerant Protestantism that helped build democratic America, to a more feeling-driven righteousness and self-righteousness, for example, among Christians of various evangelical fevers.[70] These fevers remind us of Arthur Miller's play about the Salem Witch Trials, but today, there are new scarlet letters, new apostates. Even John Kerry, failed presidential candidate with Jewish origins, reassures voters that he now regularly reads the New Testament, as a good, former altar boy should. In Israel, a secular housecleaner in her mid-twenties, when asked for whom she would vote, responds that she is waiting to hear from Rabbi Ovadia. And she is secular. Another entire religious moshav agrees that constitutions and voting are meaningless—we have Torah and rabbis tell us how to live. In recent years, single-issue matters, such as abortion, homosexuality, are code-words for religious votes and candidates.

Fromm's observations echo Erikson's[71] concern that, unlike independently-oriented European youth, American youth tended towards conformity, group, even gang thinking.

Fromm grounds us, bids us turn *within* to learn about our challenge, possibly even threat to freedom. In brief, he clarifies that internal freedom must match political (external) freedom for a true democracy to flourish. And by *internal freedom he means the freedom from the primitive anxieties about being independent, about taking responsibility for our decisions.* Because of our anxiety about responsibility, we fall back on a primitive dependency; seek out political gurus, even demagogues. A Utopian goal Fromm directs us towards, inner freedom, seeking responsibility. But, his addition to political philosophy is crucial to our understanding democracy, to establishing and maintaining this way of governance

---

[70] Leon Botstein, 2006, Jerusalem. Comments preceding a concert of Jewish American composers.

[71] Erikson, Erik. *Identity, Youth and Crisis.* New York: W W Norton & Co Ltd, 1968.

WHAT'S LEFT TO SAY: THE AUTHOR SPEAKS

and life. The *demos* is an active organism, does not continue of its own momentum, needs to be directed, coaxed periodically by its citizens, those who value democracy.

While Fromm comes to the question of democratic society and individual responsibility from a larger, historical frame, we hear embedded within his ideas Erik Erikson's work on child-rearing and cultural values. For democracy, one needs child rearing that fosters a sense of internal certitude, capacity, an ability for intimacy that does not preclude a sense of internal freedom and independence; an ability—even obligation—to speak one's mind for the sake of one's community. Democracy needs a sense of commitment to the well-being of others, motivated by a sense of self-assurance, a sense that one's early needs were well provided for.[72] That is, Erikson and Fromm write of similar concerns, as psychoanalysts, although they came to the problem of freedom from different methodological perspectives. They join the company of Bettelheim, Adorno and others. What Erikson says of child-rearing, we can extend to adolescence and young adulthood, the developmental crucible transitioning from family to society. What societal institutions—sanctioned and respected—usher youth into responsible citizenship?

These Israeli soldiers *got* it: *certitude tempered by compassion; independence balanced by responsibility.* A mother of an officer in training in an elite unit tells how he kept running out of pocket money. Given that he rarely got off base, she asks. He confesses that when the soldiers have to evict a Palestinian terrorist's family, the soldiers leave their own pocket money on the family's table. This is personal responsibility for your

---

[72] Bettelheim observed, during the 60's uprisings, that some students demanded for the needs for others out of a sense of (self-defeating) anger, a sense of personal deprivation. The demands may have sounded the same, but because they were done from a basis of anger and (emotional) deprivation, these students were generally not successful advocates for the needs of others.

actions: yes, you are ordered to evacuate the family, have the house destroyed hoping to prevent further terrorism, but you show responsibility for this family.

Israeli soldiers *get* both in childhood and, paradoxically, in the army, the ingredients and the leavening necessary for responsible citizenship in democracy. Let us explicate the paradox you have already gathered from their stories.

Army is hierarchical, autocratic. It must be, as Nehamia points out; you can't "vote" on tactics as bullets fly. But within this frame, this Israeli army adds spices given by Wingate and Sadeh and the culture of Israel that fosters a sense of responsibility for your actions, your *khevre* and ultimately for your country. This responsibility for your actions and your fellow citizens are central to democracy. (Eliaz adds that responsibility to one's country can be mangled into a form of thoughtless nationalism or chauvinism.)

The debate between "structure" (rules, stipulations) and "freedom," is misleading. In his book, *A Life in Music*, Daniel Barenboim[73] dismisses this fatuous distinction: within musical structure, its discipline, the conductor and musician make subtle decisions to bring character to musical expression, for instance, starting at the forward or back edge of a beat. Even in jazz, one of the freer art forms, Leonard Bernstein showed that the ensemble—which must listen carefully to each other—is bound together around harmonic chords, certainly around tempo, even as individuals have freedom to range. A jazz ensemble is a decent model for an army company: listening to each other; leaning on each other's talents; acting together more effectively than alone; staying on the same beat, same chord. Even their sizes are comparable: half a dozen to a dozen men can "swing" together, fight effectively as a group. Soldiers must be in accord; their lives depend on it. That is, there is a balance between structure and

---

[73]   Barenboim, Daniel. *A Life in Music*. New York: Arcade Publishing, 2003.

innovation that give fuller meaning to freedom of expression in art. Or in democracy.

About structure, rules, discipline in the army, I need not write much: every effective army, at least since Roman times, emphasizes this. There are clear command structures; clear expectations. One is literally "uniformed," not only in dress, but also in behavior. Even apparently severe, apparently arbitrary punishments—a few days in the brig for not saluting properly—should have behind it the need to maintain discipline, almost automatically, to prepare for battle.[74]

Some of the vignettes demonstrate how responsible decision-making is inherent in this army. When your officer just before a dangerous action, reminds you that someone should be prepared to take over leadership in the field should he be felled, you are reminded of each man's importance and preparedness for leadership. Small matters, such as rumpled uniforms, or addressing your officers by first name (generally after basic training, however) emphasize that formalities are not as significant as your responsibilities, your objectives and almost a palpable citizenry quality of this army. Anat chuckles when she is assigned to escort American generals—is amused at their spic-and-span polish; ironed creases, knife-sharp; snappy salutes. These do not impress her; in her eyes uniforms do not make the man, certainly not the Israeli soldier. Pinchas remembers (with eyes glistening) in armored corps, Yom HaZikaron (Memorial Day): the country stops; the tanks' guns rise to salute; the men dismount, stand silently; and his officer says *sotto voce*, "This is our strength—flesh, not steel." Nehamia, the general, asks his soldiers to call him "Nehamia," look him in the eye at the beginning of the day, so he can best read his troops.

The dead, the stories about carrying on the lives of their fallen brethren is an extreme example of responsible freedom. The soldiers in this book choose to remember their buddies, remember

---

[74] There are many examples of how this is misused in the army and other institutions. (Goffman, *Asylums*. op. cit.)

WHAT'S LEFT TO SAY: THE AUTHOR SPEAKS

them not only in thought, but also in action. This is a necessary ingredient for responsible democracy: choosing to give of yourself for others and feeling that this does not diminish yourself, rather enlarges, enriches. If they do this for their fallen *khevre*, they do it as readily for their living *khevre*. This is the kind of citizen many of us would choose to live in our democracy, in our demos.

Another timely factor of responsibility is the sense of making history. When Peretz was serving as an officer in Shomron and Judea, he was aware that his family, his kibbutz, his friends, in fact the eyes of world opinion were cast upon his actions. He had seen *his* men on CNN. He thought not only of his mission—to protect, to capture a suspect—but also of how his men acted—with a sense of restraint towards the populace (Jewish and Arab), even a sense of respect. He recalls capturing a known bomber suspect, but does not forget this man's children clinging to his pant legs, crying.

Internal initiative, independence balanced by responsibility for others: these are fundamental building blocks for the internal freedom Fromm insists is necessary to match the external freedom necessary for an enduring democracy.

Psychoanalytically, this bridge from late adolescence to young adulthood is an optimal period to effect, to foster this state of mind. I refer to *character development* for which late adolescence/young adulthood are critical periods. National service in itself tells the adolescent (and society) that something significant is expected of the citizen before he or she enters a more private life, the stages of intimacy and generativity that follow in the next few decades. Anna Freud in a prescient and classic paper, entitled simply, "On Adolescence,"[75] wrote about the extremes of mental states found in the adolescent: from asceticism, generosity, idealism on the one hand, to the pendular swing of indulgence, even Bacchanalian carousing and an ability to be self-centered in a pre-Ptolemic universe (the world revolving around the adolescent). The Israel

---

[75]   Freud, A. Adolescence as a developmental disturbance., Writings, 7:39-47, 1969

army taps into and harnesses the energy of impulses, optimal physical prowess and directs these into an other-centered quality, and into a sense of remarkable self-confidence, not only in one's body, but also in how one's state of mind can expand the body's limits. The *kravi* soldier feels confident in his body, while also connected with his buddies, and through them in a meaningful manner to his society (when things go well). One soldier recalls his early officer training, when at twenty, only weeks earlier learning how to take orders, he now rappels down from helicopters in the desert, gives orders, attends not only to his safe descent, moreso his men.

Look at this in Erikson's terms. Adolescence the period of identity formation is necessary in order to enter the next phase, intimacy (versus isolation) with a more solid sense of who one is and what one can give to another in intimacy. The army taps into and develops the bridge between identity formation and intimacy. The teen, well before *giyus*, call-up, even as young as 15, is thinking about which unit he aspires to; identity is closer to his body's development. (As opposed to many U.S. college students, who are studying in ways that may be far removed from their bodies.)

Psychoanalytic models of development, in the simplest first approximation, are the study, the understanding of how we make sense of our changing bodies. How, in the oral phase, the infant begins to trust that the world will provide well for it (or not); how the pre-toddler begins to feel it can control its sphincters (or feel controlled externally); how the toddler feels it can get its "legs," its fingers to do things, be on the make — industry (versus the sense that it is incompetent); and so forth. In this sense the army helps solidify identity. It also moves the adolescent into the next developmental stage — intimacy — with commitment to his buddies. This is not an abstract phenomenon: the young soldier needs to feel (not just think) that he can count on his comrades to save his life. This somewhat artificial experience of intimacy (after all, the young man didn't necessarily choose this unit) is a place to practice working through his ability for intimacy that he can then experience later more fully in heterosexual love, in finding a partner.

The usual American setting for a similar cohort, that is college, often complicates identity formation and intimacy with the freer access to alcohol and drugs. One American young woman spoke of the "first year's" twenty-pound weight gain—from booze—as a normative phase. In our American study, only the top segment of our highest functioning group were able to avoid "lost years" that most of the others described in drug or booze-saturated campuses.[76] In addition, none described a sense of group identity with common goals, nor a sense of giving themselves meaningfully to their societies during the college/graduate school experience. (Others did feel that they were contributing meaningfully beginning in their late twenties.) In Tallahassee, Florida, the college students speak of the highest incidence of sexually transmitted diseases of any campus in the country, this setting of bared midriffs and tank tops. This does not speak of psychological intimacy. Our Americans displayed a relative delay in capacity for intimacy.

We have this paradox: the overtly autocratic, hierarchical institution of army fosters democracy, internal freedom and commitment to others. George Washington insisted that all citizens in a republic must serve in the army. Here we have a deeper understanding to what Washington was referring. Here, our Israeli soldiers, who speak so personally to us, teach us.

*　　*　　*

What will happen as peace, hopefully, approaches? What will happen when less soldiers need to be recruited in Israel? After all, as U.S. Defense Secretary, Donald Rumsfeld has argued, a professional army and soldier prosecute wars better than less-trained and less-motivated recruits. Some of what Rumsfeld refers to may be due to artifactual differences between U.S. and Israel armies: the U.S. armies have fought offensive wars at least since W.W.II. The Israeli army has been built as a defensive force; when it has tried to

---

[76]   *Lives Across Time*, op. cit.

function as an offensive army, such as in Lebanon, it didn't work as well. As we see in Viet Nam and Iraq, however, the future may find that *in democratic societies*, particularly those with conscription, there may be shorter tolerance for offensive wars.

Is a National Service, which relies less on the physical prowess expected in the army, as meaningful to young men (and women) and consequently as successful in building personality and commitment to others? Can one construct the same *Khevrut, akhva'ut* (comradeship and fraternity) in a National Service as one can in an Army in which true brotherhood involves laying down your life for another, or more significantly, keeping your buddy safe. These questions go beyond this book, but are provoked by the stories herein. It is our challenge: not only to achieve peace, but also to build respected institutions to fit the developmental needs of our youngsters and future citizens, and the needs of a democratic society. How do we harness our youths' need and ability to be altruistic, to use their bodies meaningfully, to rely on peers, make deep and meaningful decisions for themselves and their community?

For now, let us step back and look at this band of brothers. They represent themselves well, also their *khevre*, although perhaps they do not represent all soldiers, nor Israelis. If I have done my job well enough, you will recall Yonah, who still does not know if he did right to support his knee-shattered buddy on an action, but could not have done differently; Micha, who, after killing a sniper aiming at him—his first kill—cannot stand up, asks himself if he is a soldier, a medic, a Jew; Pinchas, whose life redeems his father's teen hood in a Nazi concentration camp; Avi, devastated at the loss of his four men; Eliaz, struggling against childhood memories of friends, twin Arab brothers, when he must order to fire; Peretz, who at thirty recalls the taste of his pacifier when he was four as the kibbutz was being bombed; David, who realizes he is living out the lives of *two* fallen comrades, one whose name he bears; Aviv, who harnesses the army to overcome his mother's immolation; Yedid, who sees himself as an officer and a teacher.

They ask that you remember not them, but their fallen. I ask us to remember the living and the dead, the stories we are told and might have been told.

May their stories remain with you. May their lives give a window into their souls, the soul of this unique army, this unique country, this Israel.

Index A

A

A.D. Gordon 85

Adolescence 7, 13, 16, 19, 81, 98, 207, 210, 220, 235-6, 254, 257-8,

Adorno, Theodore 251, 254

Ahad Ha'am 85

Al ha'shechem 26

Allon, Yigal 239

Am Ha'aretz (an uneducated person) 34

Apocalypse Now 90

Arafat 13, 130, 134, 243

Aristotle 207-8, 220, 221-2, 234, 241, 251-2

Artillery 43-4, 46, 54, 77, 104, 113, 142, 243.

Ashkenazi 43, 64, 71, 108, 166

B

BAKUM 123,194

Balata Refugee Camp 40-1

Barak, Ehud 14, 81, 83, 137, 147, 238, 243

Barenboim, Daniel 255

Baruch Goldstein 126

Bedouin 18, 20, 59, 85, 110, 162, 233, 246, 247

Beersheva 59, 162,165, 248.

Begin, Menhachem 73, 149, 243

Beit Ha'neu'rim (teen's house) 193

Beit Jala 135, 189.

Beit k'nesset 107

Beit Yeladim (children's house) 77-8, 81, 187, 193

Z

BVG